THE CRISIS OF CAMPUS SEXUAL VIOLENCE

Although awareness of campus sexual assault is at a historic high, institutional responses to incidents of sexual violence remain widely varied. *The Crisis of Campus Sexual Violence* provides higher education scholars, administrators, and practitioners with a necessary and more holistic understanding of the challenges that colleges and universities face in implementing adequate and effective sexual assault prevention and response practices. In this volume, a diverse mix of expert contributors provide a critical, nuanced, and timely examination of some of the factors that inhibit effective prevention and response in higher education. Chapter authors take on one of the most troubling aspects of higher education today, bridging theory and practice to offer programmatic interventions and solutions to help institutions address their own competing interests and institutional culture to improve their practices and policies with regard to sexual violence.

Sara Carrigan Wooten is a Doctoral Candidate in Educational Leadership and Research at Louisiana State University.

Roland W. Mitchell is the Joe Ellen Levy Yates Endowed Professor and Interim Associate Dean for Research Engagement and Graduate Studies in the College of Human Sciences and Education at Louisiana State University.

THE CRISIS OF CAMPUS SEXUAL VIOLENCE

Critical Perspectives on Prevention and Response

Edited by Sara Carrigan Wooten and Roland W. Mitchell

Routledge
Taylor & Francis Group

NEW YORK AND LONDON

First published 2016
by Routledge
711 Third Avenue, New York, NY 10017

and by Routledge
2 Park Square, Milton Park, Abingdon, Oxon, OX14 4RN

Routledge is an imprint of the Taylor & Francis Group, an informa business

Library of Congress Cataloging-in-Publication Data
The crisis of campus sexual violence : critical perspectives on prevention
    and response / edited by Sara Carrigan Wooten and Roland W. Mitchell.
        pages cm
    Includes bibliographical references and index.
    1. Campus violence—United States.   2. Campus violence—United
States—Prevention   3. Sex crimes—United States—Prevention
4. College students—Crimes against—United States.   5. Universities
and colleges—United States—Safety measures.   6. Universities and
colleges—Security measures—United States.   I. Wooten, Sara Carrigan.
II. Mitchell, Roland (Roland W.)
    LB2345.C75 2016
    371.7′82—dc23
    2015009671

ISBN: 978-1-138-84940-2 (hbk)
ISBN: 978-1-138-84941-9 (pbk)
ISBN: 978-1-315-72560-4 (ebk)

Typeset in Bembo
by Apex CoVantage, LLC

Printed and bound in the United States of America by Publishers Graphics, LLC on sustainably sourced paper.

CONTENTS

FOREWORD

I want to commend the editors of and chapter contributors to this extremely important and groundbreaking work, *The Crisis of Campus Sexual Violence: Critical Perspectives on Prevention and Response*. Issues surrounding campus sexual violence are brought into the limelight in this very timely and critical book. In the book's introduction, it was not surprising to read that "research has consistently demonstrated over the past four decades that college women are at high risk of an attempted or completed rape while in college." I recalled my own experiences, as a young college freshman, when faced with sexually aggressive behaviors which, if tolerated, provide a foundation that become precursors to campus sexual violence assaults. In saying this, I do not want to belittle these types of aggressions, as all such acts violate those who experience them. I went to high school and college in the 1950s and 1960s. The topic of sexual violence was not openly discussed by my peers. Thankfully, the circumstances creating shame and fear of addressing such uncaring acts are being directly challenged, due to societal pressures speared on by examples, as noted by the book editors, "of news stories involving sexual assault scandals in higher education . . . in part due to changes in technology that have enabled survivor stories to spread swiftly through the media." The power of evidence presented in the words of those directly affected is supported by many scholars who view them as legitimate sources of knowledge of the human experience.

Contributors to *The Crisis of Campus Sexual Violence: Critical Perspectives on Prevention and Response* underscore that "the increased attention to the reality of rape and sexual assault in higher education is a major step in the right direction," but the contributors go on to point out that "institutional response to highly publicized incidents of sexual violence remains widely varied." The authors advocate for the construction of "meaningful policy that addresses the concerns of different student groups, negotiating regulations and mandates, promoting rather than discouraging reporting, and implementing effective prevention education programming." For example, within the context of detailing the health, educational, and financial consequences of campus sexual violence, the authors provide much needed information to enable the reader to: think through the consequences of conflating criminal laws with Title IX, the Clery Act, and campus administrative due process; to recognize that unique campus student populations call for varied factors essential to the development of effective campus-based sexual violence programs that are sensitive and address the needs of all, including sexual assaults, for example, within the perspectives of racial/ethnic communities, within LGBTQ communities, and within the intersections of these and other historically marginalized student campus communities; to see the importance of addressing rape-prone campus subcultures and to comprehend the resultant sense of institutional betrayal and negligence in failing to do so; to assess the promise of bystander intervention programs implemented at Title IX postsecondary schools; to critically examine how policy problems are framed rather than to pursue policy solutions based on a routinized acceptance of how a problem is defined; and to understand the important role played by institutional leaders in establishing safe campuses with a focus on prevention of sexual violence, characterized, in part, by the development of a campus-wide ethic of care and trust.

In sum, the editors and authors of *The Crisis of Campus Sexual Violence: Critical Perspectives on Prevention and Response* engage the reader in a much needed vital interrogation of higher education with a focus on the transformation of campuses as spaces where sexual violence is not accepted as inevitable. Several book contributors indicate that, while progress has been and is being made, discussions presented here are just beginning to uncover the need for much more dialogue and work dedicated to addressing this pressing issue. Nonetheless, I am impressed by the breadth and depth of this book, which not only provides nuanced perspectives on the crisis of campus sexual violence but provides voice for many silenced in the past and support to those who are currently silenced. In addition, insights provided here encourage all to participate in these discussions and to work together against acts of sexual violence, on and off campuses.

Caroline S. Turner
Immediate Past President of the Association for
the Study of Higher Education (ASHE)
Professor and Graduate Coordinator for the
Doctorate in Educational Leadership Program
California State University, Sacramento

ACKNOWLEDGMENTS

Since the formation of this project during the summer of 2013, numerous stories about campus sexual violence have been put front and center on the public stage. From the *Rolling Stone* publication of a story about a gang rape at the University Virginia—a story that became mired in controversy due to the publication's lack of investigation into the details of the gang rape and that spurred a national conversation regarding not only proper journalism practices but also why the trauma of rape can cause survivors to misremember particular details—to the Columbia University senior Emma Sulkowicz, who physically carried her dorm room mattress across campus for months as a sign of protest against the university for refusing to expel her rapist. These stories have been particularly salient for us as we have been editing, writing, and compiling this book. They reminded us of the persistent demands for a "perfect victim," of the multitude of ways in which the harm of sexual violence does not end with the acts of violence themselves, and of the power and bravery of those who are willing to tell their stories. These stories also highlight that the perceived boundaries between higher education institutions and broader society are crashing down. Higher education institutions are not spaces removed from dominant cultural attitudes about sexual violence, and so it is no tremendous surprise that just as sexual violence is an epidemic outside of the gates of higher education, so too is it a crisis within.

This book argues that it is incumbent upon colleges and universities to figure out how to meaningfully recognize, talk about, and act upon this crisis. We the editors are watching this battle play out in our own context of Louisiana. Sara has been named to a Louisiana Campus Sexual Assault Working Group, tasked with identifying how our higher education institutions are failing to protect their students. Those at the table, experts from across the state including university counsel and state legislators, engage in nuanced, complex conversations about things like what good disciplinary policy looks like for a student who is found responsible for committing a sexual assault on campus. And the conclusion of those conversations often centers on the impossibility of one-size-fits-all solutions, of the need for dramatic cultural change in addition to the formation of better policy. Those conversations have demonstrated the mission of this book, which is to highlight the competing interests, legal challenges, and ethical obligations of sexual violence prevention and response in higher education.

Thus, we are so grateful for those courageous members of leadership, administration, and faculty who have named their own institution's failures and who work tirelessly to improve the culture of their campuses. We are thankful to the members of state and federal legislative bodies like Louisiana State Senator J.P. Morrell and U.S. Senators Kirsten Gillibrand and Claire McCaskill who have put campus sexual violence at the top of their political priorities and have not shied away from hard, honest examinations of the problematic practices of our higher education institutions. We are proud of the incredible work being done by student activists across the country, who refuse to be shut out of policy conversations that directly impact them. Most importantly, we want to thank the student survivors of campus sexual violence. You are the ultimate reason for the creation of this book. You are the ones we are all writing for.

Finally, we are so appreciative of the support and home that Routledge has given to this project. Heather Jarrow has been our champion from beginning to end, offering us enthusiastic support for this book and encouragement in its development all along the way.

I, Sara, am profoundly grateful for the support I have received from my mentors at the School of Education at Louisiana State University regarding this book, including Petra Munro Hendry, Jacqueline Bach, Danielle Alsandor, and Rebecca Owens. Additionally, those scholars who supported my early foray into my research on campus sexual violence, Karen V. Hansen, Thomas A. King, and Sabina E. Vaught, have my deepest respect and thanks. Without the three of you, I would not be where I am today. My colleague, mentor, and dear friend Bruce Parker, who has been encouraging my overly ambitious leaps into academia for ten years now, is owed my deepest gratitude. Two years ago, I had the kernel idea for this volume, but without Bruce's steadfast insistence in my ability to bring that idea to fruition, this acknowledgments page likely would not even exist. Bruce, I dedicate this, my very first book, to you. To Roland Mitchell, who has always believed in my work and my ambition, I cannot express enough thanks. Without hesitation, Roland dove headfirst into this book with me and it has been an honor for me to learn from him and work with him throughout the editing process. To my truest love and husband, Dave, there are not enough expressions of thanks in the world for the unending support and faith you have given me along this book's journey from idea to completion.

The lion's share of the intellectual curiosity and scholarly commitment that I, Roland, possess today are a direct result of the overwhelming investment that my mentor, friend, and academic brother Jerry Rosiek made in me now nearly two decades ago. My drive to confront evil in all its varying forms, be it sexism, racism, homophobia, or classism, has been stoked by close and trusted colleagues Noelle Whitherspoon-Arnold, Bruce Parker, Kenneth Faching-Varner, Petra Hendry, T. Elon Dancy, Becky Atkinson, and Gerald Wood. To Sara Wooten, from our first meeting as colleagues to this very moment I appreciate that you have always brought out the best in me and truly modeled in all things school, community, and scholarship an unwillingness to turn a blind eye to injustice. Consequently, this book is not simply an academic exercise but a living proclamation of our ongoing commitments to these efforts. Without a doubt all of my passion for life and vigor are the living manifestation of Reavis and Patricia Mitchell. My brothers Reavis III, Reagan, and Roman are my backbone and my courage. Thanks to them I know I am never alone. My son Brandon Lewis has brought a joy into my life that I truly had no idea I could ever experience. And finally, I dedicate this book to my brilliant, loving, and faith-filled wife Chaunda Allen Mitchell. You center my world and model the ongoing pursuit of peace that makes these projects possible.

1

INTRODUCTION

Sara Carrigan Wooten and Roland W. Mitchell

As scholars, policymakers, administrators, and activists we find ourselves in a historical moment in the United States of increased interest in, and awareness of, campus sexual assault. Each year seems to carry with it a flood of news stories involving sexual assault scandals in higher education. This is in part due to changes in technology that have enabled survivor stories to spread swiftly through the media. The work of the Office of Civil Rights has also played a significant role in bringing Title IX violations regarding sexual violence in higher education to prominent national attention. While the increased attention to the reality of rape and sexual assault in higher education is a major step in the right direction, institutional response to highly publicized incidents of sexual violence remains widely varied. For example, colleges and universities are increasingly reliant on bystander intervention programs due to federal mandates to implement them as part of a broader anti-sexual violence strategy. Such prevention programming, while rightfully unifying the campus community in its obligation to prevent violence, also sustains the notion that sexual violence is an inevitable part of campus life. Additionally, bystander intervention programs largely remain extremely heteronormative, where the possibility of lesbian, gay, bisexual, and transgender (LGBT) student assaults are at best briefly mentioned and at worst silenced. Such programming has also been largely silent on the necessity of distinguishing between different cultural values and pressures, where concerns about reporting sexual violence may be radically different from one group to another. For example, the rationale to not report for a White, straight woman may be entirely different than the rationale to not report by a Latino, bisexual man, depending on the circumstances of their assaults.

The example of bystander intervention programs highlights the incredible complexity of sexual assault prevention. For each component of prevention and response efforts, a multiplicity of questions unfolds regarding how best to serve all students and effectively provide a safe and survivor-supportive campus. This volume attends to the difficulties that higher education institutions (HEIs) face in implementing adequate and effective sexual assault prevention and response practices. We acknowledge the plethora of concerns that HEIs must attempt to balance when considering how best to serve students and illuminate a number of questions that risk remaining unanswered in the national fervor to develop immediate, practical solutions. To this end, this book provides scholars, administrators, leadership, and practitioners with a more holistic understanding of the challenges that higher education institutions face when attempting to prevent sexual violence on campus. However, this volume goes beyond a mission of simply highlighting these difficulties. We begin with experiential and theoretical chapters that lay a foundation for chapters that offer new perspectives on pragmatic solutions. Some authors offer insights into programmatic developments that they have been a part of developing and implementing, while others take a critical standpoint in assessing the barriers to adequate prevention, education, and response efforts that exist. We argue that developing programmatic interventions that are not held in conversation with, and at times in tension with, theoretical perspectives regarding the manner in which sexual violence is being framed in higher education is to act without an appreciative understanding of the problem. Ultimately, these essays represent a political project aimed at calling attention to the kinds of institutional dynamics that make eradicating sexual violence in higher education a difficult enterprise, at best. Collectively, they constitute an honest, nuanced, and timely take on one of the most troubling features of higher education.

Sexual Violence in Higher Education

The focus of sexual violence in higher education research has typically been aimed at understanding prevalence rates, incidence types, and risk factors such as alcohol and drug use as well as party and fraternity culture. In their groundbreaking study on sexual violence in higher education, Koss, Gidycz, and Wisniewski (1987) illuminated the significant prevalence of rape during college years for women. Research has consistently demonstrated over the past four decades that college women are at high risk of an attempted or completed rape while in college (Baum & Klaus, 2005; Fisher, Cullen, & Turner, 2000; Karjane, Fisher, & Cullen, 2005; Koss, Gidycz, & Wisniewski, 1987; U.S. Department of Justice, 2002). Research on sexual violence in higher education has identified that reporting rates are consistently low when held against prevalence rates.

While this research has dramatically altered what is known about rape and sexual assault in particular, much less has been written about the role that leadership, for example, plays in developing institutional strategies for mitigating campus sexual violence or how legal mandates shape, or fail to shape, HEI responses to incidents of rape and sexual assault. Such questions are critical for those working to combat high prevalence rates of sexual violence against college students. Understanding institutional culture, priorities, and decision-making strategies reveals the at times overwhelming problems that HEIs face when developing prevention and response initiatives.

Higher education institutions in the United States reflect the dominant social norms of our culture. The theoretical standpoint of this volume identifies that culture as patriarchal, whereby violence against women by men is responded to generally in a manner that either blames women for the violence done to them or focuses on prevention strategies that identify how women can better protect themselves. Institutional culture in higher education often promotes a mission of helping women help themselves to prevent sexual violence through bystander education, self-defense trainings, warnings to not walk alone at night, warnings to not go to parties alone, warnings to always watch their alcoholic beverage so as to prevent them from being spiked with "date rape" drugs, and providing information on where to seek help in the event of an assault, rather than fundamentally altering aspects of that culture that promote violence against women.

Publicity, Strategy, and Response

In February of 2012, Boston University hockey player Max Nicastro was arrested and charged with sexually assaulting a female student on campus. This was not the first allegation of sexual violence brought against a member of the team to be made public, and a subsequent investigation commissioned by Boston University President Robert A. Brown revealed a dangerous attitude of sexual entitlement shared amongst players. Two months after Nicastro's arrest, the university announced that it was establishing a sexual violence crisis center on campus. The need for such a center was a popular initiative, one that had been called for by numerous parties over the years. The center would be responsible for implementing prevention education training and providing support for victims of violence. The university also increased its bystander intervention efforts by requiring officers of all student organizations to undergo specific bystander intervention training.

In April of 2012, the Office of Civil Rights (OCR) announced that it would be investigating Title IX violations alleged to have been committed by the University of Montana. After two sexual assaults were reported in 2011, the university conducted an independent investigation, the results of which revealed a total of nine sexual assaults of women from the fall of 2010 to the winter of 2011 that had been reported to the university and insufficiently handled. Complainants asserted that they had been discouraged from reporting due to several of the university's football players, including the quarterback, being accused. Several reforms were instituted as a result of the 2011 internal investigation, including the development of a 20-minute online training ironically[1] named Personal Empowerment Through Self Awareness (PETSA) for incoming students. Despite such action, the OCR investigation concluded that the university had violated Title IX mandates in a number of areas and entered into agreement with the university for further institutional reform.

The work done by higher education institutions to prevent sexual violence on their campuses has historically been carried out in a reactionary manner to incidents on campus or federal mandates. While federal mandates exist for all institutions receiving federal funding, the actual implementation of these mandates can be inconsistent. For example, while most institutions are in compliance with the Clery Act mandate to report crime statistics for each year, many also remain in violation of other provisions of the Clery Act such as distinguishing between forcible and nonforcible sexual assault (Fisher, Cullen, & Turner, 2000). The result of inconsistencies in sexual assault prevention, response, and reporting has been a multitude of different programmatic approaches across institutions with limited success in addressing what is understood to be an epidemic of rape and sexual assault occurring on campuses every year. In the case of Boston University, the institutional response to the violence committed by members of the hockey team was to create a fixed location within the university to handle education and prevention efforts as well as crisis intervention. For the University of Montana, reliance on a 20-minute online training for students, which they must complete before being allowed to register for classes, has been the chosen method of broadly educating students on sexual assault in the hopes of preventing such violence. Neither of these interventions, however, were part of a broader institutional effort to critically examine and alter the campus culture itself.

Addressing Institutional Culture

Changing institutional culture is an almost unthinkable goal given the basic compliance challenges that have been illuminated by the OCR investigations of Title IX violations over the past several years. In her analysis of 64 higher education sexual assault policies, Anderson (2004) concluded that HEIs often have multiple incentives for discouraging sexual violence reporting by students. This is typically carried out through a variety of implicit means. Universities and colleges have adopted archaic legal mandates such as, "prompt complaint, corroboration requirement, and cautionary instructions" (Anderson, 2004, p. 1). These mandates have a deterrent effect on sexual assault reporting by students and "may correlate with powerful institutional incentives to deter student complaints of sexual assault" (p. 7). Anderson establishes the powerful nature of rape myths regarding women and sexual violence, myths that often portray women as vindictive, conniving, and untrustworthy. These myths are so enmeshed in our cultural attitudes toward rape and sexual assault, that the manner in which campus leadership and administrators structure institutional policy may reflect a socioculturally hostile attitude toward victims, who are often, if not always, assumed to be heterosexual women.

Besides this general suspicion of women who report rape, HEIs benefit from deterring complaints in a number of ways, including preventing damage to their institutional reputation if too many incidents of sexual violence are reported via the Clery Act and preventing civil suits from being brought by students who are determined by the institution to have committed an act or acts of sexual violence. While Anderson points out that the fear of civil suits from students is extremely remote if all policies and procedures in investigating a complaint are followed precisely, the risk of harm to a university's reputation if large numbers of women report their assaults is very real. This prioritization of reputation and prestige encourages HEIs to construct a system in which the less they know about the extent of the problem on their own campus, the better. The Dear Colleague letter of 2011 and the White House Task Force to Protect Students from Sexual Assault, which produced its first report in 2014, have sought to provide more rigorous guidelines for universities and colleges regarding their responsibility to meaningfully engage the crisis of campus sexual violence. However, such policy changes and clarifications of the law have not thus far led to a dramatic rise in sexual violence reporting by students.

A Critical Approach to Sexual Violence Prevention and Response

While the literature has done much to illuminate the scope and breadth of sexual assault and rape in higher education, it has not gone far enough in exposing the multiplicity of competing interests that higher education institutions must contend with when developing and implementing sexual violence prevention and response mechanisms. Furthermore, powerful discourses about sexual violence that are informed by heteronormative and White supremacist constructions of women and ideal victimhood remain largely unquestioned within analyses of prevention policy and programming. Constructing meaningful policy that addresses the concerns of different student groups, negotiating regulations and mandates, promoting rather than discouraging reporting, and implementing effective prevention education programming are just some of the issues that the essays in this volume contend with. Rather than continuing to reproduce the same systems of thought about sexual violence that have been encoded into the literature for decades, this volume is a critical interrogation of higher education with a focus on shifting the conversation. The authors contribute a vast amount of professional experience in negotiating and observing the dynamics of sexual violence prevention in higher education that have thus far constrained essential change and ultimately make a substantial contribution to what is known about how institutions are, and are not, rising to the challenge of protecting and advocating for the safety of their students.

In Chapter 2, Susan V. Iverson conducts a critical policy discourse analysis on sexual assault policies in higher education. She contends that for institutions of higher education to truly address the problem of sexual assault,[2] in reality as much as in perception, colleges and universities must consider how the problem

of sexual assault is portrayed. Her chapter examines the text of sexual assault policies to investigate embedded assumptions and predominant meanings constructed
through the policies. Her study was designed to understand the "effects of policy
proposals and the representations they necessarily contain" (Bacchi, 1999, p. 13).
The use of assumptive concepts in language may limit a policy's effectiveness and
actually reinscribe the very problem the policy seeks to alleviate (Allan, 2007;
Allan, Iverson, & Ropers-Huilman, 2010; Bacchi, 1999; Ball, 1990; Scheurich,
1994). Iverson concludes that if the construction of solutions diverts attention
away from understanding the complexity of campus sexual assault, then incidence
of sexual assault will not be reduced.

Sara Carrigan Wooten illuminates the ways in which universities and colleges
construct and (re)produce a specifically heterosexist discourse of sexual violence
in Chapter 3. The discourse is made manifest through various "sites" in higher
education, including prevention programming materials and resources such as
rape aggression defense trainings. This chapter examines the historical production of this discourse, beginning with a discussion of foundational second wave
feminist texts that sought to raise awareness about women's experiences with rape
and sexual assault. By attending to this history, this research connects how scholarship on sexual violence became the impetus for legal and policy changes that
continue to guide present understandings of rape and sexual assault in higher
education. This chapter surfaces possibilities for more transformative and holistic
interventions into sexual violence prevention programming and policy in higher
education, as the messages contained within the discourse have material consequences for resource allocation. Ultimately, Wooten asserts that effective support
measures for all students regarding sexual violence must consider the dominant
ideologies that pervade present understandings of what sexual violence is, who can
perpetuate it, and who can experience it.

Susan Marine explores the historical and ideological specificities of the effort
to combat sexual violence in the Ivy League in Chapter 4. After serving as a
leader on the issue for ten years at both Dartmouth and Harvard colleges, she
offers a unique "insider's" perspective on the challenges and opportunities inherent in creating and advancing the work of sexual violence at two of America's
most revered colleges. The traditions and legacies of the Ivies cast a long shadow
in American higher education, and for this reason, deconstruction of the processes by which these colleges came to terms with the "problem" of sexual assault
yields important lessons about how institutional identity shapes efforts to combat
sexual violence. This chapter examines the impact that Dartmouth and Harvard
policies, practices, and political nuances have had for the execution of meaningful
sexual assault prevention efforts on college campuses nationwide. Marine demonstrates how close and public scrutiny of these institutions' practices by a diverse
set of commentators including alumni stakeholders, the Office of Civil Rights,
and local and national feminist activists had a significant impact on the shaping of policy and practice, despite abundant evidence that Ivies are inherently

patriarchal and particularly resistant to change. In addition to examining the key events, influencers, and resultant policies and programmatic developments, Marine also reflects upon her experiences working with survivors at these institutions and the social and cultural milieu that shaped (and often stunted) their ability to continue to graduation and to obtain the ultimate reward for their perseverance—a degree from an Ivy. Both the promising practices and difficult or harmful actions observed by the author comprise a complex narrative about privilege, power, and progress in the Ivy League.

In Chapter 5, Todd W. Crosset recounts lessons gleaned from his experience serving as an expert witness in three separate Title IX cases brought by women who had been sexually assaulted during their time in college by university football players. He identifies the tension between the substantial role that athletic departments play in developing the public reputation of a university at the same time that they operate in distinct ways from other campus departments, posing unique challenges for administrative oversight and management. The chapter begins by exploring the connections between a sociological understanding of sexual assault and the law. In particular the sociological contention "that group structure and processes, rather than individual characteristics, are the impetus for many rape episodes" (Martin & Hummer, 1989) and that "rape prone cultures" (Sanday, 1981) are socially constructed is considered in light of the legal concept of "hostile environment." The chapter then employs three cases to identify ways in which some institutions unwittingly contribute to the cultivation of rape-prone subcultures in their athletic departments, the ways institutions failed to address the unique issues facing athletic departments, and finally, some of the mistakes universities make when responding to complaints against athletes. The chapter concludes with suggestions of some preventative actions to mitigate the likelihood of Title IX cases resulting from athlete-perpetrated sexual assaults and to address factors inherent in college athletics, which are also associated with higher rates of sexual assault.

In Chapter 6, Alison Kiss and Kiersten N. Feeney White examine the impact of the Jeanne Clery Disclosure of Campus Security Policy and Campus Crime Statistics Act and Title IX Education Amendments of 1972, with particular emphasis on three perspectives of compliance with these two federal laws: ethical, technical, and practical. A predisposition for technical and practical application of these laws by higher education institutions indicates a narrow, procedural comprehension of the Clery Act, as opposed to an ethical commitment (White, 2013). The authors assert that incidents of sexual violence magnify the need for campus officials to adopt an "ethic of caring" in relation to campus safety in consideration of Nel Noddings' "ethic of caring" theory that there is a connection to caring, educational decision-making, and one's responsibility for morality, fidelity, and true concern for individuals (Noddings, 1986, 1988, 1992, 1994, 1995). They explore the role that institutional leadership should play in demonstrating an enhanced ethical commitment to campus safety and guiding a positive response to campus crime, in particular sexual assault (Duncan, 2011; Kiss, 2011; White, 2013). This chapter will challenge practitioners to consider developing holistic strategies for organizing a strategic plan for prevention of sexual assault and ethical, technical, and practical compliance with Title IX and the Clery Act (White, 2013).

Brett A. Sokolow, Saundra K. Schuster, W. Scott Lewis, and Daniel C. Swinton examine five of the more vexing, yet related, challenges institutions face in bringing their policies and procedures into compliance with Title IX in Chapter 7. These challenges are as follows:

- Cross-constituency complaints (student-on-faculty, faculty-on-staff, etc.);
- Several to many different processes for resolving complaints accusing students, faculty, staff, unionized employees, etc.;
- Different processes for discrimination complaints than those used to address Title IX-related complaints;
- Incorporating Title IX equity standards into employee-on-employee complaints; and
- Reconciling complaints that include both Title IX-covered behaviors and those standing outside Title IX.

The authors identify an increasingly popular approach to remedy, or at least mitigate, these challenges—the creation and utilization of campus-wide, unified policies and procedures to address all civil rights-based complaints. Making frequent reference to guidance offered by the Office for Civil Rights and Caselaw, the authors identify compliance approaches and the at times competing guidance offered by the courts and the federal government. The authors further address the relative strengths and weaknesses presented by a unified set of policies and procedures, including the implementation complications and hurdles institutions may face. This chapter concludes with recommendations for application of a unified set of policies and processes.

In Chapter 8, Nancy Chi Cantalupo discusses the consequences for student survivors of sexual violence when higher education institutions conflate civil proceedings with criminal law. Cantalupo analyzes Title IX of the Education Amendments Act of 1972, the Jeanne Clery Disclosure of Campus Security Policy and Campus Crime Statistics Act, and U.S. constitutional law precedents governing the administrative due process rights of students who are accused of perpetrating sexual violence. All three of these regimes regulate the handling by educational institutions of sexual violence committed against a school's students. None of these three legal regimes is based in criminal law, nor are they enforced by criminal courts. Rather, all are enforced by federal administrative agencies or by civil courts. However, because sexual violence often also violates state criminal laws, members of the general public, including those who serve as school officials, have a tendency to conflate and confuse these federal laws with state criminal laws. The first part of this chapter reviews in detail how this tendency to conflate and confuse has serious, negative implications for sexual violence victims and violates their rights under federal law. In order to avoid these negative consequences, in the second part of the chapter Cantalupo suggests several methods for keeping criminal proceedings separate from administrative and civil proceedings but also coordinating such parallel proceedings in the instances where a victim wishes to pursue both options for redress.

Traci Thomas-Card and Katie Eichele identify key components to consider in developing a comprehensive campus-based sexual violence program in Chapter 9. The chapter begins with an overview of critical policy and protocol development that must be implemented to ensure the longevity of sexual violence prevention in higher education, such as institutional definitions for sexual assault, dating violence, domestic violence, and stalking that the Campus SaVE Act provided. The authors identify three pillars of a successful campus-based sexual violence program: 1) direct services for victim/survivors and concerned persons; 2) topics and methods for an engaging education program; and 3) the process for developing strong peer advocates and leaders. An outline of direct services is provided that addresses crisis counseling, medical advocacy, housing advocacy, academic advocacy, reporting to law enforcement, navigating the criminal justice system, and maintaining a list of on-campus and community resources for referrals. Recommendations are made regarding successful funding strategies, outreach and community building, and program implementation.

In Chapter 10, Caitlin B. Henriksen, Kelsey L. Mattick, and Bonnie S. Fisher critically examine the effectiveness of the federal government's responses to reduce opportunities for sexual violence among college students in light of three decades of research. First, what researchers know about the occurrence of sexual violence, intimate partner violence (IPV) and dating violence (DV) and stalking experienced by college students is described to provide a context to understand responses. Strategies that have been implemented to address these concerns are detailed as well as what is (un)known about their effectiveness to reduce opportunities for sexual violence, IPV/DV, and stalking. This chapter explores the components of the newly mandated strategy, bystander intervention, and critically assesses whether bystander intervention is the "right" prevention strategy for campus administration to implement to reduce sexual violence among their students.

Finally, Rebecca Ropers-Huilman, Kaaren M. Williamsen, and Garrett Drew Hoffman close the book with their thoughtful afterword, which highlights the overlapping themes across the chapters within this volume. These themes include the multiple "scripts" that institutional leadership, educators, or survivors are often compelled to perform in relation to incidents of campus sexual violence, as well as prevention and response strategies.

Collectively, these essays point to major areas of present institutional limitations that prevent, inhibit, or challenge adequate and appropriate response to the ongoing crisis of sexual violence in higher education. They represent a new approach to understanding this crisis—that of examining the real complexity of negotiating competing interests and responsibilities, political influences, and legal mandates facing higher education leadership. By holistically examining these pressures, this volume imparts a fresh perspective and offers new insights to a growing body of work centered on how best to help students who have been raped and sexually assaulted. We hope that by situating this project within the work that has been done on prevalence rates, incidence types, risk factors, and opportunities for institutional response, we will expand and improve the increasingly public dialogue on how to combat sexual violence in higher education.

Ultimately, this volume should spur more difficult questions than it answers. How are sexual violence prevention policies impacting students of color? How are these policies serving, or not serving, lesbian, gay, bisexual, transgender, and queer students? Are male students able to access university resources that reflect their experiences of sexual assault and rape? Are we expanding locations of help within the institution beyond women's resource centers and student health centers? Beyond bystander intervention programs and incoming student seminars, how are institutions engaging in a holistic reckoning regarding campus rape culture? One book cannot stand alone in critically examining how sexual violence prevention and response in higher education is operating. We look forward to continuing a rich and generative conversation that goes far beyond the pages of this book and to being inspired by the scholarship of others who take up this call.

Notes

1. The PETSA program name places its emphasis on personal awareness, implying that sexual violence can be prevented through hyper self-vigilance of would-be victims, a trope that has been accused of reaffirming victim blaming in sexual violence prevention.
2. Iverson's use of the term "sexual assault" also refers to rape. A recent trend in sexual assault policies in higher education is to refer to such acts as sexual misconduct; this term includes rape, sexual harassment, and sexual exploitation. For the purpose of this volume, she will use the term "sexual assault" as inclusive of all of these behaviors, unless she denotes otherwise or uses direct quotes. When referring to violence against women, Iverson is including those elements covered by the Violence Against Women Office—sexual assault, relationship violence, and stalking.

References

Allan, E. J. (2007). *Policy discourses, gender and education: Constructing women's status*. New York: Routledge.

Allan, E. J., Iverson, S. V., & Ropers-Huilman, R. (Eds.). (2010). *Reconstructing policy analysis in higher education: Feminist poststructural perspectives*. New York: Routledge.

Anderson, M. J. (2004). *The legacy of the prompt complaint requirement, corroboration requirement, and cautionary instructions on campus sexual assault*. Villanova University School of Law Working Paper Series 20, Villanova, PA.

Bacchi, C. L. (1999). *Women, policy and politics: The construction of policy problems*. Thousand Oaks, CA: Sage.

Ball, S. J. (Ed.). (1990). *Foucault and education: Disciplines and knowledge*. New York: Routledge.

Baum, K., & Klaus, P. (2005). Violent victimization of college students, 1995–2002. National Crime Victimization Survey. Retrieved from www.ocpa-oh.org/Campus%20Safety/Violent%20Victimization%20of%20College%20Students.pdf

Duncan, A. (2011, December 14). Column: End double standards in sex abuse cases. *USA Today*. Retrieved from www.usatoday.com/news/opinion/forum/story/2011–12–14/penn-syracuse-abuse-investigation/51918148/1

Fisher, B. S., Cullen, F. T., & Turner, M. G. (2000). *The sexual victimization of college women* (NCJ 182369). Washington, DC: U.S. Department of Justice, Office of Justice Programs.

Karjane, H. M., Fisher, B. S., & Cullen, F. T. (2005). *Sexual assault on campus: What colleges and universities are doing about it*. Washington, DC: U.S. Department of Justice, Office of Justice Programs.

Kiss, A. (2011, November 23). Re: Campus safety rests on community engagement [Web log message]. Retrieved from http://www.educationnation.com

Koss, M. P., Gidycz, C. A., & Wisniewski, N. (1987). The scope of rape: Incidence and prevalence of sexual aggression and victimization in a national sample of higher education students. *Journal of Consulting and Clinical Psychology, 55*(2), 162–170.

Martin, P. Y., & Hummer, R. A. (1989). Fraternities and rape on campus. *Gender & Society, 3*(4), 457–473.

Noddings, N. (1986). Fidelity in teaching, teacher education, and research for teaching. *Harvard Educational Review, 56*(4), 496–511.

Noddings, N. (1988). An ethic of caring and its implications for instructional arrangements. *American Journal of Education, 96*(2), 215–230.

Noddings, N. (1992). *Challenge to care in schools: An administrative approach to education*. New York: Teachers College Press.

Noddings, N. (1994). The role of educators in combatting violence. *Religious Education, 89*(4), 568–571.

Noddings, N. (1995). A morally defensible mission for schools in the 21st century. *Phi Delta Kappan, 76*(5), 365–368.

Sanday, P. R. (1981). The socio-cultural context of rape: A cross-cultural study. *Journal of Social Issues, 37*(4), 5–27.

Scheurich, J. J. (1994). Policy archaeology: A new policy studies methodology. *Journal of Educational Policy, 9*(4), 297–316.

U.S. Department of Justice. (2002). Bureau of Justice Statistics. *National Crime Victimization Survey*. [Record-Type Files]. ICPSR22902-v2. Ann Arbor, MI: Inter-university Consortium for Political and Social Research [distributor], 2008-12-10. doi:10.3886/ICPSR22902.v2. Binghamton, NY: The Haworth Press.

White, K. N. (2013). *The influence of "Clery Act Training Seminars" on participants' ethical commitment to campus safety beyond compliance in colleges and universities* (Unpublished doctoral dissertation). Saint Joseph's University, Philadelphia, PA.

PART I
Constructions of Sexual Violence in Higher Education

2

A POLICY DISCOURSE ANALYSIS OF SEXUAL ASSAULT POLICIES IN HIGHER EDUCATION

Susan V. Iverson

Sexual violence continues to occur at an alarming rate on college campuses across the United States (Baum & Klaus, 2005; Frazier, Anders, Perera, Tomich, Tennen, Park, & Tashiro, 2009; Karjane, Fisher, & Cullen, 2005; Paul & Gray, 2011). Typical solutions to the problem of sexual violence—disciplinary procedures, educational interventions, and support services for victims—have not reduced the incidence of sexual violence. Many studies have been conducted examining the effectiveness of sexual violence prevention efforts in higher education (Ahrens, Rich, & Ullman, 2011; Exner & Cummings, 2011; Gidycz, Orchowski, & Berkowitz, 2011; Moynihan, Banyard, Arnold, Eckstein, & Stapleton, 2011). While such studies are useful in their description of prevention approaches and the effectiveness of such approaches, a gap remains in the literature regarding the role of policy as a solution to the problem of interpersonal violence (Jackson, Bouffard, & Fox, 2013) and specifically sexual violence on campus.

Policy, as a solution to sexual violence, has developed over the last two decades largely in response to federal legislation. The Jeanne Clery Disclosure of Campus Security Policy and Campus Crime Statistics Act has made a particular impact on U.S. institutions of higher education. This federal law, first enacted by Congress as the Campus Security Act in 1990, requires institutions of higher education in the United States to disclose campus security information including crime statistics for the campus and surrounding areas. Several articles regarding institutional compliance with the Clery Act (Cantalupo, 2011; Janosik & Gregory, 2009; Lowery, 1995; Murphy, Arnold, Hansen, & Mertler, 2001) have examined the efficacy of the Clery Act and provided useful insights regarding the utility of reporting and its impact on student behavior regarding safety. However, different from those legislative or policy studies, this inquiry, which employs the method of policy discourse analysis, examines what has been discursively produced by sexual violence policies.

For institutions of higher education to truly address the problem of sexual violence, in reality as much as in perception, colleges and universities must consider how the problem of sexual violence is portrayed. This chapter is designed to understand the "effects of policy proposals and the representations they necessarily contain" (Bacchi, 1999, p. 13). The use of assumptive concepts in language may limit a policy's effectiveness and actually reinscribe the very problem the policy seeks to alleviate (Allan, 2008; Allan, Iverson, & Ropers-Huilman, 2010; Bacchi, 1999; Ball, 1990; Scheurich, 1994). If the construction of solutions diverts attention away from understanding the complexity of campus sexual violence, then incidence of sexual violence will not be reduced. This chapter shares findings from an investigation of sexual violence policies[1] to uncover embedded assumptions and predominant meanings constructed through the policies.

Conceptual Framework

Policy Analysis

A variety of approaches to the study of policy exist. The dominant, conventional— sometimes called "rational"—approach to policy analysis views policymaking principally as a process of problem-solving; it involves "description, explanation, and prediction of issues" (Hawkesworth, 1988, p. 2). Policymakers employ formulaic steps in policymaking, and decisions are assumed to be "relatively straightforward" and are "clearly formulated in advance"—meaning the problem which the policy seeks to resolve is accepted as an unquestioned, objective fact, and attention is instead focused on identifying solutions to the given problem (Bacchi, 1999, p. 18).

Critiques of conventional approaches to policy analysis (Bacchi, 1999; Ball, 1990; Marshall, 2000; Scheurich, 1994; Walton, 2010) argue that such policy approaches are "responding to 'problems' that exist 'out there' in the community" rather than investigating how such "'problems' are 'created' or 'given shape' in the very policy proposals that are offered as 'responses'" (Bacchi, 2000, p. 48). Such rationalist approaches to policymaking and analysis often fail to examine underlying and often taken-for-granted assumptions about solutions embedded within how a problem is represented and the implications for these representations (Allan, 2008; Allan et al., 2010; Bacchi, 2000; Iverson, 2012). Alternatives, such as critical (inclusive of feminist) educational policy studies, have emerged.

I align with those who adopt critical/feminist approaches to policy analysis to study the *construction* of policy problems rather than the development of policy solutions with an uncritical acceptance of the problem (Allan et al., 2010; Bacchi, 2000; Bensimon & Marshall, 2003; Scheurich, 1994; Winton, 2013). Policy, from a critical/feminist perspective, is understood as "complex, inherently political, and infused with values" (Winton, 2013, p. 159). Further, critical policy analysis acknowledges policy as a site of power: policy texts "appear stable and coherent but are . . . continually up for negotiation and re-negotiation . . . [and] people in roles of educational authority . . . tend to play a larger role in policy development" (Walton, 2010, p. 136). They emerge as what Foucault (1977/1995) would call regimes of truth; they "typically posit a restructuring, redistribution and disruption of power relations, so that different people can and cannot do different things" (Ball, 1993, p. 13). Such approaches highlight ways in which power operates through policy by drawing attention to hidden assumptions or policy silences and unintended consequences of policy practices (Allan, 2003; Bacchi, 1999; Scheurich, 1994). These perspectives also help to raise important questions about the control and production of knowledge and the ways policy can be used to empower individuals to act upon/in their environment to challenge dominant ideology (Ball, 1993; Marshall, 1999). This analysis of sexual violence policies follows the work of those who conceptualize policy-as-discourse: "policies as discursive and/or textual interventions that produce effects within formal organizations" (Allan, 2008, p. 31; Bacchi, 2000; Shaw, 2010; Winton, 2013).

Policy-as-Discourse

A *policy-as-discourse* approach seeks to understand and explain "the means by which social processes and interactions shape different realities" (Shaw, 2010, p. 200). The term *discourse* is often misunderstood; it gets (mis)used as "shorthand for 'ways of talking' about an issue" (Bacchi, 2005, p. 198). Rather, my use of discourse, informed by the work of Foucault (1977/1995), signals "ways of thinking, which may overlap and reinforce each other and close off other possible ways of thinking" (Shore & Wright, 1997, p. 18).

Discourses are never neutral; some discourses are taken up more readily than others and, as such, become dominant. Dominant discourses are reaffirmed through their institutionalization and can be identified most easily by the way in which they have become taken for granted (Allan, 2003; Bacchi, 2000; Mills, 1997). For instance, Bacchi (2004) describes two competing discourses of affirmative action: a dominant discourse of affirmative action as "preferential treatment" and a less visible discourse of affirmative action as "social justice" (p. 129). Dominant discourses shape and affect policy efforts and the potential for meaningful change and can have (unintentional) "deleterious effects" and render reform efforts as ineffective (Bacchi, 2004, pp. 135–136).

Discourses both construct and constrain "possibilities of thought" (Ball, 1990, p. 2); they are "about what can be said, and thought, but also about who can speak, when, where and with what authority" (Ball, 1990, pp. 17–18). Further, Foucaldian theory of discourse constructs particular social identities, or subjectivities, that we take up. Our identity position—or subjectivity—refers to "our ways of being an individual" (Weedon, 1997, p. 21); positions we are both "subjected to" and internalize, or take up, through discourse (Foucault, 1980). For instance, mother, victim, professional, and ally are all identity positions that one might occupy. These identity positions are produced through discourse, and we inhabit or perform them (Allan, 2008).

Discursive Construction of the Problem of Sexual Violence

Several scholars have examined the ways in which discourses operate to re/produce the problem of violence against women[2] (Alcoff & Gray, 1993; Bacchi, 1999; Cahill, 2000; Eyre, 2000; Ferraro, 1996; Heberle, 1996; Hengehold, 1994, 2000; Pollack, 1990; Woodhull, 1988). Dominant constructions of sexual violence frame the problem more often as something that a woman experiences, rather than something a man does (Cahill, 2000), e.g., representing women as "victims of domestic violence [rather than] survivors of male violence" (Bacchi, 1999, p. 190). Interventions and prevention efforts tend to individualize the problem as "personal or natural behavior" (Bacchi, 1999, p. 184), rather than treat sexual and interpersonal violence as "systemic," "structural," and "institutional" problems (Bacchi, 1999; Hengehold, 1994). Additionally, as evidenced in analyses of rape prevention efforts, gender discourses shape images of men as abusers (and heroes) and women as vulnerable and victims; and (unwittingly) naturalize men's physical power to rape and women's vulnerability (Iverson, 2006; McCaughey & King, 1995; see also Fine, 1988, on sexuality education). Allan (2003) too, in her analysis of the text of women's commission reports issued at four research universities, identified (among her findings) a dominant discourse of femininity that "reinforces male dominance and heterosexism by shaping femininity in ways that promote women's appeal to and dependence on men" (Allan, 2003, p. 52); this situates women as violable, weak, fearful, and a "potential object of male anger, aggression, and violence" (Allan, 2003, p. 53).

Yet, "discourses are plural, not singular"; meaning, individuals inhabit multiple and competing subjectivities that contain "tensions and inconsistencies" but which also provide "openings for contestation" (Bacchi, 2004, p. 141). Thus, alternative discourses, and subjectivities constituted discursively, are available. For instance, several scholars have illuminated ways in which discourses can be constraining, repressive and isolating but also be resistant and oppositional (Alcoff & Gray, 1993; Heberle, 1996; Hengehold, 2000). For instance, Heberle (1996) illuminates the paradox of women's identification as victims, which reinscribes the gendered norms, enabling victimization of women. Yet, if rape is conceived of as a script (rather than an event), then it can be interrupted and rewritten. For example, women can engage in disruptive speech, e.g., including stories at Take Back the Night rallies from "women who self-identify as having successfully resisted assault" (Heberle, 1996, p. 72; see also Alcoff & Gray, 1993). Prospects for change are contingent upon "creating discursive conditions in which survivors' own voices will be heard and their views and concerns taken as legitimate" (Westlund, 1999, p. 1062).

Methods

This investigation utilized the method of *policy discourse analysis* to investigate university policies on sexual violence to understand how these documents frame the problem of sexual violence. A hybrid methodology developed by Allan (2008), policy discourse analysis is a strategy for examining policy discourses and the ways they come together to make particular perspectives more prominent than others. This approach "highlights the discursive power of policy by investigating the written text of policy documents as primary data sources . . . [and focusing] on the assumptions embedded in the naming of policy problems and solutions" (Allan, 2003, p. 49). Further, Allan (2008) explains that policy discourse analysis is "specifically designed to respond to research questions related to the discursive shaping of policy problems, solutions and images; and the ways in which discourses shape and re/produce subject positions" (p. 54).

Employing the method of policy discourse analysis, the following questions guided this study:

* What are the predominant images of women and men in sexual violence policies?
* What discourses are employed to shape these images?
* What identity positions are discursively re/produced for women and men on campus?

Sample and Data Collection

The sample for this study consisted of 22 sexual violence policies from 22 recipients[3] of 2012 U.S. Department of Justice's Office of Violence against Women (DOJ-OVW) campus grants (see Table 1.1). My rationale for this sampling strategy was that these 22 campuses, as recipients of federal funds to address sexual violence on their campuses, have (or are conducting revisions of) sexual violence policies. I did not assume these were model policies or reflected best practices; rather, these campuses are known to be committing focused (and funded) efforts to the problem of sexual violence on their campuses. Further, collecting policies from the 22 DOJ-OVW campus grant recipients enabled a cross-section of various institutional types, ranging from Christian 4-year colleges (i.e., Samford University) to an historically Black college (i.e., Virginia State University), from public research universities (i.e., University of North Carolina at Chapel Hill) to a community college (i.e., Joliet Junior College).

With the list of 22 grant recipients, I conducted a search of the web site for each campus, using the search function and keywords: sexual violence (or misconduct or assault) policy. All had content related to sexual violence (from policies to prevention efforts); however, six campuses had bad links or no evidence of a policy. Follow up emails and phone calls yielded further documents and helpful

TABLE 2.1 Sexual Violence Policies Used for Study

Institution	State	Sexual Misconduct Policies
Samford University	Alabama	Title IX Sexual Misconduct Policy (2012–13)
Humboldt State University	California	Policy Against Sexual Harassment and Sexual Assault (2005)
University of California, Merced	California	Sexual Harassment Policy (2006) and Protocol (2012)
Gallaudet University	District of Columbia (DC)	Sexual Misconduct Policy (2013–14)
Joliet Junior College	Illinois	Title IX Policy on Sexual Harassment and Assault (2012)
Loyola University, Chicago	Illinois	Sexual Misconduct Policy (n.d.)
Wheaton College	Illinois	Sexual Assault Policy (n.d.)
Clark University	Massachusetts	Sexual Violence Policy (n.d.)
College of St. Scholastica	Minnesota	Sexual Assault and Violence Policy (n.d.)
University of Mississippi	Mississippi	Sexual Misconduct Policy (2012–13)
University of Montana	Montana	Policy on Discrimination, Harassment, Sexual Misconduct, Stalking, and Retaliation (2013)
SUNY-Stony Brook	New York	Sexual Harassment Policy (2008)
North Carolina Central University	North Carolina	Sexual Violence Policy
University of North Carolina at Chapel Hill	North Carolina	Policy on Prohibited Harassment, Including Sexual Misconduct and Discrimination (2013)
Minot State University	North Dakota	Policy on Harassment (2008)
Ohio University	Ohio	Sexual Misconduct Policy (2012)
Bucknell University	Pennsylvania	Sexual Misconduct and Relationship Violence Policy (2013–14)
University of Tennessee at Martin	Tennessee	Sexual Misconduct (n.d.)
North Central Texas College	Texas	Freedom from Discrimination, Harassment, and Retaliation Policy (2010)
Old Dominion University	Virginia	Sexual Misconduct Policy (2011)
Virginia State University	Virginia	Sexual Misconduct Policy (2009)
Fairmont State University	West Virginia	Policy on Sexual Assault (n.d.)

confirmation that one-page policies I had identified were indeed the sole policy document. All 22 institutions had something, ranging from lean policies (i.e., 1–3 pages), to comprehensive policies (i.e., 23–48 pages); however, the average policy length was 8–9 pages.

Situating Self

Before describing my analytic process, I briefly describe my role as an "instrument" in the research process (Guba & Lincoln, 1981); I reveal for the reader how my personal self and experience informs the research process. For more than 15 years, I worked as an administrator at four institutions of higher education. During this time, I worked as a judicial officer, adjudicating sexual assault cases. I was also a trained victim's advocate and volunteered at a rape crisis center. I developed a victim's advocacy program at one institution and have been involved in countless educational programs and presentations about violence against women in an effort to increase awareness. I also revised or authored sexual assault policies at four institutions. My work in this arena spanned from 1989–1990, when I served on a policy development committee and helped establish a campus victim's advocate program, concurrent with the issuing of the 1990 Campus Security Act, to 2003–2006 when I worked for a project funded by a DOJ-OVW campus grant, drafting policies on sexual misconduct, stalking, and relationship abuse. I am committed to policies and educational efforts to address sexual violence on campus and view such efforts as a (potential) vehicle for change. Further, as a feminist, I am committed to ending violence against women. These experiences provided me with an "insider's" perspective for this inquiry. However, these advantages are accompanied by the limitation of potential researcher bias. Recognizing this, I worked throughout the research process to remain attentive to my assumptions in order to enhance my examination of the data.

Analytic Process

This study employed the Allan's method of policy discourse analysis (see full explanation in Allan, 2008, pp. 58–64). The first phase of the analytic process involved line-by-line analysis of each policy to identify and code *images* of women and men in the sexual violence policies. Examples of initial codes included victim, perpetrator, fear, reasonable, dependence, autonomous, scared, and intimidated. The second phase of coding involved an inductive reading of each policy for that which was meaningful to which I assigned codes that were both descriptive and interpretive (Miles & Huberman, 1994). Codes were then clustered according to common themes to generate image categories and identify identity positions that emerged from these images. I then re-read and coded all 22 documents in response to the following research question: what discourses are employed to shape the predominant images? In this phase of the analytic process, I also examined the identity positions that emerged; I asked *who* is produced?—meaning what subject positions are discursively constituted, or rather, what social identities can be taken up or inhabited by individuals. This multi-phased and layered approach to data analysis was important, enabling me to examine the data on multiple levels: reading individual policies deductively and inductively, analyzing segments of text in their original text, then out of context, and in relation to other documents provided an opportunity to see patterns and themes within and among the sexual violence policies and enabling me to examine consistencies and inconsistencies across institutions.

Findings

Analysis of the sexual violence policies revealed a discourse of risk, producing the subjectivities of being both *at-risk* and a *risk manager*. The individual (typically women) is at-risk, vulnerable to sexual violence; yet, the institution too is at risk due to the ubiquity of sexual violence on campus. Institutional agents must manage this risk by managing reporting of offenses. Further, a discourse of dependency, intersecting with the discourse of risk, constructs the *dependent victim*, reliant on the institution to keep her/him safe and provide support. Additionally, a discourse of rationality, which gives rise to the *reasonable person*, intersects with the discourse of risk, enabling the risk manager to objectively evaluate and act upon complaints of sexual violence.

Institutionalized Vocabularies

First, some observations about the policies as preface to my description and discussion of these findings. Each policy was unique. While some elements (i.e., consent-based language, protections against retaliation) and some phrases (e.g., defining sexual harassment as "unwelcome" and sexual exploitation as "intentional") were shared across most policies, these reflect "an institutionalization of . . . vocabularies" (Thapar-Bjorkert & Morgan, 2010, p. 50), rather than a standardization of policies. In fact, I was surprised by the lack of uniformity, considering that the Clery Act prescribes required elements of policies. Some institutions, for instance, do not include the basic requirements, such as procedures to be followed once an offense has occurred, disciplinary procedures and possible sanctions, and educational programming.

Institutionalized vocabularies are most evident in the adoption of consent-based language for defining sexual violence. Consent language became infamous in 1991 when Antioch College incorporated the "verbal and willing" definition into its sexual violence policy, fueling an avalanche of commentary, including even a *Saturday Night Live* parody ("Ask First" at Antioch, 1993). Consent-based definitions are nearly universal in policies today; however, (former) resistance-based definitions (e.g., use of force, against one's will), which dominate legal definitions, remain in policies as well. Sometimes these—consent and resistance—both exist in the same policy. For instance, Wheaton's policy defines sexual assault as "forcing, threatening, or coercing an individual into sexual contact against the individual's free will with or without the individual's consent." My question, however, was *who* is produced, and concealed, by policy texts; what subject positions are discursively constituted?

Discourse of Risk

A discourse of risk pervades the policies, producing the subjectivity of being both *at-risk* and a *risk manager*. Notably, these subject positions are available not only to individuals encountering sexual violence (i.e., the at-risk victim) but also institutional agents, who manage the ever-present risk of sexual violence on their campuses.

At-Risk

Sexual violence, the policies assert, is "severe and pervasive," "a serious violation," "one of the most serious violations," "a form of personal violence that affects all of us." Thus, (ungendered) individuals must prepare themselves to defend against potential violence to their bodies, which are inscribed as "always already rapable" (Heberle, 1996). Yet, those policies that provide statistics regarding who is typically a victim, reveal that "1 in 4" college women, under age 25, is the victim of sexual assault or attempted sexual assault (e.g., Bucknell University; Clark University; University of Tennessee at Martin; Virginia State University). Thus, college *women* are at-risk to "being physically or mentally incapacitated," to being "taken advantage of," to induced incapacity due to "the taking of a so-called 'date rape' drug," to "unwanted," "deliberate," "unwelcome," and "intentional" touching, contact, coercion, assault, exploitation, and numerous other offenses. A discourse of risk constructs women as physically and emotionally vulnerable: at-risk. Yet, this discourse also situates institutional agents as risk managers.

Risk Manager

Sexual violence is ubiquitous on college campuses—as on policy asserts, "sexual assault is a problem on campus" (University of Tennessee at Martin). And universities must manage the risks associated with sexual violence in the same way a fraternity is expected to manage the risk of having alcohol at a chapter event. Universities, well-educated on the rules for compliance with Title IX and Clery Act, provide education to students, but also "training and information" to university personnel and clear procedures are delineated in several policies for responding to a report of sexual misconduct, including any consequences for failure to respond (e.g., the Ohio University policy communicates to employees that it is a "criminal offense to fail to report" an incident of sexual misconduct).

Many policies assert that the university can initiate a complaint of sexual misconduct when it learns of an offense; however, this initiative is rarely (if ever) taken and the burden lies with the victim to report. The policies frame the victim's obligation in many ways, such as encouragement to report (Joliet Junior College; UNC-Chapel Hill; Wheaton College), for, as Samford's policy states, reports are "best if filed by the victim." It is also, several policies argue, in the "best interest of the community" for the victim to report (Clark University; University of Montana; College of St. Scholastica). Policies encourage reporting "ASAP" and tell victims "do NOT wait" (University of Montana; also UNC-Chapel Hill; College of St. Scholastica; Wheaton College) and observe that reporting is "worth the effort" (Gallaudet University). The discourse of risk produces the at-risk victim turning to an institutional agent seeking to manage that "risky subject." The at-risk victim then is dependent on the institution (its agents) for support—the same site that failed to keep them safe from the ubiquity of sexual violence.

The Dependent Victim: Discourse of Dependency

A discourse of dependency shapes the dependent victim subject position by providing that women need to be provided for and protected by the institution. A discourse of dependency situates victims as reliant on others, namely university personnel, to mediate their experience, support them, and keep them safe (Allan, 2003). For instance, policies, as exemplified by this data excerpt from Wheaton's policy, assert that "victims . . . [should] seek counseling and/or identify a support person. A support person plays an important role in providing personal encouragement to a victim in a crisis situation." Some, as stated in St. Scholastica's policy, advocate that victims, "Get to a safe place as soon as you can and contact a close friend who can be with you as long as you need her/him. Your friend can assist you in finding an advocate."

Advocacy for victims getting support is intertwined with institutional assurances of protection (*after* the sexual violence has occurred). For instance, Samford's policy states "the University will undertake an appropriate inquiry and take prompt and effective action to *support and protect* the complainant" (italics added). Gallaudet's policy asserts it "will not wait for the conclusion of any criminal investigation or proceedings to commence its own investigation and will take interim measures to *protect the complainant and the community*, if necessary" (emphasis added). Most policies assure victims they will also be protected from any retaliatory harassment.

Notably, the university as protector of the dependent victim emerges *after* the assault has occurred. While universities provide "preventive and risk education and training" (Gallaudet University), sexual misconduct emerges as *always already* present. Universities will provide "medical care, reporting options, and emotional support services for victims of sexual misconduct. . . . [E]mpowering victims is critical to the healing process and as such [the university] supports an individual's decision to move forward (or not) with a criminal charge, protective order, and/ or complaint of sexual misconduct" (Old Dominion University). The dependent victim then is in need of protection and rescue; is reduced to a state of passivity; the complainant's experience is contingent upon expert interpretation, requires therapeutic intervention, and must be mediated by others, ideally experts to give authority and legitimacy to the victim's experience (Phipps, 2010; Westlund, 1999). Joliet's policy exemplifies this when it invites any student to contact a Title IX officer when, "in good faith," you "believe you may have experienced harassment or assault, but are unsure of whether it was a violation of policy." Victims (women) are situated as passive and thus dependent on a masculinist organization for support and protection. This discourse of dependence, constructing the dependent (and at-risk) victim, exists in contrast with a discourse of rationality that affords reason to the risk manager.

The Reasonable Person: Discourse of Rationality

The reasonable person is a legal standard for determining:

> Whether certain kinds of behavior should be deemed harmful or offensive and thus punishable. The 'reasonable person' is supposed to represent community norms; thus whatever would offend or harm 'a reasonable person' is said to be more generally offensive or harmful.
>
> *(Ehrlich, 1999, p. 250)*

This standard of reasonableness operates in sexual violence policies as well; they adopt the "reasonable person" standard for evaluating whether offenses of sexual misconduct "would cause a *reasonable person* to feel fear" (Loyola University, italics added) or would "place the other person in reasonable fear of bodily injury or cause substantial emotional distress" (Bucknell University). One policy exemplifies how the reasonable person standard is incorporated into definitions of sexual misconduct:

> Threats exist where a *reasonable person* would have been compelled by the words or actions of another to give permission to sexual activity to which he or she otherwise would not have consented . . . [and] Intimidation exists when *a reasonable person* would feel threatened or coerced even though there may not be any threat made explicitly.
>
> *(University of Mississippi, italics added)*

The reasonable person provides an "objective" standard against which the victim's report can be held. For instance, the University of Montana's policy, in describing standards for evaluating whether an offense has occurred, states "the harassment will be considered not only from the perspective of the individual

who feels harassed, but also from the perspective of a *reasonable person* in a similar situation" (italics added).

The reasonable person, produced by a discourse of rationality, serves to offset the affective realities of sexual violence: a circumstance filled with "fear" and "distress." The objectivity of the "reasonable person" brings reason and logical, cognitive analysis to a subjective experience. As Ohio University's policy articulates, offenses constitute sexual misconduct when they are deemed "sufficiently severe or pervasive from both a subjective (the complainant's) and an objective (reasonable person's) viewpoint." Yet, the use of the reasonable person as the standard for determining offenses of sexual misconduct may have limitations or unintended consequences.

Discussion

Feminist scholars in the 1990s challenged the generalizability of the "reasonable person," arguing that men and women will experience sexual violence differently (Ehrlich, 1999; Hengehold, 1994). One court decision, *Ellison v. Brady* (cited in Ehrlich, 1999), argued that

> [B]ecause women are disproportionately victims of rape and sexual assault, women have a stronger incentive to be concerned with sexual behavior. . . . We adopt the perspective of a reasonable woman primarily because we believe that a sex-blind reasonable person standard tends to be male-biased and tends to systematically ignore the experiences of women.
>
> *(pp. 250–251)*

However, sexual violence policies do not use the "reasonable woman" standard and instead adopt the (ungendered) reasonable person.

Just as rationality dominates the literature on decision-making (Vaccaro, McCoy, Champagne, & Siegel, 2013), androcentric procedures and decision-making function to "promulgate an institution's dominant belief-system" (Ehrlich, 1999, p. 251). Gal (1991) notes that "institutions are far from neutral arenas: They are structured along gender lines, to lend authority not only to reigning classes and ethnic groups but specifically to men's linguistic practices" (p. 197; also Acker, 2006). Thus, discourses of rationality and risk are institutional discourses; however, they are not neutral. They, like the "reasonability" standard, (perhaps unwittingly) frame the criteria for evaluating whether a rape has really occurred. Sexual violence policies, it is important to recall, "represent the university's interests as opposed to any particular individual's interests" (Ehrlich, 1999, p. 251). If (when) the subjective (complainant's) experience is misaligned with the objective (reasonable) view, the "unreasonable conduct" may be reconstructed as consensual sex, or the complainant may be reconstructed as unreasonable, risky, or irresponsible.

Sexual violence also is not ungendered. Presumably in an effort to reject heteronormative descriptions of sexuality, the subjects in sexual violence policies are ungendered or neutrally gendered (meaning "s/he" is used). Sexual victimization occurs in same-sex relationships, and several policies articulate that sexual violence occurs "regardless of sexual orientation" (i.e., University of Mississippi; UNC-Chapel Hill; Bucknell University, University of California, Merced; Joliet Junior College); Clark's policy defines sexual misconduct as offenses committed "by a man or woman upon a man or woman without effective consent." Yet, empirical evidence reports that victims of sexual violence continue to be overwhelmingly female and perpetrators are almost exclusively male.[4]

Writing with the absence of pronouns, policies tend to describe victims (or "alleged victims," Bucknell University) or complainants as individuals who "allege" or "believe" sexual misconduct has been committed; rarely is the term "survivor" used (see Bucknell University; College of St. Scholastica). The "student who violates policy" is described as the "accused" (UNC-Chapel Hill), "alleged offender" (Bucknell University), the "respondent," and rarely the "attacker" (University of Mississippi). More typical are descriptions of sexual misconduct as offensive behaviors without an agent. University of Montana's policy (not uniquely) exemplifies this: "*Sexual Misconduct* includes sexual assault, inducing incapacitation for sexual purposes, sexual exploitation, and relationship violence. *Sexual Assault* means an actual or attempted sexual contact with another person without that person's consent" (italics in original). As evident in the data excerpt, the victim has subjectivity: "another person" and "that person"; however, the person committing the behaviors is invisible. Only Clark's policy situates a subject in its description of sexual misconduct: Addressing the "initiator of the sexual activity," the policy states "do not make assumptions about consent, about someone's sexual availability, about whether they are attracted to you, about how far you can go. . . . Realize that your potential partner could be intimidated by you or fearful. You may have a power advantage because of your size, strength, and/or standing or reputation at the university. Do not abuse that power."

The disembodied misconduct of the "initiator of the sexual activity" is typically little more than a list of behaviors or offenses. The individual who perpetrates sexual violence is largely absent. Consequently, in subtle and insidious ways, the victim becomes the focus of the policy and is the (sexual) subject whose behaviors are evaluated. Did s/he consent or not? Did s/he resist or not? Was s/he incapacitated? Was the sexual contact "unwelcome" or was "pressure" for sex "unreasonable"? This can situate the victim (typically a woman) as *the problem;* the burden of responsibility is placed on women for their victimization (Thapar-Bjorkert & Morgan, 2010). Further, the problem of sexual violence fails to be problematized relative to power/gender relations, and as such, perpetrators are absolved from accountability for their own actions (Allan, 2003; Phipps, 2010; Thapar-Bjorkert & Morgan, 2010).

Future Research

Further research is needed. First, this cross-section of institutional types revealed little institutional-specific considerations relative to sexual violence. For instance, Gallaudet's policy, a university federally chartered for the education of the deaf and hard of hearing, had no unique procedures. Policies for Christian campuses (e.g., Humboldt State University; Samford University) described how sexual violence was inconsistent with the Christian environment; however, professions of "moral commitment" were consistent with how all other policies asserted that sexual violence "subverts" the university mission. Only Wheaton's policy indicates it would make changes in "chapel seating" to "prevent unwanted contact." Inquiry into how, or if, campus policies and procedures for sexual violence adapt to their unique missions would be beneficial.

Expanded discourse analyses to include educational programs and judicial procedures are warranted to discern a fuller picture of the discursive construction of sexual violence on college campuses. Additionally, purposeful selection of policies (or other institutional texts) that might illuminate alternative discourses is needed. For instance, Clark's policy was the only one to explicate how power operates in gaining consent. Also, feminist discourses that give rise to the empowered subject are largely absent from the policies. Only two policies (Bucknell University, College of St. Scholastica) mentioned "survivors" (in addition to references to "victims"), and St. Scholastica's policy is written as if speaking directly to the survivor/victim, e.g., "If you are raped or assaulted, YOU ARE NOT TO BLAME!" (emphasis in original).

Identification, and deployment, of alternative discourses (i.e., empowerment) are needed to illuminate the multiple ways individuals experience sexual violence and exercise their agency. Narrow conceptualizations (i.e., at-risk, dependent victims) reify images of the "perfect victims" (Srikantiah, 2007) and "engage us in an exercise of comparison and contrast about which woman did the right thing" (Heberle, 1996, p. 72). A range of subjectivities exist (i.e., empowered, resistant, assertive, decisive) and must be brought forward to illuminate that individuals respond to incidents of sexual violence in a multiplicity of ways (Iverson, 2006).

In sum, the purpose of this investigation was to enhance understanding of the discourses circulating in sexual violence policies and how these discourses contribute to shaping particular identity positions for men and women to assume. Further, this inquiry adds to the scholarship about how the problem of sexual violence is gendered (Martin & Hummer, 1989; Vandiver & Dupalo, 2013). Hopefully, this chapter will inspire further research about the discursive construction of men and women in sexual violence policies.

Notes

1. My use of the term "sexual violence" is inclusive of rape, sexual assault, sexual exploitation, among other forms of sexual misconduct. Policies in higher education that codify

these behaviors tend to refer to such acts as sexual misconduct. For the purpose of this chapter, I will use the term "sexual violence" as inclusive of all these behaviors, unless I denote otherwise or I use direct quotes. When referring to violence against women, I am including those elements covered by the Violence Against Women Office—sexual assault, relationship violence, and stalking.

2. Broader than sexual violence, the term "violence against women" is inclusive of sexual harassment, rape, domestic violence, stalking, and sexual exploitation.
3. List of grant recipients retrieved July 31, 2013, from www.ovw.usdoj.gov/fy2012-grant-program.htm#2
4. Growing literature (Straus, 2004, 2009) attests to female abuse of males in domestic violence that is disrupting normative assumptions about primarily (or exclusively) male-against-female abuse in relationships (and is even positing that gender symmetry exists in relationship abuse, Straus, 2010); however, perpetration of sexual violence remains male-dominated.

References

Acker, J. (2006). Inequality regimes: gender, class and race in organizations. *Gender and Society, 20*(4), 441–464.

Ahrens, C. E., Rich, M. D., & Ullman, J. B. (2011). Rehearsing for real life: The impact of the InterACT sexual assault prevention program on self-reported likelihood of engaging in bystander interventions. *Violence Against Women, 17*(6), 760–776.

Alcoff, L., & Gray, L. (1993). Survivor discourse: Transgression or recuperation? *Signs: Journal of Women and Culture, 18*(2), 260–290.

Allan, E. J. (2003). Constructing women's status: Policy discourses of university women's commission policy reports. *Harvard Educational Review, 73*(1), 44–72.

Allan, E. J. (2008). *Policy discourses, gender and education: Constructing women's status.* New York: Routledge.

Allan, E. J., Iverson, S. V., & Ropers-Huilman, R. (Eds.). (2010). *Reconstructing policy analysis in higher education: Feminist poststructural perspectives.* New York: Routledge.

"Ask First" at Antioch. (1993, October 11). *New York Times.* Retrieved from www.nytimes.com/1993/10/11/opinion/ask-first-at-antioch.html

Bacchi, C. (2000). Policy as discourse: What does it mean? Where does it get us? *Discourse, 21*(1), 45–57.

Bacchi, C. (2004). Policy and discourse: Challenging the construction of affirmative action as preferential treatment. *Journal of European Public Policy, 11*(1), 128–146.

Bacchi, C. (2005). Discourse, discourse everywhere: Subject "agency" in feminist discourse methodology. *Nordic Journal of Women's Studies, 13*(3), 198–209.

Bacchi, C. L. (1999). *Women, policy and politics: The construction of policy problems.* Thousand Oaks, CA: Sage.

Ball, S. J. (Ed.). (1990). *Foucault and education: Disciplines and knowledge.* New York: Routledge.

Ball, S. J. (1993). What is policy? Texts, trajectories and toolboxes. *Australian Journal of Education Studies, 13*(2), 10–17.

Baum, K., & Klaus, P. (2005). *Violent victimization of college students, 1995–2002* (NCJ 206836). Washington, DC: U.S. Department of Justice, Office of Justice Programs, Bureau of Justice Statistics.

Bensimon, E. M., & Marshall, C. (2003). Like it or not: Feminist critical policy analysis matters. *Journal of Higher Education, 74*(3), 337–349.

Cahill, A. J. (2000). Foucault, rape, and the construction of the feminine body. *Hypatia, 15*(1), 43–63.

Cantalupo, N. (2011). Burying our heads in the sand: Lack of knowledge, knowledge avoidance and the persistent problem of campus peer sexual violence. *Loyola University Chicago Law Journal, 43*, 205.

Ehrlich, S. (1999). Communities of practice, gender, and the representation of sexual assault. *Language in Society, 28*(2), 239–256.

Exner, D., & Cummings, N. (2011). Implications for sexual assault prevention: college students as prosocial bystanders. *Journal of American College Health, 59*(7), 655–657.

Eyre, L. (2000). The discursive framing of sexual harassment in a university community. *Gender & Education, 12*(3), 293–308.

Ferraro, K. J. (1996). The dance of dependency: A genealogy of domestic violence discourse. *Hypatia, 11*(4), 77–91.

Fine, M. (1988). Sexuality, schooling, and adolescent females: The missing discourse of desire. *Harvard Educational Review, 58*(1), 29–54.

Foucault, M. (1980). Truth and power. In C. Gordon (Ed.), *Power/knowledge: Selected interviews and other writings 1972–1977 by Michel Foucault* (pp. 109–133). New York: Pantheon.

Foucault, M. (1995). *Discipline and punish: The birth of the prison* (2nd ed.) (A. Sheridan, Trans.). New York: Vintage Books. (Original work published 1977)

Frazier, P., Anders, S., Perera, S., Tomich, P., Tennen, H., Park, C., & Tashiro, T. (2009). Traumatic events among undergraduate students: Prevalence and associated symptoms. *Journal of Counseling Psychology, 56*(3), 450–460.

Gal, S. (1991). Between speech and silence: The problematics of research on language and gender. In Micaela di Leonardo (Ed.), *Gender at the crossroads of knowledge* (pp. 175–203). Berkeley: University of California Press.

Gidycz, C. A., Orchowski, L. M., & Berkowitz, A. D. (2011). Preventing sexual aggression among college men: An evaluation of a social norms and bystander intervention program. *Violence Against Women, 17*(6), 720–742.

Guba, E. G., & Lincoln, Y. S. (1981). *Effective evaluation: Improving the usefulness of evaluation results through responsive and naturalistic approaches.* San Francisco, CA: Jossey-Bass.

Hawkesworth, M. E. (1988). *Theoretical issues in policy analysis.* Albany: State University of New York Press.

Heberle, R. (1996). Deconstructive strategies and the movement against sexual violence. *Hypatia, 11*(4), 63–76.

Hengehold, L. (1994). An immodest proposal: Foucault, hysterization, and the "second rape." *Hypatia, 9*(3), 88–107.

Hengehold, L. (2000). Remapping the event: Institutional discourses and the trauma of rape. *Signs: Journal of Women and Culture, 26*(1), 187–214.

Iverson, S. V. (2006). Performing gender: A discourse analysis of theatre-based sexual violence prevention programs. *NASPA Journal, 43*(3), 547–577.

Iverson, S. V. (2012). Constructing outsiders: The discursive framing of access in university diversity policies. *Review of Higher Education, 35*(2), 149–177.

Jackson, R. D., Bouffard, L. A., & Fox, K. A. (2013). Putting policy into practice: Examining school districts' implementation of teen dating violence legislation. *Criminal Justice Policy Review, 1–22.*

Janosik, S. M., & Gregory, D. E. (2009). The Clery Act, Campus Safety, and the perceptions of senior student affairs officers. *NASPA Journal, 46*, 208–227.

Karjane, H. M., Fisher, B. S., & Cullen, F. T. (2005). *Sexual assault on campus: What colleges and universities are doing about it.* Washington, DC: U.S. Department of Justice, Office of Justice Programs.

Lowery, J. (1995). Complying with the congressional mandates and the practice of student affairs. *College Student Affairs Journal, 15*(1), 16–25.

Marshall, C. (1999). Researching the margins: Feminist critical policy analysis. *Educational Policy, 13*(1), 59–76.

Marshall, C. (2000). Policy discourse analysis: negotiating gender equity. *Journal of Education Policy, 15*(2), 125–156.

Martin, P.Y., & Hummer, R.A. (1989). Fraternities and rape on campus. *Gender & Society, 3*(4), 457–473.

McCaughey, M., & King, N. (1995). Rape education videos: Presenting mean women instead of dangerous men. *Teaching Sociology, 23*(4), 374–388.

Miles, M., & Huberman, A. M. (1994). *Qualitative data analysis: An expanded sourcebook of new methods* (2nd ed.). Newbury Park, CA: Sage.

Mills, S. (1997). *Discourse.* New York: Routledge.

Moynihan, M. M., Banyard, V. L., Arnold, J. S., Eckstein, R. P., & Stapleton, J. G. (2011). Sisterhood may be powerful for reducing sexual and intimate partner violence: An evaluation of the bringing in the bystander in-person program with sorority members. *Violence Against Women, 17*(6), 703–719.

Murphy, R. K., Arnold, W. H., Hansen, K. R., & Mertler, C. A. (2001). The effects of the campus security act on the perceptions of safety and safety behaviors of first year students. *Journal of College and University Student Housing, 29*(2), 31–35.

Paul, L. A., & Gray, M. J. (2011). Sexual assault programming on college campuses: Using social psychological belief and behavior change principles to improve outcomes. *Trauma, Violence, & Abuse, 12*(2), 99–109.

Phipps, A. (2010). Violence and victimized bodies: Sexual violence policy in England and Wales. *Critical Social Policy, 30*(3), 359–383.

Pollack, W. (1990). Sexual harassment: Women's experience vs. legal definitions. *Harvard Women's Law Journal, 13*, 35–85.

Scheurich, J. J. (1994). Policy archaeology: A new policy studies methodology. *Journal of Educational Policy, 9*(4), 297–316.

Shaw, S. E. (2010). Reaching the parts that other theories and methods can't reach: How and why a policy-as-discourse approach can inform health-related policy. *Health, 14*(2), 196–212.

Shore, C., & Wright, S. (Eds.). (1997). *Anthropology of policy: Critical perspectives on governance and power.* New York: Routledge.

Srikantiah, J. (2007). Perfect victims and real survivors: The iconic victim in domestic human trafficking law. *Boston University Law Review, 87*, 157–211.

Straus, M. A. (2004). Women's violence toward men is a serious social problem. In R. J. Gelles & D. R. Loseke (Eds.), *Current controversies on family violence* (2nd ed., pp. 55–77). Newbury Park, CA: Sage.

Straus, M. A. (2009). Why the overwhelming evidence on partner physical violence by women has not been perceived and is often denied. *Journal of Aggression, Maltreatment & Trauma, 18*(6), 552–571.

Straus, M. A. (2010). Thirty years of denying the evidence on gender symmetry in partner violence: Implications for prevention and treatment. *Partner Abuse, 1*(3), 332–362.

Thapar-Bjorkert, S., & Morgan, K. J. (2010). "But sometimes I think . . . They put themselves in the situation": Exploring blame and responsibility in interpersonal violence. *Violence Against Women, 16*(1), 32–59.

Vaccaro, A., McCoy, B., Champagne, D., & Siegel, M. (2013). *Decisions matter: Using decision making framework with contemporary student affairs case studies.* Washington, DC: NASPA.

Vandiver, D. M., & Dupalo, J. R. (2013). Factors that affect college students' perceptions of rape: What is the role of gender and other situational factors? *International Journal of Offender Therapy and Comparative Criminology, 57*(5), 592–612.

Walton, G. (2010). The problem trap: Implications of policy archaeology methodology for anti-bullying policies. *Journal of Education Policy, 25*(2), 135–150.

Weedon, C. (1997). *Feminist practice and poststructuralist theory* (2nd ed.). Oxford: Blackwell.

Westlund, A. C. (1999). Pre-modern and modern power: Foucault and the case of domestic violence. *Signs, 24*(4), 1045–1066.

Winton, S. (2013). Rhetorical analysis in critical policy research. *International Journal of Qualitative Studies in Education, 26*(2), 158–177.

Woodhull, W. (1988). Sexuality, power, and the question of rape. In I. Diamond & L. Quinby (Eds.), *Feminism and Foucault: Reflections on Resistance* (pp. 167–176). Boston, MA: Northeastern University Press.

3

HETEROSEXIST DISCOURSES

How Feminist Theory Shaped Campus Sexual Violence Policy

Sara Carrigan Wooten

Sexual violence is a pervasive problem in higher education and one that has been made increasingly public through the use of social media. But, what do we even mean when we say "sexual violence"? What kinds of imagery are brought to the forefront of our collective imagination when we hear about it? In this chapter, I seek to address these questions by tracing the impact of feminist theory on our contemporary understandings of sexual violence in higher education. I begin with a discussion of five pivotal second wave feminist texts and the ways in which they came to define rape specifically. It is my contention that second wave feminist theory on rape produced an extremely powerful discourse of sexual violence that not only impacted the law and policy but also continues to shape our present understandings of sexual violence today. I will conclude with what I understand to be the consequences of this discourse for lesbian, gay, bisexual, transgender, and queer (LGBTQ) students in higher education, who do not fit within dominant constructions of victims or perpetrators of sexual violence.

The 1960s and 1970s in the United States brought dramatic change in cultural attitudes regarding women, the workplace, sexual harassment, divorce, etc. Of particular note was the work of feminist scholars in bringing cultural consciousness regarding sexual violence against women to the forefront of popular knowledge. Where rape had once been dismissed as an act committed by deranged men or deviant men (read: men of color, poor men, etc.), the work of feminist theory during this time illuminated rape as a form of gendered violence against women, often committed by husbands, partners, soldiers, strangers, and male family members with the effect of controlling women through a system of fear and domination. It is my assertion that the characterization of rape produced during this time continues to dictate sexual violence policy broadly, and such policy in higher education, specifically.

Framing Patriarchy

Attitudes, beliefs, and power structures connected to sexual violence are constantly (re)produced on a societal level and manifest in colleges and universities across the country. Such understandings of sexual violence are in the service of a particular hegemonic ideology. Hegemony, a concept theorized by Antonio Gramsci as a dominant worldview used to support those in power and control the masses (Gramsci, Hoare, & Nowell-Smith, 1971), functions in the United States through the normalization of Whiteness, heterosexuality, masculinity, and middle-class forms of cultural capital (Bourdieu, 1984), among other things. Heterosexuality and masculinity are particularly important here, as both are made manifest through patriarchy, which normalizes men as dominant over women. According to Caringella (2009):

> Entitlement, or the righteously held prerogative to free and full access to a woman's body, is observed in the male belief in the right to have sex and the use of force and violence in order to do so, whenever and wherever a man has the urge.
>
> *(p. 64)*

This tenet of patriarchy is thus deeply connected to acts of sexual violence, which have been theorized as a physical reaffirmation of patriarchal power by men over women (Block, 2006; Burt, 1991; Iglesias, 1996). Due to these hegemonic constructions of the perpetrator and victim in situations of sexual violence, it is not surprising that the population that has received the most attention from those investigating and intervening in campus rape culture is White, heterosexual, cisgender[1] women (Wooten, 2014, p. 436). This identity is reflected in feminist theory, particularly second wave constructions of sexual violence, which I will discuss in the following sections.

Feminist Theory

Feminism is generally understood as a social movement directed at the full enfranchisement of women in all sectors of life including political, economic, and social. Feminism within the United States has been largely characterized by three distinct "waves": the suffragette first wave during the late 19th and early 20th centuries; the sexual revolution second wave spanning from the 1960s through the late 1970s; and the ongoing multicultural/transnational third wave from the mid-1990s to present. Feminism is not unique to the United States—there exist thousands of feminist movements across the world, including transnational and intranational movements.

Feminist theory serves as a philosophical extension of feminism within primarily academic, but also activist, discourse and practices. Feminist theory has been grounded in the field of women's studies and its offshoots gender studies, feminist studies, and sexuality studies. Within the United States, there are numerous articulations of feminism, some of which are complementary and some of which are oppositional. Cultural, liberal, and radical feminisms are examples. Black feminism and Chicana feminism are examples of postcolonial feminisms that have distinguished themselves from the White cultural priorities of the previous three.

One of the common threads that runs through feminist organizing within and outside of the United States has been the recognition and condemnation of sexual violence against women. However, White feminist organizing in the United States has historically prioritized the denouncement of sexual violence against women over many other oppressive realities that women experience. The second wave of White feminism in the United States is particularly noteworthy for its achievements in bringing national attention to the reality of sexual violence against women and for substantial legal shifts in the treatment of rape in particular. This is not to say that Black feminist and womanist scholars of that time, for example, were silent on issues of sexual violence. To the contrary, much scholarship was produced[2] on the distinct experience of sexual violence for Black women and how those experiences were rendered invisible by the "common oppression rhetoric" of White feminism (La Rue, 1995). For example, Angela Davis (1972) described the condition of slave women in the southern United States as that of being forcibly reduced to "female animal[s]" through their systematic rape by White men. An antebellum narrative of slave women as wild, animalistic, and hypersexual developed to further dehumanize them and justify the violence they lived. Unlike White women in the United States, rape for African American women is tied to specific histories and continuing legacies of chattel slavery that have rendered them lascivious and ultimately unrapable. Despite this, and the collaborative anti-rape activism that Black and White women did together during the 1960s and 1970s, the discourse of sexual violence that has arisen from second wave feminism is a decidedly Whitened, homogenizing experience across disparate communities of women.

The following discussion centers on five canonical pieces of feminist literature that arose from the second wave of feminist activism. These pieces had a direct impact on cultural and legal attitudes regarding sexual violence, and in some cases produced material changes in the law. However, they are also responsible for creating powerful imagery of both victims and assailants, imagery that I will argue continues to be reflected in sexual violence policy in higher education.

Second Wave Feminist Literature

Before I begin my discussion and subsequent analysis of the five foundational pieces used to advance my theory of the impact of feminist theory on the discourse on sexual violence that pervades the United States and particularly our college campuses, I cannot overstate the intellectual and material contributions that the highlighted authors have made to what is known about the reality of sexual violence against women and its patriarchal and misogynistic roots. This chapter does not seek to argue a revisionist narrative for these pieces—I am not attempting to engage in an outright strict critique of these pieces regarding the ways in which they characterize rape and violence against women by men. Rather, this chapter seeks to identify the ways in which the descriptions of sexual violence that originated with 1970s feminist literature and have proliferated in the literature for decades thereafter continue to dominate our present discourse of sexual violence in ways that are consequently heterosexist. I do not believe the descriptions of rape in particular as contained within these texts were intentionally heterosexist. On the contrary, I believe they were revolutionary in their brash confrontation of power in relation to rape and referenced centuries-old understandings of women as the sole victims of rape, rather than creating new archetypes. Nevertheless, it is the goal of this chapter to identify the heterosexist construction of rape from these pieces and to surface how that construction has limited the ways in which rape and sexual assault are conceptualized as fundamentally heterosexual phenomena, thereby entering into a more complicated conversation with these pieces and opening up possibility for more nuanced contemporary engagement with, and interrogation of, the discourse on sexual violence.

Each of these five texts was part of a sustained movement of feminist action in the United States. The authors here are part of the U.S. feminist canon, their work regularly featured on women's studies syllabi, and they have had a lasting impact on popular perceptions of rape and sexual violence. Brownmiller's book in particular had an immense effect on cultural understandings of rape as a common experience amongst women. The book was included on the New York Public Library's list of Books of the Century for its impact (Diefendorf & Bryan, 1996).

Dialectic of Sex

Shulamith Firestone's *The Dialectic of Sex* (1970) begins with a brief discussion of the tensions between Marxism and feminism, particularly Marx and Engel's pithy acknowledgement of the division of labor along gendered lines. Women, she contends, have always been at a biological disadvantage in terms of power and control. Rather than being able to exercise agency, women prior to the advent of birth control have always been trapped by their bodies, particularly in relation to pregnancy, childbirth, and childrearing. Biology rendered women completely dependent on men for survival. Thus, an entrenched biological and labor dichotomy between men and women is at the core of gender inequity even in our contemporary moment. Firestone cites four central manifestations of this dependency:

1) That women throughout history before the advent of birth control were at the continual mercy of their biology—menstruation, menopause,

and 'female ills', constant painful childbirth, wetnursing and care of infants, all of which made them dependent on males (whether brother, father, husband, lover, or clan, government, community-at-large) for physical survival.

2) That human infants take an even longer time to grow up than animals, and thus are helpless and, for some short period at least, dependent on adults for physical survival.

3) That a basic mother/child interdependency has existed in some form in every society, past or present, and thus has shaped the psychology of every mature female and every infant.

4) That the natural reproductive difference between the sexes led directly to the first division of labour at the origins of class, as well as furnishing the paradigm for caste (discrimination based on biological characteristics).

(1970, pp. 8–9)

Given that humanity has moved well beyond the time of cave-dwelling, Firestone argues that it is no longer acceptable to defend discrimination along supposedly "natural" characteristics. Humanity has long distinguished itself from the class of animals.

Firestone establishes rape as a fundamentally heterosexual form of violence by first making men's and women's relationship to one another ultimately about sexual contact. By overemphasizing the sexual dynamics between men and women, she leaves little room for rape to be anything but biological destiny, and the relationship between men and women to be forever and always a hostile one. While her discussion of the biological division of labor is absolutely compelling, it is also a pointedly dehumanizing analysis. By painting premodern women as helpless victims of their own bodies and inescapably tied to their children, she ignores kinship bonds and community relationships that foster communal caregiving and nurturance. Firestone seems to agree with such arguments regarding the biological weakness of women, where women's ability to give birth is seen as a detriment and vulnerability, rather than a source of power. The dichotomy between men and women is thus concretized, with one having freedom of movement and power while the other is constrained and victimized. The foundation for understanding men as *always* sexual aggressors and women as *always* sexual victims has been sufficiently laid. If women are fundamentally vulnerable, then progress between the two sexes can only come about from men resisting their biological predilections. While she ends her biological history with the assertion that humanity has the capacity to defy nature, Firestone nevertheless remains sold on the idea that women are the inherently disadvantaged sex rather than arguing a counter discourse. Instead, it is incumbent upon modern humanity to rise above the biological weaknesses of women.

Against Our Will

Susan Brownmiller's *Against our Will: Men, Women, and Rape* (1975) begins with a discussion of her perception of the lack of rape in the animal world. Brownmiller rationalizes rape as a unique feature of humanity due to our lack of formal mating season and accompanying rituals. From there she asserts that:

> Man's structural capacity to rape and woman's corresponding structural vul-nerability are as basic to the physiology of both our sexes as the primal act of sex itself. Had it not been for this accident of biology, an accommodation requiring the locking together of two separate parts, penis into vagina, there would be neither copulation nor rape as we know it.
>
> *(1975, pp. 13–14)*

The vulnerability of women that Brownmiller identifies produces a disciplin-ary function, where, "[Rape] is nothing more or less than a conscious process of intimidation by which *all* men keep *all* women in a state of fear" (Brownmiller, 1975, p. 15, emphasis in original). Brownmiller then sets off a number of rape scenarios involving primitive humans. The archetypes discussed include a woman fighting off a man who attempts to rape her and male bonding through gang rape of a woman.

In chapter eight, Brownmiller briefly discusses male prison rape, analyzing such scenarios as ones that are inevitably about power and of constructing the role of the woman within an all-male system. She cites multiple descriptions of the process of "womanization" that occurs for young men or men with slight builds (1975, p. 261). She turns to a general discussion of sadomasochism in homosexual male communities. Brownmiller also briefly mentions what she calls "lesbian rape" in women's prisons but asserts that such violence occurs at significantly lower rates than in men's prisons.

Susan Brownmiller, by immediately referencing the presumed nonexistence of rape within animal species, implies that rape is a specific manifestation of violence in humanity. She asserts that rape is made possible due to the absence of a formal biological mating period and of the anatomy of men and women, which involves a penetrator and a receiver. The vagina is the only receiver discussed, despite rape being a series of violent acts that involve other parts of the body, both men's and women's. Thus, women are rendered physically vulnerable at all times. This argument of course ignores the very real physical vulnerability of male genitalia, located outside of the body, exposed and subject to harm. Is the power of the male sex really so, or are feminist theorists supporting and even promoting patriarchal notions of the power of the male body and the weakness of the female body, when physical evidence points to the contrary?

Henderson (2007) problematizes this naturalization of rape by radical feminist literature when held against Foucault's provocative question of why rape should be punished more severely than other forms of physical violence:[3]

> In suggesting that feminism rethink naturalized versions of sexual violence, I mean specifically those conceptions of rape in which: sexual injury is always, already the worst form that violence can take; sexual injury is universally self-shattering and selfhood is unrecoverable; men are always positioned as violent subjects, unaware of their own vulnerability, while women are positioned as universally vulnerable and anchored in their own fear; and lastly, the identities of rapist and rape preexist rape itself.
>
> *(p. 227)*

Foucault, while asking a question that is itself rooted in a place of privilege and male power, nevertheless raised salient points regarding how rape and sexual violence are framed by radical feminists in ways that appear to agree with patriarchal and misogynistic ideology about women's bodies. In illuminating sexual violence as a gendered form of violence against women, is Brownmiller also contributing to a reified understanding of women as inherently weak and subject to violence? How does such an argument exist outside of a patriarchal understanding of sex? Both Firestone and Brownmiller's arguments are curiously biologically determinant, where biological determinance has historically been used to justify the superiority of men over women (Dworkin, 1993). As Butler (1990) asserts, "The return to biology as the ground of a specific feminine sexuality or meaning seems to defeat the feminist premise that biology is not destiny" (p. 30).

Radical feminist articulations of sexual violence during the second wave are steeped in a heterosexist understanding of this violence. This is in some sense unavoidable, as rape and other forms of sexual violence are tactics fueled by patriarchy as a means of controlling women. How can one highlight this point without being heterosexist? By acknowledging that rape is not a form of violence unique to women but instead is a form of violence overwhelmingly, but not exclusively, committed against women. Rape and other forms of sexual violence are not made inevitable for a particular group because of biology but through sociocultural structures that are premised on the notion that particular bodies are more vulnerable to violence. Thus, *anybody* can experience sexual violence but heterosexist patriarchy and radical feminist theory has collapsed cisgender female bodies with inherent vulnerability to such violence, where to be cisgender and female is to be always and forever under the threat of rape. When instances of sexual violence that exist outside of a heterosexual binary get repackaged in heterosexual terms, the heterosexism of this radical feminist discourse of sexual violence is revealed. Brownmiller's discussion of prison rape and homosexuality affirms this point. The title of the chapter, "Prison Rape: The Homosexual Experience," and the use of "lesbian rape" is particularly noteworthy and provides insight into Brownmiller's own conceptualizations of sexual violence. First, being raped in prison does not necessarily involve either person identifying as homosexual, gay or lesbian. Secondly, this is where Brownmiller pointedly makes the connection between rape and heterosexuality, however unintentionally. Throughout her discussion, rape is tied to markers of sexuality for men and women. She continually maps a heterosexual binary onto male-on-male or female-on-female dynamics in prison. She identified that younger, slightly built men are often victims of gang rape in prison. This often leads to these men forming sexual relationships with other men in order to be protected from the threat of gang rape. These men are often described as *women*, or in terms evoking femininity, as a means of solidifying their status as submissive. Brownmiller does not question these articulations of submissive men but rather supports the notion that all male systems eventually recreate gendered relationships that necessitate "female" actors. In other words, someone always has to play the woman in same-sex prison relationships and sexual violence.

While I applaud Brownmiller's inclusion of nonheterosexual forms of sexual violence in her book, she does so in a manner that does not legitimate these experiences as true forms of rape. This is indicated by the lack of these stories in her chapter on "Victims," which is exclusively focused on women who have been raped by men. Rather, these cases are treated as outliers, anomalies in the common phenomenon of rape, or surrogates for "true" rape where each person plays a heterosexual role. They are not interrogated for their own uniquely gendered power structures, and Brownmiller does not question the narrative of the male prison rape dynamics as involving a "womanized" man. Those forms of sexual violence are not tied to sociocultural messages about sexual violence and power. Rather, the men's experiences of rape are written off as a manifestation of masculinity that has no proper outlet, and the women's experiences are all but uninvestigated altogether. It is not surprising that Brownmiller did not engage in a discursive analysis of sexuality and gender in relation to these other instances of sexual violence given her larger project. I merely point to these absences as a means of indicating how nonheterosexual rape does not fit neatly into a sociocultural discourse of sexual violence. It does not connect as easily to forms of popular culture or dogma. They are vexing outliers that can only be understood, both by Brownmiller and the people she interviews, through a lens that reasserts an aggressive male/vulnerable female trope.

Compulsory Heterosexuality and Lesbian Existence

At the outset of "Compulsory Heterosexuality and Lesbian Existence" (1980), Adrienne Rich outlines her primary frustrations regarding cultural heterosexism:

> I am concerned here with two other matters as well: first, how and why women's choice of women as passionate comrades, life partners, co-workers,

lovers, tribe, has been crushed, invalidated, forced into hiding and disguise; and second, the virtual or total neglect of lesbian existence in a wide range of writings, including feminist scholarship. Obviously there is a connection here. I believe that much feminist theory and criticism is stranded on this shoal.

(p. 632)

Thus, Rich seeks in part to address what she understands as the heterosexist silencing of lesbian existence within feminist literature. Rich's text is part of a powerful radical feminist movement toward political lesbian identity that took place during the 1960s and 1970s as a response to male sexual domination and patriarchal control. All sexual relationships with men came to be viewed as fundamentally oppressive, as Rich explains, male power is derived:

By means of rape (including marital rape) and wife beating; father–daughter, brother–sister incest; the socialization of women to feel that male sexual "drive" amounts to a right; idealization of heterosexual romance in art, literature, media, advertising, etc.; child marriage; arranged marriage; prostitution; the harem; psychoanalytic doctrines of frigidity and vaginal orgasm; pornographic depictions of women responding pleasurably to sexual violence and humiliation (a subliminal message being that sadistic heterosexuality is more "normal" than sensuality between women).

(1980, pp. 638–639)

Lesbian separatism was thought to offer relief for women who had up until then lived their lives stifled within the confines of heteronormativity. Lesbian existence was at the heart of sexual revolution and resistance. Rather than being natural, heterosexuality had to be understood as a political institution just like any other, one that was demarcated, policed, socioculturally reinforced and individually internalized.

Rich, who specifically attends to the existence of lesbian relationships, does not acknowledge the possibility of rape and sexual violence within those relationships. Instead, lesbian existence is both a political and spiritual escape from patriarchy. Rich herself identifies the heterosexism found in assertions regarding the "deviant" nature of lesbian existence in the literature of the 1960s and 1970s: "The assumption made by Rossi, that women are 'innately sexually oriented' toward men, or by Lessing, that the lesbian choice is simply an acting-out of bitterness toward men, are by no means theirs alone; they are widely current in literature and the social sciences" (1980, p. 632). Thus, lesbian existence is rendered a means of heterosexual women acting out, rather than a legitimate sexuality and political identity.

Rejecting this characterization of bonds between women, Rich states, "Lesbian existence comprises both the breaking of a taboo and the rejection of a compulsory way of life. It is also a direct or indirect attack on male right of access to women" (p. 649). Lesbian existence, then, is a means of escape for women who have lived their lives constrained by the expectations and demands of a heterosexist patriarchy. However, missing from Rich's discussion of the opportunities of lesbian existence is any theorization of the ways in which patriarchy may manifest itself within woman-centered relationships. She addresses in one sentence the less than ideal dynamics that can and have occurred within lesbian existence:

> But it is more than these, although we may first begin to perceive it as a form of nay-saying to patriarchy, an act of resistance. It has of course included role playing, self-hatred, breakdown, alcoholism, suicide, and intra-woman violence; we romanticize at our peril what it means to love and act against the grain, and under heavy penalties; and lesbian existence has been lived (unlike, say, Jewish or Catholic existence) without access to any knowledge of a tradition.
>
> *(1980, p. 649)*

Even these difficulties only exist in relation to compulsory heterosexuality—they are the consequences of male-identification over female-identification. The absence of any discussion of sexual violence within lesbian relationships essentializes the hetero-rape assumption and "the characterization of female sexuality as radically distinct from a phallic organization of sexuality remains problematic" (Butler, 1990, p. 30). Rich romanticizes lesbian relationships as fundamentally empowering and free from patriarchal power but fails to account for the complexity of gender and sexuality within those relationships and how patriarchal ideology continues to move within them. Instead:

> Woman-identification is a source of energy, a potential springhead of female power, violently curtailed and wasted under the institution of heterosexuality. The denial of reality and visibility to women's passion for women, women's choice of women as allies, life companions, and community; the forcing of such relationships into dissimulation and their disintegration under intense pressure have meant an incalculable loss to the power of all women to change the social relations of the sexes, to liberate ourselves and each other.
>
> *(1980, p. 657)*

If lesbian existence is the liberation Rich makes it out to be, how then do we explain the simultaneous existence of sexual violence within lesbian relationships? From where does such violence spring? If one rejects Brownmiller's characterization of sexual violence in nonheterosexual relationships as simply reproducing a heterosexual dynamic, where one person is always the "woman" and the other always the "man," from what power and dominance framework can we understand rape committed by one woman against another? As Butler (1990) concludes, "This utopian notion of a sexuality freed from heterosexual constructs, a sexuality beyond 'sex,' [fails] to acknowledge the ways in which power relations continue to construct sexuality for women even within the terms of a 'liberated' heterosexuality or lesbianism" (p. 29).

Rape: On Coercion and Consent

Catherine MacKinnon's "Rape: On Coercion and Consent" (1989) is specifically concerned with how the law functions in relation to the crime of rape. The role of "force," in both the act and the definition of the act, is central to MacKinnon's analysis of how the judicial system disenfranchises rape survivors. She makes a connection between violence, sex, and rape, asserting that the power relationship between men and women is fundamentally unequal and ultimately questions whether women can ever actually give consent. Consent, she maintains, presumes that the power relationship between men and women is equal to begin with. Sexual relationships between men and women are centered on conquest and domination, rather than equality of pleasure or control. Social media and pornography, both of which portray men as aggressors and women as victims more often than not, regularly enforce the construction of sex as an act of domination. MacKinnon maintains that, "The deeper problem is that women are socialized to passive receptivity; may have or perceive no alternative to acquiescence; may prefer it to the escalated risk of injury and the humiliation of a lost fight; submit to survive" (1989, p. 48). Coercion, rather than consent, is at the heart of power relations between men and women, particularly in the realm of sex and sexual violence.

MacKinnon's perspective on women and rape is clear from the very start of her piece when she states:

> If sexuality is central to women's definition and forced sex is central to sexuality, rape is indigenous, not exceptional, to women's social condition. In feminist analysis, a rape is not an isolated event or moral transgression or individual interchange gone wrong but an act of terrorism and torture within a systemic context of group subjection, like lynching.
>
> *(1989, p. 42)*

Rape here implicitly means heterosexual rape—rape committed by men against women within a patriarchal system. This statement on rape is unqualified, rendering rape a specifically female experience of violence. She continues, "Men and women are unequally socially situated with regard to the experience of rape. Men are a good deal more likely to rape than to be raped. . . . Women are more likely to be raped than to rape and are most often raped by men whom they know" (1989, p. 47). Again, the rape that women commit and that men experience here is couched in a heterosexual framework. Women are unlikely to commit rape against a man, and men are unlikely to be the victims of rape by a woman. But what of violence outside of those constructs? Both may be statistically accurate, with the caveat that rape overall is the most underreported crime, but what of nonheterosexual rape? This question is ignored by MacKinnon.

MacKinnon argues that rape is virtually indistinguishable from sex under male supremacy and, because of this, consent for women is a fictitious and impossible ideal. This is due to the fundamentally unequal power relationship between women and men as well as the manners in which violent and forceful sex has been eroticized. In support of the view, MacKinnon renders women, assumed here to be heterosexual women, as having no agency or strength in relation to men. The fact that women can and do say no to sex and are heard is a moot point, "To be rapable, a position that is social not biological, defines what a woman is" (p. 49). Anytime a woman acquiesces (I say "acquiesces" here to indicate MacKinnon's position) to a man's sexual desire, she is ultimately being presented with a false choice. As such, MacKinnon asserts that women, as, "gender objects," are the only ones who can truly experience rape (1989, p. 49).

Pornography and Male Supremacy

Andrea Dworkin was one of the preeminent radical feminists, best known for her abrasive and assertive writing style regarding the relationship between patriarchy, rape, and pornography. In *Pornography and Male Supremacy* (1993), Dworkin pushes her readers to understand the inherently violent relationships between men and women that are found in pornography, which she views as a form of rape, and certainly a significant medium in the glorification of violence against women and the sexual abuse of women. She cites the Latin word *rapere* as the root of the word "rape" and concludes that rape has historically been "First abduction, kidnapping, the taking of a woman by force" (1993, p. 239). This has resulted in "the sexual colonization of women's bodies [being] a material reality: men control the sexual and reproductive uses of women's bodies" (1993, p. 239). Male supremacy only allows for sex that is phallic/penetrative in nature. Dworkin rejects biological determinism, which would locate women's primary function as one of service to men.

Female sexuality is culturally read as inherently provocative and sluttish to be responded to by men (p. 237). Pornography especially depicts women as whores and the sexuality of women as seductive and teasing, thus providing a justification of rape. Pornography for Dworkin is the link between rape and prostitution, a male industry that has been built on the sexual debasement and violation of women. Dworkin asserts that:

> Pornography as a genre says that the stealing and buying and selling of women are not acts of force or abuse because women want to be raped and prostituted because that is the nature of women and the nature of female sexuality.
>
> *(1993, p. 240)*

Thus, Dworkin rejects misogynistic assumptions regarding femininity and the welcoming of violence by women.

Dworkin's interpretation of pornography as a manifestation of rape is worth serious consideration. The idea that pornography depicts the sexual degradation of women is of course not a particularly surprising or stunning one. Pornography has a long history of violent imagery toward women. However, it is Dworkin's treatment of women involved in pornographic industries that is troubling here. She describes women as devoid of agency, as ultimate victims. And if porn is simply an extension of the everyday rape of women, this victimization narrative is then mapped onto those women as well. Dworkin, like Firestone, is also guilty of using dehumanizing language in relation to women, at one point referring to them as "caged animals" (1993, p. 243). Finally, Dworkin defines rape specifically as, "the act of physically forcing a woman to have sexual intercourse" (1993, p. 239). Sexual intercourse, here, is understood as penile-vaginal penetration, indicating that the one doing the forcing must be a man. Rape is thus conditioned on there being an aggressive man and a helpless woman. Rape outside of these conditions is not mentioned, nor, I would argue, imaginable as such.

Impact of Feminist Theory on Law and Policy in Higher Education

The five feminist texts highlighted in this chapter contain a myriad of distinct as well as overlapping theoretical assumptions about the origins and manifestations of rape. Central to all five is the understanding that rape is a fundamentally heterosexual form of violence. Where lesbian existence is theorized, sexual violence within such an existence is silenced. Rape, as a reality of queer relationships, remains outside of the discourse instilled by these texts—a discourse that constructs men as rapists and women as victims. This notion of rape and more broadly of sexual violence against women had a profound cultural impact in the 1970s, and I argue remains with us today, particularly in higher education policy, programming, and prevention regarding sexual violence.

The National Organization for Women (NOW) was a key player in the anti-rape movement that arose as the result of feminist scholarship on sexual violence during the 1960s and 1970s. NOW organized a Rape Task Force that is widely credited with having spurred drastic changes in legislation regarding rape trials. The Rape Task Force heavily lobbied individual state legislatures and worked with Michigan to create a model of rape reform legislation (Caringella, 2009). The Criminal Sexual Conduct Code (CSC) specifically addressed forcible rape statutes:

> Michigan's governor signed the Criminal Sexual Conduct Code in 1974; it became effective on April 1, 1975 (BenDor, 1976, p. 149). The law defined graduated steps or degrees of criminal sexual conduct (CSC). Instances of

CSC in the first and third degrees are crimes of criminal sexual penetration, and occasions of CSC in the second and fourth degrees are crimes of criminal sexual contact. CSC in the first degree (CSC_1) and in the second degree (CSC_2) are differentiated from CSC_3 and CSC_4 by aggravated conditions of (1) victims who are minors; (2) blood affiliation, same household, or power/authority/trust position of assailant; (3) commission of another felony; (4) the presence of weapons; (5) force/coercion or victim incapacitation along with injuries; or (6) force/coercion or incapacitation and multiple offenders.

(Caringella, 2009, p. 13)

Michigan's actions inspired other states to make similar changes. The most common changes made to rape laws across the country were: changing the definition of rape to be gender neutral and thus allow for the possibility of male victims, the abolishment of third party corroboration, the abolishment of physical resistance requirements, and the implementation of Rape Shield Laws (Horney & Spohn, 1991). Rape Shield Laws limit the ability of the defense in a trial to use the alleged victim's sexual history as a means of creating doubt within the jury. In all, "fully thirty-six state rape statues underwent change between 1976 and 1978 alone" (Field & Bienen, 1980, p. 153, as cited in Caringella, 2009, p. 13).

These changes were without a doubt both necessary and tremendously important. However, the legacy of rape law reforms has not been in any way what those who fought for those reforms anticipated. Once these changes were adopted, "the liberal and radical feminist reform movement that was so engaged in critique transformed into more of a social service delivery bureaucracy that grew dependent on government funding to survive, which seriously dampened its critical edge" (Miller & Meloy, forthcoming, p. 286, as cited in Caringella, 2009, p. 2). Likewise, while the law in most states gives a gender-neutral definition of rape, the overwhelming archetype of those who experience sexual violence remains entrenched in the discourse referenced by Brownmiller, MacKinnon, and Dworkin—that of women as victims. As rare as it remains for a woman to successfully bring charges of rape against a male assailant, the incidents of men bringing charges against men or women or of women bringing charges against women remain all but nonexistent. Where the gender identity and sexuality of victims become more complex, the lack of representation is even more profound. What these reforms have done is set a precedent for policy changes as the penultimate measure of success for anti-rape activism.

Impact of Discourse on Sexual Violence Research

Sexual Violence in the United States

Due to the success of second wave feminist anti-rape activism in the United States, the discourse of sexual violence as an inherently female experience has infiltrated the research and literature that has been produced on sexual violence. Even where assailants are men and victims are women, it is important to acknowledge that not all women who are raped or sexually assaulted self-identify as "straight" or heterosexual and that such identification may make their experience of sexual violence differ in unique ways from heterosexual women. Race is another intersectional factor important to consider. As Wooten (2014) notes:

> As studies on sexual violence against women have at times failed to identify the race or ethnicity of their participants, it is also important to acknowledge that these women are also not always White nor that the construction of sexual violence produced by White feminism in the United States is shared by all women. The literature on the role of race and ethnicity as related to the experience of sexual violence makes evident that the manner in which race breaks down in studies of sexual violence is always significant and in need of publication (Cossins, 2003; Crenshaw, 1991; Nash, 2008; Razack, 1994). The publication of how race breaks down even in those studies that are not specifically focused on race has the immediate effect of resisting the normalization of Whiteness and the othering of non-White identities. Whiteness becomes an important and distinguishing feature of the data. Additionally, sexual violence is not a uniform set of experiences. Rather, sexual violence is experienced in distinct ways that are specific to one's cultural background. The ways in which a White, heterosexual, cisgender, upper-middle-class sorority woman may understand her experience of rape will inevitably be distinct from the ways in which a Black, queer, working-class, transgender man will understand his experience of rape. The specific act of rape itself may be interpreted differently by both of these people, given their sociocultural locations.
>
> *(p. 429)*

However, the heterosexist discourse on sexual violence that continues to be employed has created powerful associations, where one cannot speak of rape in a general sense without thinking of women assaulted by men.

Sexual Violence in Higher Education

In their groundbreaking study on sexual violence in higher education, Koss, Gidycz, and Wisniewski (1987) illuminated the significant prevalence of rape for women and are credited with the reporting the "one in four" statistic regarding those college women who have experienced an attempted or completed rape during their lifetime. The research done on campus sexual violence over the past several decades has consistently shown that college women are at high risk of an attempted or completed rape while in college (Baum & Klaus, 2005; Fisher, Cullen, & Turner, 2000; Karjane, Fisher, & Cullen, 2005; Koss, Gidycz, & Wisniewski, 1987; U.S. Department of Justice, 2002). However, while women are at the center of the literature on campus sexual violence, their sexuality is rarely a point of analysis. Women in campus rape literature are often presumed to be heterosexual, as are their assailants. Even when the possibility of other forms of sexual violence outside the discourse of heterosexual women assaulted by heterosexual men is allowed, the prospect of women assaulting women is unthinkable. Bohmer and Parrot (1993) demonstrate this blind spot in the rationale at the beginning of their book on campus sexual assault, saying, "It is possible for men to be raped by male assailants—or, more rarely, by female assailants—but because the vast majority of acquaintance rapes involve male assailants and female victims, this book will primarily focus on this type of sexual assault" (p. 19). Female assailants assaulting female victims is not a form of sexual violence allowed for in the discourse.

Where the literature is not focused on prevalence and incidence rates, it is alternatively focused on the causal role that alcohol, party culture, and fraternity culture play in the incidence of sexual violence on campus (Armstrong, Hamilton, & Sweeney, 2006; Boswell & Spade, 1996; Ehrhart & Sandler, 1985; Finley & Corty, 1993; Martin & Hummer, 1989; Sanday, 1992). Fraternity rape culture has been a particular and logical focus, given the rituals associated with fraternity life, namely, "the pressures of group think, masculinity, degradation of the feminine/female body, and continuous initiation and/or reaffirmation of loyalty" (Wooten, 2014, p. 430). Implicit in this research is a presumption of heterosexuality in the interactions between fraternity brothers and women, and thus, a normalization of rape as a heterosexual activity. Sexual orientation and gender identity are rarely factors of inquiry with participants. It is not my intention to deny the very real and established existence of a misogynistic rape culture that is a significant component of Greek life, although it has been suggested that not all fraternities are inherently dangerous for nontransgender, heterosexual women (Boswell & Spade, 1996). Rather, the established literature on campus rape culture continues to utilize a discourse of sexual violence that portrays men as ultimate aggressors and women as ultimate victims.

Heterosexism and the New Federal Push for an End to Campus Sexual Violence

Since the release of Vice President Joe Biden's and Secretary of Education Arne Duncan's Dear Colleague letter in 2011, the federal push for sweeping campus sexual violence policy reform has only increased. New Title IX guidelines, the Campus SaVE Act amendment to the Jeanne Clery Act, and the White House Task Force to Protect Students from Sexual Assault are just some of the interventions that have been instituted. The increased national dialogue on the crisis of sexual violence in higher education fueled by the surge of federal legislative and policy updates led Senator Claire McCaskill to conduct a survey of 440 higher education institutions regarding their policies and practices for preventing and responding to campus sexual violence. The results of the study demonstrate that higher education institutions are failing disastrously to effectively address campus sexual violence. For example, the report found that schools do not understand the full scope of the problem on their campuses, fail to encourage the reporting of sexual violence by students, fail to provide sexual assault response training for faculty and staff, and fail to provide adequate sexual assault training for students (U.S. Senate, 2014).

All the pieces of legislation and policy referenced here have historically focused on the assault of gender normative, heterosexual women in college. Senator McCaskill's survey instrument offers a number of options for participating institutions to select regarding where students might seek help in the aftermath of an assault. Choices included the mental health office on campus and the campus women's center. An LBGTQ resource center, which is an increasingly common feature of campuses, was not a provided choice. The Campus SaVE Act was originally written expressly for the protection of women on campus (Shapiro, 2014). However, increased scrutiny regarding the inclusiveness of federal policy for LGBTQ people has resulted in some shifts in these policies. For example, the Campus SaVE Act revised its language to be gender neutral in order to allow for same-sex assaults to come under its protections as well. It is worth noting that the limited discussion of this change has collapsed same-sex with gay male experiences of sexual violence, where lesbian students' experiences, for example, remain silenced (Shapiro, 2014).

The *Not Alone* (2014) report produced by the White House Task Force to Protect Students from Sexual Assault includes a footnote regarding college men's experiences of sexual violence, a note in parentheses that LGBTQ student organizations should be included in conversations regarding the development of sexual misconduct policies, and a note that the Johns Hopkins University School of Nursing will be conducting a study about sexual assault in intimate partner relationships among students and that this study will include LGBTQ relationships. These three references comprise the most significant points of departure in the document for sexual violence relating to gender normative, heterosexual women, but they do signal that the conversation is changing slightly. However, the dominant discourse of sexual violence as an experience that happens to women by men continues to be reinforced in these new initiatives. For example, the White House designed a national public service announcement featuring President Obama, Vice President Joe Biden and a number of male celebrities like Daniel Craig to educate men about consent, using language like "if she doesn't consent—or can't consent—it's a crime" (White House Task Force to Protect Students from Sexual Assault, 2014, p. 10).

Conclusion

While feminist theory and activism has produced incredible policy changes in higher education, it has done so at the expense of a multitude of students, administrators, and researchers who have bought into the heterosexist discourse of what sexual violence is, who can experience it, and who cannot. Thus, the normalization of sexual violence as a heterosexual experience has had the effect of limiting the research on sexual violence itself as well as dictating the framework of federal policy on campus sexual violence. Among the consequences of this are a severe lack of knowledge regarding how LGBTQ students and other historically marginalized student communities experience sexual violence, as well as the limiting of prevention and response resources to heterosexual women. This point is perhaps the most important in this discussion of discourse—that discourse produces material consequences. Beyond a denial or severely inadequate recognition of nonheterosexual experiences of rape and sexual assault, LGBTQ students who have had those experiences are often left without advocates who understand them or resources that reflect their identities.

Notes

1. *Cisgender* refers to a person whose gender identity aligns with the sex they were assigned at birth (e.g., a person who was assigned "female" at birth and identifies as a woman).
2. See the work of: Combahee River Collective, Mary Ann Weathers, Third World Women's Alliance, Angela Davis, Audre Lorde.
3. Michel Foucault, during a roundtable at the Change Collective, put forth the provocative question of why the crime of rape should be punished more severely than any other form of physical violence. This caused a stir among feminist communities during the 1970s, which accused him of forgetting his own discussions of power and their impact on the body.

References

Armstrong, E. A., Hamilton, L., & Sweeney, B. (2006). Sexual assault on campus: A multi-level, integrative approach to party rape. *Social Problems, 53*(4), 483–499.

Baum, K., & Klaus, P. (2005). Violent victimization of college students, 1995–2002. National Crime Victimization Survey. Retrieved from www.ocpa-oh.org/Campus%20 Safety/Violent%20Victimization%20of%20College%20Students.pdf

Block, S. (2006). *Rape and sexual power in early America.* Chapel Hill: University of North Carolina Press.

Bohmer, C., & Parrot, A. (1993). *Sexual assault on campus: The problem and the solution.* New York: Lexington Books.

Boswell, A. A., & Spade, J. Z. (1996). Fraternities and collegiate rape culture: Why are some fraternities more dangerous places for women? *Gender and Society, 10*(2), 133–147.

Bourdieu, P. (1984). *Distinction: A social critique of the judgment of taste* (R. Nice, Trans.). Cambridge, MA: Harvard University Press.

Brownmiller, S. (1975) *Against our will: Men, women, and rape.* New York: Ballantine Books.

Burt, M. (1991). Rape myths. In A. Parrot & L. Bechhofer (Eds.), *Acquaintance Rape: The Hidden Crime* (pp. 26–40). New York: John Wiley and Sons.

Butler, J. (1990). *Gender trouble.* New York: Routledge.

Caringella, S. (2009). *Addressing rape reform in law and practice.* New York: Columbia University Press.

Cossins, A. (2003). Saints, sluts and sexual assault: Rethinking the relationship between sex, race and gender. *Social Legal Studies, 12*(1), 77–103.

Crenshaw, K. (1991). Mapping the margins: Intersectionality, identity politics, and violence against women of color. *Stanford Law Review, 43*(6), 1241–1299.

Davis, B. (1972). Reflections on the Black woman's role in the community of slaves. *Massachusetts Review, 13*(1/2), 81–100.

Diefendorf, E., & Bryan, D. (1996). *The New York Public Library's books of the century.* New York: Oxford University Press.

Dworkin, A. (1993). *Letters from a war zone.* Chicago, IL: Lawrence Hill Press.

Ehrhart, J. K., & Sandler, B. R. (1985). *Campus gang rape: Party games?* Washington, DC: Project on the Status and Education of Women, Association of American Colleges.

Finley, C., & Corty, E. (1993). Rape on the campus: The prevalence of sexual assault while enrolled in college. *Journal of College Student Development, 34*(2), 113–117.

Firestone, S. (1970). *The dialectic of sex.* New York: William Morrow.

Fisher, B. S., Cullen, F. T., & Turner, M. G. (2000). *The sexual victimization of college women* (NCJ 182369). Washington, DC: U.S. Department of Justice, Office of Justice Programs.

Gramsci, A., Hoare, Q., & Nowell-Smith, G. (1971). *Selections from the prison notebooks of Antonio Gramsci.* New York: International.

Henderson, H. (2007). Feminism, Foucault, and rape: A theory and politics of rape prevention. *Berkeley Journal of Gender, Law, & Justice, 22,* 225–253.

Horney, J., & Spohn, C. (1991). Rape law reform and instrumental change in six urban jurisdictions. *Law and Society Review, 25*(1), 117–154.

Iglesias, E. M. (1996). Rape, race, and representation: The power of discourse, discourses of power, and the reconstruction of heterosexuality. *Vanderbilt Law Review, 49*(4), 871–886.

Karjane, H. M., Fisher, B. S., & Cullen, F. T. (2005). *Sexual assault on campus: What colleges and universities are doing about it.* Washington, DC: National Institute of Justice.

Koss, M. P., Gidycz, A., & Wisniewski, N. (1987). The scope of rape: Incidence and prevalence of sexual aggression and victimization in a national sample of higher education students. *Journal of Consulting and Clinical Psychology, 55*(2), 162–170.

La Rue, L. (1995). The Black movement and women's liberation. In B. Guy-Sheftall (Ed.), *Words of fire: An anthology of African American feminist thought* (pp. 163–174). New York: New Press.

MacKinnon, C. (1989). Rape: On coercion and consent. In C. MacKinnon (Ed.), *Toward a feminist theory of the state* (pp. 171–183). Cambridge, MA: Harvard University Press.

Martin, P. Y., & Hummer, R. A. (1989). Fraternities and rape on campus. *Gender & Society, 3*(4), 457–473.

Nash, J. C. (2008). Re-thinking intersectionality. *Feminist Review, 89*(1), 1–15.

Razack, S. (1994). What is to be gained by looking White people in the eye? Culture, race, and gender in cases of sexual violence. *Signs: Journal of Women in Culture and Society, 19*(4), 894–923.

Rich, A. (1980). Compulsory heterosexuality and lesbian existence. *Signs, 5*(4), 631–660.

Sanday, P. (1992). *Fraternity gang rape: Sex, brotherhood, and privilege on campus.* New York: New York University Press.

Shapiro, J. (2014). Campus sexual assault law now includes language on same-sex violence. *National Public Radio.* Retrieved from www.npr.org/2014/10/01/352757107/campus-sexual-assault-law-now-includes-language-on-same-sex-violence

U.S. Department of Justice. (2002). Bureau of Justice Statistics. *National Crime Victimization Survey.* [Record-Type Files]. ICPSR22902-v2. Ann Arbor, MI: Inter-university Consortium for Political and Social Research [distributor], 2008–12–10. doi:10.3886/ICPSR22902.v2.

U.S. Senate. (2014). *Sexual violence on campus: How too many institutions of higher education are failing to protect students.* Washington, DC: U.S. Senate Subcommittee on Financial and Contracting Oversight.

White House Task Force to Protect Students from Sexual Assault. (2014). *Not alone.* Retrieved from www.whitehouse.gov/sites/default/files/docs/report_0.pdf

Wooten, S. C. (2014). Critical interventions: Addressing the reality of LGBTQ sexual violence in higher education. In E. J. Meyer & D. L. Carlson (Eds.) *Handbook on Gender and Sexualities in Education.* New York, NY: Peter Lang Publishing.

PART II

Power and Reputation in Institutional Decision Making

4

COMBATING SEXUAL VIOLENCE IN THE IVY LEAGUE

Reflections on Politics, Pain, and Progress

Susan Marine

Our cohogs; they play one; they're all here to spoil our fun
(chorus) with a knick-knack, paddywhack, send the bitches home
Our cohogs go to bed alone . . .
Our cohogs, they play six, they all love those Tri Kapp dicks . . .
Our cohogs, they play seven, they have ruined our masculine heaven
                    "Our cohogs," Sung at a Dartmouth spring sing
                    competition in 1978 (Merton, 1979, p. 60)

One of my earliest childhood memories involves sitting at a dinner party with my mother where she proudly announced to the other guests that she, along with my father, had attended Columbia University in New York City. The other adults at the table nodded and murmured admiringly, and I suddenly knew that there were some colleges—like theirs—that were just *better* than others, whose students carried prestige with them long after their time enrolled. I also recall knowing intuitively that my parents, both college professors, bore the seal of approval of a place I would never be wealthy enough or bright enough to attend. While I never dared to aspire to attend an Ivy League school as a student, their glimmering aura was stamped in my brain, and when I was offered a position as the sexual abuse awareness program coordinator at Dartmouth College in 1996, I entered the world of the Ivy League with excitement and more than a bit of pride. I felt I would finally truly understand the mysteries of power and belonging that such privileged institutions conferred and that in a place of such vast concentrated wealth and so many brilliant minds, I would surely make headway in the social problem I most cared about: ending sexual violence. What I learned from those four years, and the nine that followed at Harvard College, led me to understand in deeper ways how power functions in these institutions, and how I naïvely believed that such power can and will be reconfigured when logic and data are abundantly shared and understood. This is the story of that journey, and what I learned to be true about the realities of sexual assault at the two Ivies where I once worked.

Sexual Assault in the Ivy League: A Brief History

Campus rape is a serious problem across the United States, and it's worth wondering what makes the Ivy League different in terms of addressing serious problems of sexual abuse between students. I believe the answer lies with the interweaving of three distinct factors: their histories, their prestige, and the degree of resistance to public scrutiny of these institutions, particularly when any weakness of their vaunted characters is exposed.

The Ivy League[1] institutions were among the first colleges and universities in America, founded in New England, New York, and Pennsylvania in the 17th and 18th centuries explicitly for the education of (mostly) well-to-do White landowners and "gentleman farmer's" sons. Their early curricula included civics, mathematics, and Latin, and they primarily existed for the cultivation of Protestant religious values into public life and leadership (Thelin, 2011). For more than 200 years, this was the purpose of these institutions; yet over time, this purpose gave way to a more robust program of preparation for civic and social leadership, particularly in business, law, and medicine. While Cornell University welcomed female students in 1870, just two years after its founding, and the University of Pennsylvania admitted women in 1880, all of the other Ivies were men's colleges until the late 1960s and early 1970s (A Survey of Coeducation, 1974). Arguably, the most selective of the Ivies—Harvard, Princeton, and Yale—became coeducational as a result of the groundswell of support for women's equal education during the second wave of feminism beginning in the 1960s. While prestigious women's colleges such as Smith and Wellesley long "stood in" for the Ivies in terms of quality of education and rigor, many believed that until women had access to the Ivies, they would not truly be able to access the same quality of education and privileges as men attending these vaunted institutions (Solomon, 1985).

While women were not permitted to attend most of the Ivies until the 1970s, it should not be assumed that they were absent from the campus scene, particularly from male students' social lives. Occasionally granted special permission to study at an Ivy, women from local women's colleges were far more likely to be bused in to the all-male Ivies to attend mixers and teas on weekends, then shuttled back to their campuses via buses still known colloquially as the "fuck truck" and the "cuddle shuttle" (Gutierrez, 2006). Alcohol-fueled social events, combined with the irregularity of the shuttle, meant that these "coeds" were vulnerable to pressures to spend the night or to both drink and identify a male "host" rapidly in an effort to maximize time at the men's colleges—both certain conditions for unwanted or coercive sex. Much of what passed for "drunken hooking up" in the years prior to coeducation would today be legally (if not ethically) considered rape, yet it was not until the national wave of awareness of the 1990s that the Ivies, along with most other colleges, were put on notice that student-on-student rape was a crime and must be treated as such.

Which brings me to the second factor that sets the Ivies slightly apart: the prestige of these institutions. Prestigious colleges, designed for and replete with legions of wealthy, intellectually curious young men and women, are not typically places that are associated with the commission of crimes, particularly violent felonies. There is something so unseemly about asserting that a handful (never mind a significant number) of students who have the intellect, wealth, and connections inherent to attending such colleges might be sexually felonious; indeed, it defies the collective imagination, given over as it is to stereotypes of the rapist as furtive, often "dark" (either literally or figuratively, as racism shapes and configures our imaginations) stranger. Such villains are presumed to be constitutionally unable to conceal their sociopathic nature among the rigors of elite college life. The prestige, of course, also shapes the ways that members of these communities—including faculty and staff—may be unwilling to recognize rape when it happens, alongside their own beliefs about themselves (and the others around them) as "special" and "chosen." Such prestige, imbued by generations of wealthy donors' support, confers a veil of protection upon these institutions' choices and policies. How could they have otherwise endured for centuries, unless their leaders in fact consistently show *impeccable* judgment?

The truth is, even those who lead Ivy league institutions are human beings, subject to the same fallibilities as any others reared within rape culture.[2] But to those on the outside, those who never belonged and who are not invited into the circle, there is something delectably satisfying when the inevitably errant judgments of Ivy leadership are on full display in the public domain, a phenomenon that one astute dean at Harvard characterized to me once as the joy that both the media and the general public take when "the mighty look silly." Recent allegations of poorly handled reports of sexual abuse at Harvard, Yale, Columbia, and Princeton remind us that when powerful institutions are perceived to fail their constituents, the public embarrassment tax that is levied is swift, vocal, and viral (Perez-Pena, 2013). This public scrutiny takes the wind out of the sails of these institutions, and even if only for a moment, they are revealed to be vulnerable and imperfect, like every other. Ultimately, the Ivies' histories, prestige, and resistance to scrutiny create a complex mix of accountability and imperviousness to it that I came to understand gradually through my decade and a half in their midst.

My Years at Dartmouth College: 1996–2000

Dartmouth College is nestled in the bucolic Upper Valley of New Hampshire and is often referred to lovingly as "the college on the hill." Dartmouth's founder, Eleazar Wheelock, founded the college in 1769 for the education of Native Americans to "spread civilization and Christianity among the savages" (Childs,

1957, p. 1). By all accounts, Dartmouth became coeducational reluctantly. Holding fast to its identity as a college for men, many students reacted with hostility to the 1971 Trustee Vote to usher in coeducation, lamenting that "175 years is a long time to hold out against the onslaughts of the female" (Forcier, 2004, p. 154).

According to Regina Barreca (2005), one of the first women to enroll at Dartmouth, "Being a woman at Dartmouth College in the 1970s was like having a double major. You were not only a freshman, you were also a coed . . . as if having more estrogen in your system changed everything . . . you were graded not only by your professors, but also by the boys on fraternity row" (p. 5). It is difficult to underestimate the resistance young women faced as they attempted to break the coeducational barrier at Dartmouth—enduring taunts of being called "the enemy" and "dirty whores," while a dean awarded a spring sing prize to a group of students who penned the previously quoted anthem, "Our cohogs"—a pejorative play on the word "coed" (Hernandez, 2012, p. 1). Simultaneously, women students were viewed as objects of sexual conquest—one surefire strategy for ensuring that they would not be taken seriously in the classroom.

Dartmouth has long been believed to be a bastion of conservatism, owing not only to its largely White and until recently disproportionately male student body, but also to its notoriously conservative student newspaper, *The Dartmouth Review*, which produced a number of famous pundits including Dinesh D'Souza and Laura Ingraham. Friends and relatives who knew me to be a socially progressive feminist wondered aloud at whether I had some kind of professional death wish when I decided to take the job at Dartmouth. Tackling issues of sexual violence on campus was hard enough—did I really need to do so in the "belly of the beast"? The power of Dartmouth's Greek system—parodied in the film *Animal House*—was undeniable. Still, my visit to the campus on a snowy February night in 1996 reassured me, as the strong turnout for my interviews and the open student forum suggested that there was a core group of racially diverse activists, many of whom were queer-identified, ready to take on the school's legacy of sexism. Deans, faculty, and senior student life administrators were also fully engaged throughout my selection process, suggesting that the college was ready to move the prevention of sexual violence beyond the interests of the stalwart group that frequented the women's resource center. When I asked the students at the open forum what was most needed at the time, I distinctly recall one young woman who clearly opined, "we need someone who can talk the boys' language and yet be approachable so that survivors will not feel afraid to disclose." I wondered if I had the mettle to provide the needed compassion while steeling myself for dismantling the resistance.

It is important to say that Dartmouth in 1996 had one of the most well-established and funded sexual assault prevention programs in the nation. Ably led first by counseling psychologist Heather Earle and then by alumna Liza Veto, the program I inherited in 1996 had many features that other colleges had not yet dreamed of. Dartmouth offered student survivors a 24-hour response system, annual training in effective response to student disclosures for all student affairs staff, a protocol that included a coordinated police and medical care response, and a consistently applied adjudication process. Students were organized into a peer response group (sexual assault peer advisors or SAPAs) and an education committee, and the annual Take Back the Night March routinely drew 200 or more participants.

Dartmouth during the mid- to late 1990s was mired in a significant cultural transformation prompted by a spate of anti-immigrant legislation, most notably California's proposition 209 (Trounson, 2006). The legislation, which prohibited considerations of race and gender in college admissions and hiring at California's public universities, touched nerves on campuses nationwide, particularly those like Dartmouth where students of color and women had always occupied second-class status positions. Progressive student activists at Dartmouth sponsored rallies, debates, and protests as the typically slumbering conservative bloc suddenly rose up to decry what they saw as falsely laid blame for discrimination. In the words of one member of the Conservative Union at Dartmouth, "students regardless of color will be more likely to fail if placed into situations for which they are not qualified" (Horowitz, 1996), implying that by definition those whose civil rights were protected by affirmative action laws were ill-suited for selective college life. The deep and mounting frustration of radical students determined to push back against any vestiges of privilege—but particularly those associated with White male patriarchy—was vivid, urgent, and palpable during that year. Attending these events, I was moved by the vision of coalition-building in action. Young women and queer people of all genders, ethnicities, and races were walking the talk, bringing serious and sustained attention to intersectional cultural and social change across the campus, knowing that in doing so, no singular or isolated effort to any violence in any form would suffice.

The warm glow cast by the fires of anti-Prop 209 activism, however bright, did not occlude the glaring truth that Dartmouth's student culture was rife with serious issues that contributed to the occurrence of sexual violence, such as a heavily gender-stratified social system that revolved around membership in fraternities and secret societies, a subtly oppressive code of silence around issues of women's belonging and agency, and students' relentless devotion to the game of Beer Pong. "Pong," as it continues to be affectionately called, enabled rapid drinking under the guise of a modified ping-pong game and is hailed both as the social glue of an otherwise disparate and scattered student body and a balm for soothing the long northern New Hampshire winters (Knight, 2013). Pong, and other drinking games, were the center of the action in the fraternity house basements, where the vast majority of drinking and socializing happened on campus, since the national sororities' charters prohibited drinking.

I arrived on campus only months after the revelations of a more nefarious aspect of Dartmouth's student culture resurfaced: rampant hazing. Two videos secretly made in the late 1980s—one named "Hell Night," the other named "Sex Room"—depicted fraternity pledges being forced to recount their sexual histories while sitting bare-bottomed on blocks of ice and being forced to perform fellatio on an ejaculating dildo. Others were shown drinking copious amounts of alcohol while being screamed at and beaten. These videos were shown publicly in the campus center, followed by a discussion led by Tom Luxon and Ivy Schweitzer, professors of English literature. One fraternity member attending the event was quoted as saying that men participate in these aspects of fraternity life because it is the one place "where you can express penisness" (Grey, 1994).

While current members of the two fraternities in question denied participation in such actions, the tapes had left an indelible mark on the campus' psyche and had revealed the brutally compulsory masculinity circulating in Dartmouth's fraternity system. This system, almost exclusively populated by White men, was fighting mightily against rumors of its irrelevance, while more and more students began to question the logic (and desirability) of a system that so clearly perpetuated White male dominance. As I began my work there, I decided that whether I felt ready or not, I had to spend many hours in conversations with students and faculty about what the tapes meant and what the larger culture of Dartmouth's White and male-centered social system might also mean for all students' ability to negotiate relationships safely and to be taken seriously in this environment. I was determined to make some headway, any at all, by actively seeking out opportunities to interact with men's social groups and to provide education and awareness.

These outings were admittedly precarious, and I wondered what I was doing showing up at fraternities to advocate for a shift in their cultures and practices. Nervously scouting out the nearest exit, lest I should be shouted down, I began each of these visits by calmly relaying to the members of the fraternity some of the stories I had heard that day, week, or month about women's experiences in the social scene at Dartmouth. They sat listening, usually politely, while I described to them the scenarios: woman visits party, eyes the guy she has been interested in from class, they drink and dance until she feels tired, he offers to walk her upstairs where they can be alone and she gamely agrees. Kissing is fine, even welcome, but her pleas to refrain from removing clothing and from having sex with her without her permission fall on deaf ears. There is often crying, physical struggle, and verbal protest, unless she is too drunk to speak (and often, she is—from playing Pong or from punchbowls filled with mysterious concoctions whose odorless alcohol is difficult to detect). There is rarely a scene made, rarely a way for others to hear her through the closed door and loud music of the party. She returns home the next day, bruised, afraid, and shaken, unsure of what to do next and whom to tell. She sees him, walking with his brothers; she knows, intuitively, that being invited to the house, and to their social gathering, is a prize for which she is expected to be grateful. She tries to forget what happened but reminders abound. She spends her days fighting the fog of memory and fear; she retreats from her own life, her own joys, everything that made her glad to be at Dartmouth. She waits for things to get better, while she also senses the slippage in her grades, her weight, the color in her cheeks. Ultimately she resigns herself to one of two fates: pushing her way through, trying to forget the experience and the weight of the judgments around her, or leaving, trying to forget the value of what she left behind, the prize of the privilege of being there.

To their credit, I was never in fact shouted down when I visited the Dartmouth fraternities. Many times, the young men's faces changed, from hard denial to curiosity to reluctant recognition—they had indeed seen or heard of this scenario or one like it, many of them, from women friends or from girlfriends who'd had the bad luck to encounter the "wrong guy" in the "pig house." What they lacked was the language and the necessary moral courage to see it and call it rape; the tools to see imminent danger and stand up for the safety of women who were vulnerable in their own house. I suspect that some may have even recognized themselves as perpetrators in the stories I relayed. Eventually, one brave soul would often speak up, hesitantly, and ask what they could do to help. The story part was easy; I more often blundered my way through the solution, mixing my pleas for vigilance with a concomitant urging not to see women as victims, not to assume women need their intervention to ward off their own vulnerability. I worried deeply about sending a sex-negative message that would imply that women can never act on their desires affirmatively when drinking is obscuring their judgment. The prevention message was thus the part that was less fluid, less sanguine. In those early years, I rarely landed in a place of confidence regarding their role in rape's elimination. Were they to step in or respect women's sexual desire and agency? Were they to learn signs of predatory behavior, and if so, what might they be? Were they to recognize their brothers as sexist, what exactly should they say or do to shift the needle of consciousness toward respect? And perhaps most intractably, if they persistently refused to own up to their own cultures of domination evident in the "Sex" and "Hell" tapes, what then could I do to persuade them that domination in any form is wrong? Sometimes they would surprise me with their own initiative, as in the case of the Zeta Psi fraternity, who decided to make the issue of rape prevention their pet cause one year, bringing resolutions to the Greek council to require safety monitors at every party, responsible for ensuring that dark corners were monitored and furtive exits with those who were compromised by alcohol were intervened in. In these moments I would feel hope, forward movement, and a momentary abatement of the unresolved questions.

But these and other questions haunted me in my four years of work at Dartmouth. I began to read voraciously about rape and its causes: Could *ever* be a gender-stratified social system that was safe? Unlikely, given what anthropologists have told us about rape supportive culture (Reeves-Sanday, 1992). Could women *ever* both express their sexuality freely and feel certain that such expressions would not be mistaken as invitations to rape? Depends, said the sociologists examining how rape has and has not changed over millennia (Brownmiller, 1993; Schwendinger & Schwendinger, 1983). Noting the fervor with which the student activists of the Prop 209 moment insisted that all subordination is linked, I began to examine and actively transform the composition of the peer educator and peer responder corps, seeing that White students occupied those groups disproportionately. Consulting the work of scholars of African American studies showed me that rape and its aftermath affects communities of color differently (Gunning, 1996), particularly when they coexist in a predominantly White (and, therefore, racist) institutional backdrop. Despite these efforts to integrate knowledge and data into my work, the truth was that the more I read, the more circular the argument in my own head became. If we truly do not know what causes and prevents sexual violence on college campuses, if even the questions are more complex than we ever imagined, than how can we shift the needle—even when surrounded by intelligence, resources, and determination?

For me, the answers were certainly elusive but continually pointed back to one unresolved issue: we do not truly understand perpetration. The work of David Lisak and Paul Miller (2002)[3] has unquestionably helped us to better understand the mind of what they term the "undetected" rapist on the college campus. But it is clear to me that we have overinvested in critiquing rape culture supportive elements like gender segregated group dynamics, Beer Pong, and some young women's burgeoning interest in participation in things like "Girls Gone Wild," while neglecting the most fundamental of all questions: Why do perpetrators— particularly perpetrators of privileged backgrounds—rape, and what can we do to stop them? What courage of intellect and imagination do we need to muster when sitting across the table at a judicial hearing from a well-dressed, well-spoken young man, an alleged rapist, pleading to return to his carefree life at an Ivy League school? What enables us to determine his sincerity, when he insists he did not cause the anguish that the young woman in the other room claims was his doing and her undoing? This vexing problem is where my heart and head landed in my four years at Dartmouth, and this was and continues to be, to my mind, the most critical question perched at the apex of the power, privilege, and history of the Ivy League.

In my final year at Dartmouth, I began to notice a troubling pattern in the makeup of students reporting sexual violence—nearly one-third of the reports I received within a 3-year span of time were made by Asian and Asian American women, primarily of East Asian descent. I recall making a hesitant phone call to Nora Yasumura, the Asian Pacific Programming Liaison (and later Assistant Dean of Asian American Student Life) to discuss the trends. I was acutely aware that the data would alarm many within the community, as well as without. I was familiar with the extensive body of literature on the deeply harmful, otherizing phenomena of Asian fetishsizing promulgated by White men (Cho, 1997; Mohanty, Russo, & Torres, 1991; Rivers, 1990). I wasn't sure of why this was happening, or even who was perpetrating the violence, as I rarely asked the perpetrators' identity (since so few students were willing to disclose). Despite my misgivings that I, as a White woman, was not equipped to interpret or even respond to this phenomenon, I was certain that the numbers implicated a concerning trend that needed to be addressed. Soon after my call to Yasumura, a student panel and formation of a committee followed. Signaling the profound uncertainty of what a meaningful intervention in this issue would be, the only concrete outcome I recall of bringing this truth to light was the elevated fear that Asian women at Dartmouth openly expressed to me during this time. To this day, I have been haunted about why— and how—the dynamics of race and racism were shaping Dartmouth's social culture in this particular way and how impotent I (and others) felt in its wake.

Though I now understood the enormity of what it would take to effect the kind of change that would feel tangible, I left Dartmouth in the year 2000 willingly, following my partner to the slightly warmer climes and urbanity of Boston. At my going-away, a young woman whom I had supported after she was raped by a popular lacrosse player came up to me and told me that she had decided not to transfer after all and to make the Dartmouth experience her own, in spite of what she had been through. The same day, I received a letter in the mail inviting me to become an honorary member of the class of 2000, voted in by a jury of senior class students who had admired my efforts. Admittedly, the lure of both "helping" and "belonging" was very palpable.

That glow lasted only briefly. A few months after my departure, I received a phone call from the past president of the Zeta Psi fraternity, asking me if I would be willing to vouch for the group with the Dartmouth administration. It seemed the fraternity members had circulated a newsletter in a recent chapter meeting that included "date rape techniques." It was meant to be a joke, he said, but the college is taking it seriously. Could I tell the college how much they had supported my office and how many times I visited them to discuss the seriousness of rape?

Whatever satisfaction I felt as an honorary member of a Dartmouth class, who had helped a young woman find her place and voice beyond the terror of rape, drained from my heart that day. I was officially, now and always, a part of this community, but it was a community where unspeakably harmful acts were continuing, in places where I thought I had made a difference. I refused his request, hung up the phone, and cried for days.

The Harvard College Years: 2002–2006

Two years after my relocation to Boston, I received an email one day from an Assistant Provost at Harvard, Marsha Semuels, whom I had met when guest speaking at a panel discussion on campus rape. After a recent rash of high-profile rapes resulting in criminal convictions, Harvard was beginning a year-long process of examining its culture and reporting mechanisms related to sexual assault (Maytal, 2002). Marsha asked if I would be interested in serving as a consultant for the university and bringing my expertise from Dartmouth to bear on the problems facing Harvard. Admittedly, I was eager to try again. The wounds of failures to create change at Dartmouth had healed over enough to make the challenge enticing: I wanted to know if the potential for change that was unrealized at Dartmouth could truly happen at Harvard, which was undeniably even more well-resourced and less hampered by its own history of coeducation, which I assumed had been far smoother.

My first day at Harvard, October 10, 2002, started auspiciously. I attended a dinner at the Faculty Club where I met the other members of the Committee to Address Sexual Assault at Harvard (CASAH), or the Leaning Committee, named after its formidable chair, Jennifer Leaning (Crimson Staff, 2003). The conversation at the table was initially convivial but soon fell somber: Harvard had a serious problem with how students perceived its willingness to confront rape, and the committee's charge was to understand why that was happening and what could be done to address it. The committee was densely populated with senior faculty, all heavy hitters in the influence department, and I immediately sensed that what was happening at Harvard, where the stakes for visible change in ending campus rape were higher than anywhere else, would be profound.

The next day, I met privately with the student activists whose relentless commitment to change sparked the college's responsiveness. Sarah Levit-Shore, Alisha Johnson, and Ellenor Honig, among many others, played a pivotal role in demanding accountability for recent events. They told me how their persistent and steady work had resulted in hard-won changes but that much remained to be done. Their continued advocacy through the campus anti-rape group, The Coalition Against Sexual Violence (CASV), was sparked by an unmet list of demands that had been sent to the administration the previous year, including better response services for survivors, a women's center, and a more swift and sensitive response to complaints through the college's Administrative Board. I learned that over the last four decades, many such iterations of student demands and administrative responses had failed to adequately address perceptions about how Harvard handled rape (Doshi, Franken, & Kitchen, 2001). Now, these activists made clear, they were demanding more and better from the CASAH.

In order to better understand the activists' concerns, I began to unearth the recent history of Harvard related to rape. The 1999 dismissal of student Joshua Elster, who had recently been convicted of two counts of assault and battery and three counts of rape in the Middlesex County courts, was rare for Harvard, although the faculty had voted one month previously to also expel D. Drew Douglas, also was convicted in the courts of rape. At the Douglas deliberations, five faculty introduced a failed motion to lessen his punishment to five years' probation, rather than full dismissal (Helderman, 1999). Some 350 students protested outside the faculty meeting that same day about a range of social issues, including the ongoing perception that Harvard was soft on rape, drawing public attention to the gaping wound in Harvard's social contract with students. Months earlier, an unnamed undergraduate, presumably fed up with the inaction of the school to take on these issues in a more systemic manner, filed a complaint with the Office of Civil Rights. Harvard College had recently decided to require "corroborating evidence" of a rape, and the complaint sought to reverse that decision and to restore "prompt and equitable" grievance procedures (Sombuntham, 2002).

Morale among the activists was low: the general feeling on campus was that despite all of the evidence, the college was unconcerned about rape, and if it pretended to be, it was only to protect its vaunted image of itself.

This perception was one that the CASAH was determined to understand and change. What I remember of that year was attending a dizzying circuit of meetings, as we reached out to every conceivable corner of student life to learn more about what students, faculty, and alumni thought and understood about the issues. Many showed up to these gatherings and spoke, but their tones were typically measured and polite. In contrast, the formidable pressures brought to bear on Harvard during this era were significant and primarily external. Nationally recognized legal scholars and feminist activists, like Wendy Murphy, put Harvard on notice: We are watching, and we will hold you accountable for observing the law, specifically, the mandates of Title IX (Dusky, 2003). Thanks to a well-publicized email account set up for gathering the perspectives of alumni, stories trickled in of women who had experienced assault, had brought complaints forward, and had felt dismissed. Faculty, deans, and other response personnel were named by these alumni as inherently unapproachable, fostering an environment—primarily with careless, victim-blaming words and actions—that had made it impossible to come forward and to hold their perpetrators accountable.

Taking all of this in, I was busy making myself known and available to as many student groups as possible, in the hopes that survivors would seek out my support and allow me into their trusted circle so that I could connect them with resources. Reflecting on it now, I can imagine the very real mistrust a student, particularly one whose trust had been so egregiously violated by a peer, would have had for an unknown older adult who had been hired to ostensibly bolster the school's image around responsiveness to sexual assault. But surprisingly, many did come forward for support, and I began to formulate a picture of sexual violence at Harvard that was not unlike that at Dartmouth.

Most assaults were committed by someone the student knew and knew well. Once again, the oppression of a gender-stratified social system—in this case, promulgated by Harvard's all-male, mostly White and affluent final clubs—created a common context for heavy drinking and minimal safeguards for women, who were only allowed to partake of drinks if they were brought to her by a male member. While some students spoke to me about assaults happening in these clubs' premises, I learned that just as many assaults took place in students' rooms, before, after, or never having visited a final club party. For the first time, I began hearing stories of assault in the LGBTQ community, and quickly learned that my own outness as a lesbian was essential to these students' willingness to come forward into the light of day. In nearly every case, the students were vigilantly wary of reporting the crimes to any campus or local police departments and refused to confer with me if they perceived this would be obligatory. In the rare cases when they wanted to pursue the crimes in local courts, more often than not, they were told by prosecutors and police that the "nuances" of their cases—a known perpetrator, alcohol or drug involvement, and a hazy memory of exactly what had happened—would render their cases "unprosecutable" and that it would be regrettably impossible to convince an unsympathetic jury of the students' plight.

Many are quick to criticize colleges and universities—especially those with everything at stake in terms of their reputation and public image—for taking on cases of rape and sexual assault internally, through their own college judicial systems (Favot, 2011; McNamara, 2013). But what I witnessed during my time at both Dartmouth and Harvard was that the criminal court system was persistently unwilling, even in cases with a determined survivor, to take on the typical cases seen on college campuses, leaving the students I supported with no choice but to pursue their complaint through the college's channels. Because these processes bring the risk of exposure and the potential for a disappointing verdict, most chose not to pursue them at all. Meanwhile, rapists who otherwise masquerade as bright, privileged, and high-achieving—a handful of the vast majority of the kind of students who go to these colleges, after all—continue to rape with impunity, as the (broken) system serves their interests.

It was against this backdrop of dead-end "options" that I came to understand something else, something that was previously quietly obscured about Harvard survivors' impossibly complex choices. The lifetime of hard work and commitment to excellence that the survivors I worked with had spent earning their coveted spot at Harvard was an agonizing thing to let go, and yet survivors often did, feeling the impossibility of continuing. The stress of seeing the perpetrator, feeling he or she had lost nothing, while feeling their own lives at Harvard collapsing in around them was simply too much to bear. For those who left, the sting of this loss never fully diminished and symbolized the greatest injustice of all. Their belonging to this privileged place, the belonging that promised to provide them with a lifetime of opportunities and connections, had slipped through their hands. The institution, and their trust in it, failed them in ways from which they would never be able to fully recover. The weight of this institutional betrayal, though noted by scholars in the field as something that can be fixed (Freyd & Birrell, 2013), typically was not, and left the survivors I worked with at Harvard with a deep and visceral sense of abandonment that was impossible to fully redress.

The CASAH continued its work through the rest of 2002 and into 2003, eventually releasing a lengthy report of findings that included a clear statement of need for significantly expanded awareness and prevention education, a nod to the fact that the vast majority of Harvard students did not know or understand the legal definition of rape (Seltzer, 2003). The committee also recommended the establishment of a trained "fact finder," an attorney specializing in sexual harassment law, to conduct investigations of cases brought to the Administrative Board, a subtle but clear indication that the long-held practice of having resident deans—academics serving in student support roles—conduct investigations and gather all relevant information was insufficient for getting at the truth of the matter. The report also called for the establishment of the Office of Sexual Assault Prevention and Response (OSAPR) and provided funding for three professional positions and a 24-hour hotline, a significant investment of human and capital resources at the time. As the OSAPR's founding director, I encountered both support and frustration in building a new system to serve survivors and to begin to make headway in the more problematic elements of the student culture, including the final clubs. Due to the fact that the Harvard administration "released" them to independence a decade prior, relinquishing any institutional oversight, the clubs' sense of obligation to participate in educational programs or to adopt additional safety monitoring was miniscule. My colleagues and I traded on their goodwill to make this happen, but it was a far cry from the days of working with the Greeks at Dartmouth, bolstered by the institutional support for mandating education for all such groups. My colleagues Heather Wilson and Gordon Braxton made admirable headway in the effort to reach some of the clubs, but ultimately, these clubs' commitment to ending their ages-old practices that reduced women to mere "guests" in their dwellings was (and remains) patently insincere.

Still, I was proud of the work we did as a committee and proud of the structures we built to respond to the cavernous need for more education, serious prevention, and a reporting and adjudication system that would represent fairness and equity for all. But I was troubled by one glaring omission from the CASAH report and from the work we were doing as a committee and continue to feel that it limited the effectiveness of our approaches. Quite simply, the decades of feminist theorizing, activist strategies, and promotion of a *gendered* awareness of interpersonal violence that had emerged since the 1970s was routinely silenced or ignored in this era at Harvard. While Harvard has produced (as students) and employed (as scholars) a small army of noted feminists who have written copiously on the topic of men's violence against women, these analyses were mistrusted and muted from the analysis of the issues at Harvard, as many preferred to position rape and assault primarily as an issue of alcohol abuse, female collusion in unsupervised, male-controlled social spaces, and the absence of a consistent narrative from survivors.

Such explanations were drained of relevant feminist and pro-feminist thought, emanating from Harvard and Radcliffe alumni and faculty like Susan Faludi, Katha Pollitt, Debra Prothrow-Stith, Jackson Katz, Judith Herman, Diane Rosenfeld, and numerous other scholars, journalists, and writers whose thinking has shaped what we know to be true about the intersection of violent masculinity and sexual subordination. It seemed to me that "going there"—truly calling for an examination of the culture, and mining the effects of almost 400 years of male-centered ideology and leadership at Harvard, was untenable. I once again began to understand that the period surrounding the college's process toward coeducation was rocky, and that women were, in many ways, still catching up. There might not have been an "our cohog" sense of open hostility, but Radcliffe alumnae across generations spoke of feeling like second-class citizens on their own campus, even as they eventually became integrated into Harvard proper (Rimer, 1997). Women of past eras had eloquently spoken and written of what it was like to become part of Harvard (Ulrich, 2004), but the narratives I was hearing from young women in the early 2000s suggested that not much—certainly not enough—had changed. I was discouraged, again and again, from bringing that analysis into the frame, from asking those questions, even though much of this rich thinking had emerged from "Harvard's own."

While at Harvard, I continued to be deeply troubled by the lack of attention paid to perpetration. I attempted to articulate the urgency of this matter in an essay published in the *Chronicle of Higher Education* (Marine, 2004). I note now how measured my own language was—how easily I lapsed into the less-politicized, more clinical language of "public health," a sure sign of my own complicity in the neutering of the issue at hand. In this essay, I wrote:

> True prevention (as we know from other public-health initiatives) would involve identifying the causes of rape, testing interventions with high-risk groups and individuals, and widely disseminating information about successful results . . . we must face a sobering reality: Sexually coercive and violent men attend our classes, play on our teams, and even graduate with honors from our colleges. . . . Establishing effective policies for responding to a rape is not enough. We must redouble our efforts to prevent rape before it happens.
>
> *(Marine, 2004, p. B5)*

Feminist analysis of this seemingly intractable social problem was, and continued to be, mistrusted at Harvard. But even as I struggled with that reality, I was reminded daily of its necessity in the stories of the survivors I worked with, survivors trying to make sense of why everything and everyone around them seemed complicit in their silence. And I still vividly recall being asked one day, by a respected senior faculty member, what the OSAPR was doing to help young men understand their risk of being falsely accused of rape by women. I still think about that, and I still wonder what she meant.

Weaving Together the Ivy: Reflections in Conclusion

In the three years since I left Harvard (where I served as the director of the women's center from 2006–2011, after leaving the OSAPR), I have had many opportunities to reflect on the experiences I had there as well as those I had at Dartmouth. Despite the abundant resources, the commitment of many tireless activists, and the support of many in the faculty and in the administration, I have been particularly struck by how little forward movement has been made, collectively, in ending campus sexual violence at Ivies or any other college. All indications are that rape and other forms of sexual violence are alive and kicking at colleges across the country. The past two years have seen an explosion of high-profile cases reported at Ivies, including Dartmouth and Yale, and many other colleges. For several months, it seemed each time I tuned into the news I would see feminist attorney Gloria Allred standing next to a tearful young woman, recounting yet another tale of institutional negligence in response to her experience of assault. The good news is that survivors now feel legitimate in speaking out; the bad news is, as I saw first-hand, their speaking out exacts a high price on them and their educational futures.

In conversations with others about my time at Dartmouth and Harvard, I often encounter assumptions that are unfounded and that must be challenged. There's a persistent belief that because these institutions are enormously wealthy, that all *students* at Ivies are wealthy, powerful, and privileged and that all have the family support and material resources to withstand any adversity. Thanks to programs that have rendered these institutions far more accessible to low-income and first-generation students, this is not always the case—many of the students I worked with lacked the wealth and subsequent social capital to thrive at Harvard while surviving the harrowing experience of rape. The public perception that "what Harvard and Dartmouth (and schools like it) do, others will follow" is also mistaken. Ivy League leadership on the issue of sexual assault is largely due to the resources these schools can marshal in the service of student support and less about the inherent superiority of any of their own prevention or harm reduction approaches. Given that there is still so much we don't know about nonsociopathic perpetrators—about their motivations and about interrupting them—such institutions would do well to devote more of their abundant resources to answering this urgent question. Most of all, the belief that the kind of people who rape do not find their way to, and succeed in, elite institutions must be studied, countered, and changed. I now understand that the kind of tacit approval that people everywhere, including my parents' friends, attribute to the Ivies occludes courageous confrontation of this very real problem.

In June of 2013, Yale University released a report of recently adjudicated cases in which a student was charged with "nonconsensual sex"—critics swiftly charged this was an overly polite euphemism for what is actually rape and expressed outrage at the fact that the offending student was issued a written reprimand (Kingkade, 2013). Language that attempts to redefine rape as a vaguely aberrant departure from "normal" human sexual behavior is unhelpful. There is something so patrician about changing the word rape to "nonconsensual sex"—a subtle shift that feels familiar to me, as someone who benefited enormously from the many perks of living among and working in the Ivies for more than a decade. This kind of politeness and civility are the calling cards of such places; a long-cultivated kind of gentility circumscribes the way that everything—including, it seems, life-altering social phenomena—is interpreted and responded to. It quietly erodes the power of personal revelations of suffering, of pain, of "weakness" affecting one's march toward success via academic achievement. Such disclosures, I learned, are unwelcome, bordering on distasteful.

But we're talking about rape here. It's distasteful. It's demeaning, and it's ugly. As this book goes to press, new allegations of inattention to the seriousness of sexual assault in the Ivies have surfaced. A Title IX violation has been levied against Dartmouth, Harvard and 90 other colleges currently under investigation for mishandling student reports and providing insufficient assurance of redress (Anderson, 2014). A survivor-led activist alumni group, Dartmouth Change, is applying increased pressure and attention to the ways that the college has permitted the problem to continue unabated (Dartmouth Change, 2014). The recently inaugurated President Philip Hanlon has called for Dartmouth students to "clean up their act" (Potter, 2014) and has allocated additional resources to the founding of a Center for Community Action and Prevention (Platt, 2014). Perhaps most promisingly, a conference bringing together activists, researchers, legal experts, and social change advocates was convened on the campus in July 2014. I participated in this event and the working groups meetings that followed, and for the first time in many years, feel that the ground is shifting in terms of resolve to address the issues at a meaningful, national, and coordinated level.

Down the road in Cambridge, Harvard made the list of institutions under question for Title IX violations, at both the undergraduate college and the law school. In response, President Drew Faust recently convened a Sexual Assault Task Force, chaired by Provost Steven Hyman and including prominent faculty, legal experts, and student activists, to determine the best courses of action. Their work has culminated in a preliminary report allocating additional resources to the OSAPR, including additional funding for education and prevention, and a Harvard-specific campus climate survey ("New resources," 2014). It is encouraging to see the most influential leaders at these colleges—presidents and provosts—taking an active role in these matters. It is even more encouraging to see the inclusion of scholars who bring a historicized analysis of gendered power relations to the task. This is the factor most likely to bring about real and substantial change, to transform these institutions from being players in these matters to being leaders.

And the truth is, whether it is openly acknowledged or not, America has a social contract with the Ivies, which goes something like this: We permit you to define and deploy the operations of your particularly elitist institutions (relatively) unquestioned, and you in turn take on and solve the kinds of human problems that can only be mastered with significant amounts of money and the well-channeled brilliance of those who teach, conduct research, and study in your midst. These institutions have met and exceeded that agreement on a vast array of the causes of human suffering: cancers we previously thought untreatable, human trafficking, addiction, famine, and corporate malfeasance, just to name a few. Campus rape awaits the same fate.

Notes

1. The Ivy League colleges are Harvard, Princeton, Yale, and Columbia Universities, the University of Pennsylvania, and Dartmouth, Brown, and Cornell Colleges.

2. Rape culture refers to the backdrop of current social norms that normalize sexual violence and permit rapists to rape with impunity (e.g., Buchwald, Fletcher, & Roth, 2005).
3. Lisak and Miller conducted interviews with college-age men who acknowledged manipulating vulnerable women, especially freshmen, into overconsumption of alcohol, to facilitate sexually assaulting them. Their study has shaped what we understand about the rapist who is not apprehended or incarcerated but instead operates freely in the college domain.

References

Anderson, N. (2014, May 1). 55 colleges under Title IX inquiry for their handling of sex violence claims. *Washington Post*. Retrieved from www.washingtonpost.com/local/education/federal-government-releases-list-of-55-colleges-universities-under-title-ix-investigations-over-handling-of-sexual-violence/2014/05/01/e0a74810-d13b-11e3-937f-d3026234b51c_story.html

Barecca, G. (2005). *Babes in boyland: A personal history of coeducation in the Ivy League*. Hanover, NH: University Press of New England.

Brownmiller, S. (1993). *Against our will: Men, women, and rape* (2nd ed.). New York: Fawcett Books.

Buchwald, E., Fletcher, P., & Roth, M. (2005). *Transforming a rape culture* (2nd ed.). Minneapolis, MN: Milkweed.

Childs, F. L. (1957). A Dartmouth history lesson for freshmen. *Dartmouth Alumni Magazine*. Retrieved from www.dartmouth.edu/~library/rauner/docs/pdf/FAQ_DC_History.pdf?mswitch-redir=classic

Cho, S. K. (1997). Converging stereotypes in racialized sexual harassment: Where the model minority meets Suzie Wong. *Journal of Gender, Race, and Justice, 1*(1), 177–211.

Crimson Staff. (2003, April 21). Leaning towards reform. *Harvard Crimson*. Retrieved from www.thecrimson.com/article/2003/4/21/leaning-towards-reform-the-committee-to/

Dartmouth Change. (2014). Retrieved from www.dartmouthchange.org

Doshi, M. M., Franken, T. D., & Kitchen, K. E. (2001, November 8). Rape happens at Harvard. *Harvard Crimson*. Retrieved from www.thecrimson.com/article/2001/11/8/rape-happens-at-harvard-on-april/

Dusky, L. (2003, Spring). Harvard stumbles over rape reporting. *Ms. Magazine*. Retrieved from www.msmagazine.com/mar03/dusky2.asp

Favot, S. (2011, April 29). Official calls mishandling of sexual assault cases staggering. *Center for Public Integrity IMPACT Report*. Retrieved from www.publicintegrity.org/2011/04/29/4420/impact-official-calls-mishandling-sexual-assault-cases-staggering-0

Forcier, M.F.D. (2004). "Men of Dartmouth" and "the lady engineers": Coeducation at Dartmouth College and Lehigh University. In L. Miller-Bernal & S. L. Poulson (Eds.), *Going coed: Women's experiences in formerly men's colleges and universities* (pp. 153–181). Nashville, TN: Vanderbilt University.

Freyd, J. J., & Birrell, P. J. (2013). *Blind to betrayal*. Indianapolis, IN: Wiley and Sons.

Grey, C. (1994, March 3). Greek video sparks discussion. *Dartmouth*. Retrieved from http://thedartmouth.com/1994/03/03/news/greek-video-sparks-discussion

Gunning, S. (1996). *Race, rape, and lynching: The red record of American literature, 1890–1912*. London: Oxford University Press.

Gutierrez, A. (2006, February 22). The girls next door: A night on the town at Wellesley College. *Harvard Crimson*. Retrieved from www.thecrimson.com/article/2006/2/22/the-girls-next-door-what-are/

Helderman, R. (1999, March 10). Faculty votes 119–19 to dismiss Douglas. *Harvard Crimson*. Retrieved from www.thecrimson.com/article/1999/3/10/faculty-votes-119–19-to-dismiss-douglas/

Hernandez, R. (2012, October 7). Two paths through Dartmouth meet in a US Senate race. *New York Times*, A17.

Horowitz, D. (1996, November 19). Students debate Proposition 209. *Dartmouth*. Retrieved from http://thedartmouth.com/1996/11/19/students-debate-proposition-209/

Kingkade, T. (2013, August 8). Yale fails to expel students found guilty of sexual assault. *Huffington Post*. Retrieved from http://www.huffingtonpost.com/2013/08/01/yale-sexual-assault-punishment_n_3690100.html

Knight, C. (2013, November 12). Why Dartmouth Beer Pong is so dangerously fun. *Business Insider*. Retrieved from http://www.businessinsider.com/dartmouth-beer-pong-guide-2013–11

Lisak, D., & Miller, P. (2002). Repeat rape and multiple offending among undetected rapists. *Violence and Victims*, 17(1), 73–82.

Marine, S. (2004, October 26). Waking up from the nightmare of rape. *Chronicle of Higher Education*, B5.

Maytal, A. (2002, November 19). Educate against sexual assault. *Harvard Crimson*. Retrieved from www.thecrimson.com/article/2002/11/19/educate-against-sexual-assault-last-may/

McNamara, E. (2013, February 11). Deans are out of their depth: Sexual assault on college campuses. *Cognoscenti, A Blog of National Public Radio*.

Merton, A. (1979, June 19). Hanging on (by a jockstrap) to a tradition at Dartmouth. *Esquire*, 57–67.

Mohanty, C., Russo, A., & Torres, L. (1991). *Third world women and the politics of feminism*. Bloomington: Indiana University Press.

New resources for office of sexual assault and prevention (2014, May 14). *Harvard Gazette*. Retrieved from http://news.harvard.edu/gazette/story/2014/05/new-resources-for-office-of-sexual-assault-prevention/?utm_source=SilverpopMailing&utm_medium=email&utm_campaign=05.15.daily%2520%281%29

Perez-Pena, R. (2013, March 19). College groups connect to fight sexual assault. *New York Times*, A14.

Platt, B. (2014, February 7). New center to focus on sexual assault prevention. *Dartmouth Now*. Retrieved from http://now.dartmouth.edu/2014/02/new-center-to-focus-on-sexual-assault-prevention/

Potter, C. (2014, April 17). Dartmouth college president speaks out against violent campus culture. *Chronicle of Higher Education*. Retrieved from http://chronicle.com/blognetwork/tenuredradical/author/cpotter/

Reeves-Sanday, P. (1992). *Fraternity gang rape: Sex, brotherhood, and privilege on campus* (2nd rev. ed.). New York: New York University Press.

Rimer, S. (1997, February 24). Radcliffe women, once docile, prod Harvard sharply on equality of the sexes. *New York Times*. Retrieved from www.nytimes.com/1997/02/24/us/radcliffe-women-once-docile-prod-harvard-sharply-on-equality-of-sexes.html

Rivers, T. (1990). Oriental girls. *Gentleman's Quarterly*, 158.

Schwendinger, J. R. & Schwendinger, H. (1983). *Rape and inequality*. Thousand Oaks, CA: Sage.

Seltzer, S. M. (2003, June 5). Leaning committee signals major changes in sexual assault policy. *Harvard Crimson*. Retrieved from http://www.thecrimson.com/article/2003/6/5/leaning-committee-signals-major-changes-in/?page=1

Solomon, B. M. (1985*). In the company of educated women: A history of women and higher education in America.* New Haven, CT: Yale University.

Sombuntham, N. (2002, June 5). Complaint filed on sexual assault change. *Harvard Crimson*. Retrieved from www.thecrimson.com/article/2002/6/5/complaint-filed-on-sexual-assault-change/

A survey of coeducation in the Ivies. (1974, October 4). *Harvard Crimson*. Retrieved from www.archives.upenn.edu/histy/features/women/chron3.html

Thelin, J. R. (2011). *A history of American higher education* (2nd ed.). Baltimore, MD: Johns Hopkins University Press.

Trounson, R. (2006, November 3). UCLA students protect race and gender policies. *Los Angeles Times*. Retrieved from http://articles.latimes.com/2006/nov/03/local/me-ucla3

Ulrich, L. (2004). *Yards and gates: Gender in Harvard and Radcliffe history.* New York: Palgrave-Macmillan.

5

ATHLETES, SEXUAL ASSAULT, AND UNIVERSITIES' FAILURE TO ADDRESS RAPE-PRONE SUBCULTURES ON CAMPUS

Todd W. Crosset

On many college and university campuses, the athletic department is the face of the institution. Ironically, the athletic department is often the most distinct department. The culture and practices of the athletic department developed separately from the rest of campus. As such, athletic departments operate in a manner that is quite different than other departments.

The dissonance between athletic departments and the rest of campus can seem particularly acute around the issue of sexual assault. The sex–segregated and sometimes violent culture of collegiate sport can foster an environment that is threatening for women (Murnen & Kohlman, 2007). When the athletic department operates distinctly and differently from the rest of campus, it complicates the managerial goal of preventing sexual assaults and/or responding appropriately to the reporting of a sexual assault.

This chapter draws on lessons learned from my vantage point as an expert witness in three Title IX/sexual assault cases. Each case was brought against a university after women were sexually assaulted by varsity athletes or recruits. Each case had unique aspects. I will as much as possible confine my comments to issues that were common to all three in an effort to draw general conclusions about sexual assaults and athletics in higher education.[1]

My intent is to share knowledge gained in an effort to make campuses safer for students. The motivation for some who choose to read this chapter may be less noble—institutional preservation. It is understandable that some will turn to this chapter to learn how to "protect" an institution. Title IX court cases are costly. They absorb considerable time and energy. They damage the reputation of an institution in the short term. University and college upper management and coaches' failure to respond appropriately to charges of sexual assault can result in termination.[2] However, the collateral damage from sexual assault Title IX cases extends to staff and employees. The university, through their lawyers, will question the professionalism and practices of their own employees. The process of defending a university can embitter counselors, campus police, and residence hall staff. Good employees sometimes decide to leave an institution after being deposed. The motivation of the reader, however, is beside the point. In the end the outcome will be the same. Taking steps to proactively protect the institution from Title IX suits and expert witnesses like myself will also be steps to creating a safer campus.

On Becoming an Expert Witness

I did not set out to be an expert witness. In retrospect, the way my career unfolded I should not have been surprised. For a good part of my young adulthood, I was a part of the college athletic world. I am a former athlete and college coach. For a time, I was a college athletic administrator. I am now a sport sociologist. I was involved in some early research on college athletes and violence against women (Crosset, Benedict, & McDonald, 1995; Crosset, Ptacek, McDonald, & Benedict, 1996). I currently work in a school of management, where I prepare students for jobs in the sport industry. These attributes, along with a recommendation from a colleague to a rather persuasive lawyer, led to my first stint as a legal expert.

That first case was brought by Lisa Simpson against the University of Colorado in 2003. It was a long, complicated legal battle. I worked with Simpson's lawyers, in particular, teaching them about the "world" of college athletics. They in turn taught me about our system of justice and the job of expert. Eventually the university settled with the plaintiff. Along the way, the National Collegiate Athletic Association (NCAA) passed a series of recruiting reforms, including the prohibition of all-female recruiting clubs that colleges used to seduce young men into signing with their football program. Thankfully, none of the cases I worked on went to trial. I never took the stand. All cases were settled out of court. In each case, to varying degrees, the women filing suits against a university won.

The job of an expert witness is to review various court documents, including depositions and exhibits, in light of the scholarly research. Then they write a report based on their knowledge and their research. Experts may be deposed— questioned by lawyers for hours, who try to poke holes in their report and question their reputation, while other lawyers shout objections to questions. I can't say that I enjoy the work. However, the position of "expert" does afford an inside view into the operations of universities. While it is important to recognize that information gleaned from court cases is not necessarily fully truthful, people called to testify cannot stray far from the truth while arguing for their perspective. They do not want to be accused of perjury. As such, Title IX sexual assault court documents provide a unique window into higher education crisis management and sexual assault prevention.

Social science intersects with Title IX sexual assault cases around the legal concept of "hostile environment." Peggy Sanday (1981) discovered that in some environments, rape was more prevalent than in others. She coined the phrase "rape-prone cultures" to capture this social variation. Sanday's groundbreaking, cross-cultural research on tribal societies and, later, her research on college fraternities (Sanday, 1990), demonstrated that rape is fostered by particular cultural configurations. She identified three factors that increased the risk of rape: interpersonal violence, male domination, and sex segregation. Sociological research on sexual assault builds on Sanday's central point—"that group structure and processes, rather than individual characteristics, are the impetus for many rape episodes" (Martin & Hummer, 1989). These sociological concerns are generally framed by the legal context of Title IX cases, the promotion of hostile environment and/or institutional knowledge of and failure to respond to a hostile environment.

Those early studies that found an association between varsity athletes and violence against women have held up. Research continues to suggest that members of all-male groups on campus, particularly sport teams and fraternities, are more likely to commit sexual assault than nonmembers (Murnen & Kohlman, 2007). However, most collegiate sports teams do not constitute rape-prone cultures. Particular institutional structures, team culture and practices, combine with the male-privileged, sometimes violent, and sex-segregated world of collegiate sport to create a rape-prone culture. I focus on four factors that contribute to creating a team environment prone to promoting sexual assaults: peer support for violence against women; normativity of interpersonal violence; institutional support for male privilege; and institutional practices that fail to hold athletes accountable for criminal behavior.

When taken individually, incidents that fall within these four categories would not be evidence of a hostile environment. If they appear collectively and repeatedly, however, they can represent a constellation of acts that can constitute a hostile environment for women. To make this assessment, I review various court documents, including depositions and exhibits, in light of the scholarly research on the association between sexual assaults and college athletes. In addition, I examine the public record related to past incidents at the institution, especially the accused perpetrators' team, incidents with the head coach's previous teams, and past incidents of the accused perpetrators either in high school or in another college. My question is: Do coaches recruit perpetrators of sexual assault? I look for evidence that might indicate that individuals in a program engaged in ongoing sexual harassment or had a history of sexual assaults and/or sex discrimination. I examine policies and practices that might foster or tacitly encourage a rape culture. Included in this research is the athletic department's record of holding student athletes accountable for rule violations and the universities' response to students who file complaints against athletes.

Critical in these Title IX legal cases is notification and response. Did university staff and coaches know of a threat to women? And then, did the university take remedial action to decrease that threat? There are two lines of inquiry for this research when the assault is perpetrated by a varsity athlete. One, does the university acknowledge that sex-segregated groups on campus are more likely to constitute rape-prone cultures and thus require special attention? Second, did university actors know a particular practice, program, or person posed a threat to women? And then, if they knew of a threat, how did they respond?

Elements of a rape-prone culture are revealed in the program's history and current practices. They might also become apparent in the actions of university officials in the wake of a student's complaint. For example, does the university move to protect the woman from retaliation? Does the school make special effort to support the accused athletes?

In my legal research, I pay particular attention to the communication between the university staff and athletic department personnel. Managerial issues are complicated by assumptions of accountability. Student athletes may feel most accountable to the athletic department. Teams are experienced by athletes and understood by other university officials as "total institutions." Sports consume the majority of the focus, time, and energy of student athletes and athletic departments meet most of their needs. Athletic departments provide health care, academic advising, and support financial aid. They may even have their own admissions process.

Coaches are far more than teachers of a sport. They act as mentors, career advisors, and moral guides. Often they take on roles that are far beyond their job descriptions. Not surprisingly, coaches are assumed to be responsible for athletes' behavior and academic performance by other administrators. Coaches, for better or worse, have the most power to shape student athlete behavior and to hold them accountable for their actions. However, campus staff often have first-hand knowledge of threatening behavior by athletes. Due in part to the "distance" between the athletic department and the rest of the university and assumptions about the role of the coach and athletic administrators, the coordination of a response to an assault perpetrated by an athlete is sometimes muddled by university officials.

In times of crisis, like accusations of sexual assault, there can be misunderstanding regarding accountability. Coaches and athletic administrators sometimes continue operating like a total institution. They provide advice and arrange legal support. Athletic department concerns for a team's reputation and/or record, the welfare of the accused, or meeting NCAA requirements can conflict with the university's responsibility to respond appropriately to complaints about student behavior. However, my experience suggests the opposite is just as likely. Coaches, who prior to the crisis offered student athletes personal advice, moral leadership, and counseling, suddenly follow university protocol and distance themselves from athletes accused of sexual assault. Yet, university officials may still assume that coaches and athletic administrators act on behalf of the men they recruited. In either case, unless communication between the athletic department and the rest of campus is robust, sexual assault complaints against college athletes are easily mismanaged.

Institutional Knowledge and Response: Institutional Practices That Fail to Hold Athletes Accountable for Criminal Behavior

For a Title IX case to be successful for the plaintiff, her lawyers must demonstrate that university officials either knew or should have known about a threat to women and then did not take steps to remedy the situation. College and university administrators generally acknowledge that athletes, along with fraternities, marching bands, and other male-dominated campus groups can become rape-prone subcultures on campus. In examining whether a university is in violation of Title IX, I first look for educational prevention programs designed for sex-segregated groups on campus—in particular programs for male athletes. Then I look for evidence of knowledge of and response to specific individuals or practices. Did university officials know that an individual, team, or team practices present a threat to women on campus? If they did know of a threat, did they take steps to address that threat?

While it seems like common sense to have educational programs tailored to all-male groups on campuses (Moynihan, Banyard, Arnold, Eckstein, & Stapleton, 2010), there can be resistance to these programs from within the athletic department. Coaches, in particular, may feel athletes are already (and unfairly) held to a higher standard than other students and/or athletes are too frequently stigmatized as a problem. Within collegiate athletic administration, there is an ideology that athletes, as much as possible, should be treated as a typical student. For example, NCAA rules prohibit isolated athlete-only residence halls and cafeterias. The NCAA limits practice time to 20 hours a week (which is the average time students spend on extracurricular activities) to ensure that student athletes have some time to be "regular" students. Yet, athletes have to meet higher standards than other students. For example, they are tested for recreational drug use, and they are forced to declare a major and make steady progress toward graduation to remain eligible. The 20-hour practice rule is understood by all to be a public relations fiction. Athletes spend considerably more than 20 hours a week on their sport. The 20 hours does not include prep/taping prior to practice, postpractice therapy, games, travel, or even pregame practices. Simply put, athletes are not like regular students. As a result, folks working with athletes have an aversion to programs that add to their burdens and further divide them from the general student body.

Another reason some folks push back against programs on sexual assault specifically for athletes is that it may be felt as an unfair stigmatization. Coaches and administrators know that the majority of athletes are good people. They believe what collegiate sport offers young people, for the most part, is a positive experience. Athletes and college sport, they argue, are not the problem. The problem is a public relations issue. Folks working in athletics already feel athletes are over-exposed and an easy target for criticism. Their argument will run something like this: regular students regularly drop out of school, transfer, or are asked to take time off for academic reasons. This is not news. When a star athlete fails to return to campus, however, it is news. Such publicity, they will argue, unfairly perpetuates the dumb jock stereotype. Athlete-specific sexual assault educational programs may be seen as a product of unfair assumptions about athletes. Sexual assault is a general problem, coaches and administrators may argue, and student athletes should be incorporated into the sexual assault prevention programs that are offered to the rest of the student body.

The structure of sport, however, fosters some of the characteristics of a rape-prone culture. Athletes are arranged in sex-segregated groups, which are often patriarchal, privileged, and sometimes violent. These attributes are distinct from the rest of campus. As such, athlete-specific sexual assault prevention education is appropriate. Further athlete-specific programs are not in conflict with athletic department practices. Athletic departments sponsor various athlete-only programs (athletic academic counseling is the most obvious) that attempt to mitigate the structural burden of being an athlete and a student.

In each of the three court cases, universities seemed to acknowledge that male athletes posed a problem on campus, yet failed to address that issue. In one of the cases I reviewed, the university had won funding to start an athlete-specific prevention program. During the 3-year period the university sponsored this educational initiative, no athletes were reported for sexual assault. However, when the "start-up" funding ended, the program was abandoned. The next year, a freshman male athlete assaulted a woman on campus. In another case, the university provided reams of material on their educational prevention programs for university students—especially the programs offered during freshman orientation. The athletic department argued that they attempted to treat their athletes as if they were "typical students," but the athletic department's rhetoric didn't match their practice. The football team held practices during the orientation sexual assault prevention program. Freshman football players were not mandated to attend the program, like the rest of the incoming freshman. They were mandated to be at practice—even "red-shirt freshman."[3] The football players, who committed sexual assault later that semester, had not been able to attend the prevention program. In the third case, the team incorporated educational material into the team's orientation. However, the information was out-of-date and inaccurate. The topic was addressed by the head coach who had no training in the area of sexual assault and was presented in conjunction with a police "ride around" exercise. The program enabled team members to ride with police officers while on duty. Regardless of the intent of the program, the players understood this program to be a way to make a connection with law enforcement officers so they would have a "friend" within the force when they got into trouble.

The lack of effective prevention programs is not in and of itself evidence of a hostile environment. Rather it is presented as a piece of evidence in a larger portrait of a team's culture. Because university officials acknowledged that athletes constituted a higher risk group on campus and failed to offer any or effective educational training, I was able make the case that the failure was one act in a constellation of acts that contributed to the cultivation of a rape-prone culture.

The second aspect of knowing about and failing to address a threat to women relates to specific threats. Did someone in an official capacity know a particular student athlete (based on previous behavior) or an athletic department practice posed a threat. Research suggests that the person most likely to commit a sexual assault is the person who has already committed a sexual assault (Jackson, Veneziano, & Riggen, 2004). As such, it is critical for university and college administrators to provide those who have already demonstrated a proclivity for violence toward women with meaningful prevention education or to remove them from campus. In each of the three cases, someone in an official capacity had prior knowledge that the accused perpetrator posed a threat to women on campus prior to the assault on the plaintiff. And in one case, the university had been notified that a particular recruiting practice was problematic.

In the first case, coaches and athletic staff went to great lengths to construct a high school transcript for the eventual perpetrator so that he would meet (albeit just barely) the minimum eligibility requirements of the NCAA. University officials, including members of the athletic department, aware of the difficulties the rigor of the university presented for the student athlete, recommended that the student attend a summer bridge program. The program was intended to acclimate low-income and rural students to college life. The student athlete, however, was kicked out of this program as a result of a series of incidents that threatened women. The athlete had a tendency to behave in an inappropriate manner in academic settings and when confronted (particularly by women in authority), he had a tendency to be defensive and threatening. The athlete told the director of the summer bridge program, an employee in the undergraduate dean's office, that he believed women "needed to fear him and should know their place in order to have his respect." His actions indicated that he was a threat to his fellow students and teaching assistants and residential staff, particularly if they were female.

Members of the athletic department had frequent contact with the director of the summer bridge program and understood and respected the reasoning that led to the decision to dismiss the student athlete. An athletic department administrator, in a memo to other athletic administrators, including the head football coach, acknowledged that "we will have to have a plan to deal with [this athlete]'s 'issues' when he returns in the fall." Clearly the undergraduate dean's office and the football program were aware that this young man posed a threat to women. But neither the university staff nor members of the athletic department provided the young men with special counseling or education. The undergraduate dean passed the problem along to the athletic department, assuming they would address the issue, or at the very least be able to constrain this young man. The athletic department did not have the means or the desire to do the hard work to help this man make changes. Not surprisingly, back to campus without either support or being held accountable, he committed a sexual assault during his first semester on campus.

In the second case, the coaching staff knew that an eventual perpetrator had been accused of sexual assault while in high school. Employees of the athletic department recruited an alumnus and a booster to provide the incoming freshman with legal support. They did not, however, inform the university of the accusation against the recruit, choosing instead to keep it a secret from the rest of the university. Keeping the "problem" out of the public eye and away from campus officials also precluded reaching out for help. No one took any steps to address this young man's past behavior outside of offering legal support. He was not provided special counseling or education. This man later committed a sexual assault against a fellow student athlete.

In addition to recruiting an athlete accused of sexual assault, the university was notified that a particular recruiting practice posed a threat to women. Notification was never more obvious. The university and the athletic department were informed by the District Attorney's Office that their recruiting practices were resulting in sexual assault complaints from women. The District Attorney's Office met with the chancellor, the athletic director, and a representative of the university's counsel. The context of the notification was a charge of sexual assault against a recruit. Although the state did not bring charges, due to the victim's inability to identify the perpetrators, district attorneys did put the university and the athletic department on notice about this team's recruiting practices.

The District Attorney's Office expressed concern that the football program had institutionalized the practice of providing sex to high school recruits as part of recruiting weekends. The District Attorney's Office advised the university that they should adopt a "no alcohol" and "no sexual contact" policy for recruiting visits. Further, there should be written policies and procedures that required close supervision of the high school students who were being recruited for the football team. Additionally, the District Attorney's Office advised the university that they should provide training around issues of sexual harassment and sexual assault and even offered to assist in that effort. The District Attorney's Office also offered to assist the university in reviewing any policies and procedures developed around the issues of alcohol, sex, and recruiting weekends.

In sum, the university officials were given concrete and specific notice by high-ranking law enforcement officials that its football recruiting practices were dangerous to women. Yet, the university officials, possibly relieved to hear that the district attorney was not going to press charges, did not feel compelled to make changes. The team continued to offer alcohol and sex as part of their recruiting trips. Indeed, the football program facilitated the practice by selecting football players they called "partiers" (including the young man who committed a sexual assault in high school) to serve as hosts to recruits. A couple years after the meeting with the District Attorney's office, when recruits sexually assaulted a woman while on a recruiting visit, the district attorney encouraged the victim to sue the university under Title IX because she had previously notified the university of the issue.

In the third case, it was a bit harder to make the case that the university had received notice because the players were not named. University residential life staff had received a sexual assault complaint against "two football players." Staff then informed upper management of residential life and the university police force that a complaint had been lodged against "two football players." Given the nature of sport on college campuses, team cultures, and the accountability of players to coaches, residential life staff could have reached out to the football program for assistance. Coaches have strong ties to the students in their program and could have intervened even without knowing which players posed a threat. But no one reached out to the athletic department or the football coaching staff. Two months later these two men committed another sexual assault.[4]

In all three cases, university officials were aware that a particular student athlete, athletes, or athletic department-sponsored activities posed a threat to women and that university administrators did not take appropriate action once they had knowledge of a specific threat.

Rape-Prone Culture

The structure of college sport can lay the foundation for rape-prone sub-cultures within a university. Men's sports are usually sex segregated, and often patriarchal, and male privileged. However, these attributes, while they increase the likelihood of teams becoming rape-prone cultures, are not evidence of that culture. Other attributes must be expressed before one can make the case a team poses a threat to women. University officials can, albeit unwittingly, contributed to the fostering of a rape-prone culture. As such, they may contribute to creating or perpetuating a hostile environment for women.

Peer Support

One of the strongest predictors that an individual will engage in sexual assault is expressed support for violence against women by peers (DeKeseredy & Kelly 1995; Kreager, 2007). Direct evidence of peer support (locker room conversations, witnessing behaviors at team functions) is difficult to attain from afar. So the evidence of peer support is inferred via the public record and depositions. For example, is the perpetrator a part of a team that has members who have committed sexual assault? If yes, what was the extent of their punishments; were they able to remain a part of the community? Has the coach recruited men (either out of high school or from another college) who have been accused of sexual assault? People who have committed sexual assault are very likely to bring to the team the myths and ideology that supports their behavior.

In one case, the perpetrator, a freshman, joined a football team with at least three other men who had been violent toward women and remained on the team. One athlete, the team's leading rusher, assaulted a 15-year-old on his high school campus. Outside of red shirting his first year on campus, he did not receive remedial interventions. Another, the leading wide receiver, arrested for damaging his ex-girlfriend's car, did not receive counseling or punishment from the university or the athletic department. The third, another leading running back, had a series of problems with women starting shortly after his arrival on campus. He broke the wrist of a female employee of the athletic department from whom he received payments in violation of NCAA rules. He threatened a female gymnast. Two coaches of women's teams complained to the head football coach about this athlete's behavior toward their athletes. No remedial steps were taken or offered by the football staff, the athletic department, or the university to address this student athlete's threatening behavior directed toward women. He did receive counseling, however, to address his fear of being injured while playing football.

In another case the accused athletes were on a team with a player who was charged with assaulting his pregnant wife and subsequently pleaded guilty. Although this was a very serious crime, he was allowed to continue playing for the team, receiving only suspensions from spring practice and two games. This team had a female place kicker. She reported that she had been verbally harassed in an extremely sexually derogatory manner. The players harassing the place kicker received a talking to by the coach but no real consequences. From this evidence, I was able to make the case that the accused athletes were on a team in which his peers expressed attitudes and behaviors supportive of violence against women and were able to do so with little or no consequences.

Interpersonal Violence as Normative Behavior

Sanday (1981) noted that violent cultures are more prone to rape. Therefore, I take into account other incidents of off-field interpersonal violence by members of the team in my assessment of team culture. If team members are reported for a series of violent acts, it may indicate that off-field violence is normative behavior. For example, in one case I reviewed, teammates of a perpetrator had recently shot a gun into the air at a night club, and two football players came to physical blows in a dispute about rent. One was arrested. The other attacked a student who broke up the fight with a butcher knife. Two other players were charged with aggravated assault and criminal trespass after breaking into a fellow student's apartment, brutally beating him, and destroying property. Incidents like this suggest that the training to use force on the field has spilled over into other areas and violence in this community is a norm, rather than confined to a game.

In a second case, research revealed that the football coach tolerated off-the-field violence by hiring a coach with a history of violence as a player. He had assaulted an employee in a subsequent trip to campus after he graduated. The university had banned him from campus. However, when the coach hired him as an assistant the university waived the ban. Additionally, the football handbook used overly-violent language, encouraging players to "beat" an opponent "to death" in the fourth quarter. In both these cases, I was able to argue that violence (well beyond the instrumental violence associated with the game of football) was a norm of these programs. Violence was a part of the daily off-field lives of the athletes.

Sex Segregation and Male Privilege

Men living in sex-segregated, male-privileged environments are more likely to engage in sexual assaults (Sanday, 1981). Sport can go a long way to creating that space. However, the university is a diverse place. Athletic departments or teams would have to extenuate these attributes of sport if one were to make the case for male privilege and segregation. For example, in the second case, the university amplified the sex-segregated and male-privileged atmosphere of a big time college football program by supporting a group of 25–40 female volunteers (often called hostesses) to assist in the recruiting of football players. This student recruiting club was all-female. These women volunteers attempted to lure the recruits to "sign" with the football team by sponsoring parties with underage drinking and sometimes with sex. Official, all-female, university-sponsored recruiting squads have been disbanded by the NCAA as a result of this case. However, recent incidents suggest that the practice of using women to woo top recruits has not stopped and is still informally encouraged by coaches.[5]

In the three cases I reviewed, the perpetrators were either recruits or freshman. However, were I to investigate cases involving upper classman, I would look for institutional support for or the turning of a blind eye toward team houses. These sex-segregated, team exclusive, off-campus living arrangements can foster rape-prone athletic subcultures.

Institutional Failure to Hold Men Accountable

Men are more likely to engage in sexual assault if they believe that they will not be held accountable for their actions (Muehlenhard & Linton, 1987). Members of an all-male group on campus are more likely to commit a sexual assault if they think the consequences will be minimal and/or there are people with power on campus that will protect them. College athletes' most significant contacts with the university are their coaches. Coaches are very involved in the overall welfare of the football players and take it upon themselves to assist athletes with their problems and to hold them accountable for their transgressions. So when I begin to research this area of concern, I look into the ways and the extent to which coaches and athletic staff hold men accountable for their behavior.

In one case, the coach and his staff promoted a "family culture." Throughout the football handbook, players were encouraged to view their team as a family and to value loyalty to each other. Although cohesion is a goal for any athletic team, the negative consequence of the manner in which this football program fostered its family-centered approach was the creation of a "culture of silence."

"What is said in here stays in here" was a motto of this team. As such, players were discouraged from reporting misbehavior by other teammates. Moreover, players got the message that how they treated each other was far more important than how they treated people outside of the program. They were sanctioned far more severely for intra-team misbehaviors, such as stealing from a teammate, than they were for misbehaviors directed toward members of the public, where a "wait-and-see" how the university or the courts would respond preceded team disciplinary decisions.

In another case, the athletic department, and the football program in particular, had a practice of protecting their athletes and giving them second chances, particularly if they were "impact"[6] players. In this case, the athletic department did not report incidents that were threatening to women either internally or to the broader university community. Not only did the football program have a practice of failing to report criminal activity, threatening activity, and other infractions—choosing instead to deal with problems internally by temporarily suspending players—but the coach repeatedly gave impact players second and third chances. Starters all received second chances after serious violations of team rules or criminal behavior just prior to or during the time the perpetrator was a member of the football program.

These two cases, where it was quite easy to argue coaches contributed to a hostile environment for not taking violence against women seriously, can be contrasted with the third case. The head coach held his players accountable for violence against women. He was far more tolerant of intoxication, drug use, and fights between teammates than attacks against women. For example, he dismissed immediately two players after they were arrested for sexual assault. This action demonstrated his commitment to hold men accountable for violence against women when placed in contrast to his treatment of a player with an addiction issue. He too was dismissed from the team but only after his third alcohol/drug-related arrest. In this case, the failure to hold men accountable did not reside with the coach but elsewhere in the athletic department and related to the speed (lack thereof) with which the case was adjudicated.

Slowing the Pace of Adjudication of College Athletes

The speed with which a university/athletic department responds to an accusation of sexual assault contributes to an athlete's perception of institutional support. There are, of course, some good reasons for a university to move cautiously once presented with a sexual assault case. Issues of due process and concerns about interfering with a criminal investigation can slow a coach or university officials from taking immediate action. However, failure to respond in a timely fashion contributes to a hostile environment. Schools should not wait for the conclusion of a criminal investigation or criminal proceeding to begin their own Title IX investigation (Ali, 2011).

Athletics presents universities with a powerful tool with which to hold men accountable. Coaches and athletic departments maintain jurisdiction over an athlete's access to sport and can act far more quickly than can a university or the legal system. Athletic departments and teams are tiny private governments with their own sets of rules and punishments. In the case of poor grades, petty theft from a teammate, or showing up late to a workout, an athletic department or coach is quite capable of investigating and meting out a punishment. Ironically, they are often quite a bit swifter at sanctioning minor offenses than they are criminal ones. Athletic departments will sometimes wait for a criminal case to be adjudicated in the courts before they take final action, even when their own investigations reveal violations of team rules. We sometimes hear coaches and athletic administrators argue that athletes should not face "double jeopardy" or that the athletic department is waiting for the results of a police investigation. The logic here fails, of course. Athletic departments and universities are quite capable of adjudicating criminal complaints against athletes internally that are not reported to the police. The two systems (team rules and public laws) are separate. The standard of proof, the punishments, and the processes within an athletic department are quite distinct from our legal system.

In the cases I reviewed, athletes were suspended or dismissed from teams, yet remained members of the athletic department while their cases were adjudicated in the courts or by the university. In other words, while they were kicked off the team, they continued to have access to the academic support services available to all athletes and they remained on scholarship.

Consider, for example, the case in which the housing staff and police were notified that two unnamed football players were involved in a sexual assault but did not inform the football coach. Here the head football coach, upon being presented with the evidence, dismissed both players from the team. He then abdicated responsibility for further punishments to the athletic director (continuation of scholarship), to the dean of students (expulsion), and the housing director (denial of University housing.). The head coach's actions seemed appropriate. University officials, however, took their time in adjudicating the case despite an admission of guilt by one of the student athletes. The athletic director, in particular, contributed to the slow pace. He wanted, he said, to rely on the courts for a determination of guilt before acting to revoke scholarships or to permanently dismiss the student athletes from the athletic department. Had the university followed the athletic director's wishes, the university would not have acted to expel the athletes for a year. But the athletic director's tactics probably had very little to do with the court ruling and more about the academic calendar. By deferring to the courts, the athletic director was able to delay a university hearing until after the completion of the semester.

Both men remained on scholarship through the spring semester. Both assailants took classes on campus, and both men were officially student athletes (although no longer members of the football team) and as such had access to the resources of the athletic academic center. The tactic worked. The athletic director exploited the slow pace of the courts, which enabled the athletes to finish out the semester in good academic standing (at least a 2.6 GPA).

The delay in holding the perpetrators accountable led the victim to think the worst of the university. She was suspicious of the players receiving support from university at the same moment she was experiencing a lack of support. The athletes were expelled from the dorms; an appropriate response. However, one of the perpetrators found off-campus housing with a university employee. The employee also acted as the athlete's tutor. The victim brought this living arrangement to the attention of university officials. However, no one informed the athletic department. Instead the officials determined that the employee was leaving the university at the end of the semester, which would eventually make the matter moot. Had university officials communicated with the athletic department, they might have recognized that free housing provided by a university employee was an impermissible benefit under the terms of the athletic scholarship. The athletic department could have addressed the victim's concern.

In the end the victim felt, and rightly so, that the university was going out of its way to support the perpetrators. At the same time, a new dean of students unfamiliar with university policy and ill equipped to respond to the victim's concerns boggled the complaint. In the end, I was able to argue that the combination of the lack of appropriate support for the victim, the deliberate delay of adjudication by the athletic director, and the continued support for the perpetrators, all interfered with the victim's access to education.

There are a host of reasons that an athletic department is reluctant to enforce its own rules if the athlete is involved in a criminal case. One reason is that athletic departments have a vested interest in moving slowly. Even if coaches and administrators come to the conclusion that certain athletes committed sexual assault and they want the athletes off the team and expelled from the university, they may delay adjudication until the end of a semester. NCAA rules, intended to promote academic integrity (the Academic Progress Rate [APR] index) encourage schools to have any "expelled" athlete finish the semester in "good academic standing" and transfer to another school.

The expressed intent of the APR index is to encourage graduation. The APR credits teams points for each athlete who returns to campus and is in good academic standing at the end of each semester. Teams with low APR ratings can lose scholarships or be banned from postseason play. If an athlete is expelled from school mid-semester, a team will not receive any points. However, teams are not penalized for losing players via transfer so long as those players maintain good academic and transfer to a new institution the next semester. Delaying adjudication to the end of the semester enables athletic departments to both expel students from their own campus, protect their APR rating, yet facilitates the transfer of the perpetrator to another institution. This practice limits the punishment athletes face for sexual assault. Kicked out of one school, they can continue their playing career and education at another institution. Additionally, this practice communicates to other athletes that the consequences for sexual assault from the athletic department are fairly mild.

Officials are adept at making it appear that they are holding the men accountable by expelling or suspending the athlete from the team. To justify their continuing status as a scholarship athlete, university officials might say something like, "we are holding the young men accountable for their academics," or "we are keeping an eye on them, while the legal process unfolds." However, within the college sport, it is generally understood that the department is working with the athletes to make progress toward a degree and to maintain at least a 2.6 GPA in an effort help the student transfer. Further, the athlete understands (or comes to understand) that the easiest way for them to continue their athletic career is to leave in "good standing." Athletes dismissed from teams generally "stick it out" academically until the end of the semester.

Policies and practices that slow university adjudication and enable perpetrators to remain on campus or finish the semester provide athletes with a sense of protection and further burden the victim, who may also be attempting to continue her education.

Conclusion: Creating a Safer Campus With Varsity Athletics

One take-away from this experience is the need to recognize that student athletes are different from most other students. Universities offer athletes special locker and weight rooms, medical care (trainers), tutoring, and life skills programs. All of these spaces and programs acknowledge and support their difference. I am not suggesting that administrators give up on their attempts to integrate athletes, as much as possible, into the rest of campus. Rather it is to acknowledge that those efforts will not be fully successful. Athletes, particularly highly committed ones, have obligations, constraints, and relationships that are unlike other students. Further, male athletes on campus spend much of their time and energy engaged in a sex-segregated, male-dominant, and sometimes violent activity—the very characteristics that are also the foundation of rape-prone subcultures. It makes sense, then, to provide prevention education programs specifically designed for athletes.

Second, the athletic department's adjudication of incidents does not necessarily depend on the university's process or the state's judicial process. Rules for student athlete behavior necessary to retain a scholarship and to be a part of the athletic department are not the same as for remaining at the university. Losing the position of "athlete" does not deny a student athlete the position of student. It is not double (or triple) jeopardy to dismiss an athlete from a team or from the athletic department and for the university to expel a student from housing or campus and the state send him to jail for a period of time. Students (like all people) are accountable to various groups and communities, and they need to be held accountable in each one.

Deferring to an adjudication process outside of the athletic department both abdicates responsibility and protects perpetrators. Athletic departments in many ways are the best mechanism through which to hold men accountable. Athletes care deeply about athletics. The team and athletic department can and do (when they choose to) act more swiftly than the university or the state. The consequences, particularly dismissal from the team, loss of scholarship, and expulsion from campus housing, have serious consequences and communicate to other athletes that coaches and teams can and will hold athletes accountable.

Coaches and athletic administrators would do well to adjudicate violence against women complaints quickly and in a coordinated fashion. Athletic department punishments that are the outcome of team rule violations do not replace those that result from the slower university or legal processes. Nor should a coach or athletic administrator wait for those processes to conclude to administer team and department punishments. Significant loss in playing time, suspension, or expulsion from the team can be quickly imposed. More importantly, athletes expelled from teams for violent offenses can also be denied athletic department support and athletic-related scholarships. Athletic departments should not facilitate the transferring of athletes with a history of violence against women to another school. The current common practices, which encourage athletes to "finish out the semester" and to transfer, passes a problem along to another school, promotes a rape-prone culture by not holding men accountable for their actions, and can create a hostile environment for the victim who must share the campus with the athlete or know he is receiving support.

Some may argue that a young man's future should not be ruined by one mistake. And some coaches sincerely think they are doing some good by helping an athlete in trouble to get a fresh start at another school. Enabling a perpetrator to move on without serious consequences perpetuates the social problem of men's violence toward women.

Further, university officials need to disabuse themselves of the myth that sport is, by its very nature, an activity that promotes character and develops men in positive ways. In particular, we need to push back against claims by coaches and athletic administrators that college sport or tutelage under a particular coach will help men with a history of violence against women to change. Coaches pull on these mythic qualities of sport when it is convenient for them—usually when recruiting a problematic albeit highly talented athlete. Varsity athletics is not a crime prevention program.

Finally, schools fail both athletes and female students when they fail to communicate and coordinate across departments. These communication failures are not unique to sport. However, the isolation and the distinctiveness of the athletic department complicate matters. Most egregious were athletic departments that did not inform university officials of complaints against the men they recruited out of high school or from other schools and residence programs. If universities are willing to engage in the hard work necessary to help men make changes, it will require open communication, a coordinated effort, and an environment in which education takes precedence over spectator sport.

Notes

1. I do not identify the facts with specific cases to avoid potential breach of confidentiality. The cases I worked on were *Simpson vs. the University of Colorado; JK vs. Arizona State University*; and *Harris vs. University of Northern Iowa*.
2. For example, the Lisa Simpson case against the University of Colorado resulted in the termination or reassignment of the chancellor, the president, the athletic director and the head football coach.
3. "Red-shirt freshman" is a term used to describe a first-year student athlete who is ineligible to play. These student athletes practice with the team but cannot play in games. This is usually the result of their failure to meet basic academic standards coming out of high school or due to an injury.
4. The woman who made the original complaint identified the two men as her assailants after their arrest.
5. The rape case at Vanderbilt University (2013) involving football players is one illustration. It has been reported that the victim was recruited by the coach to gather attractive women to party with recruits. See Ganim (2014).
6. "Impact player" is a term used to describe very good players, the team's stars, and many of the starting players. The absence of these players will have a detrimental effect on the quality of the team's performance.

References

Ali, R. (2011, April 4). Assistant Secretary for Civil Rights, U.S. Department of Education, Office of Civil Rights. Dear Colleague Letter: Sexual Violence. Retrieved from http://www2.ed.gov/about/offices/list/ocr/letters/colleague-201304.pdf

Crosset, T. W., Benedict, J. R., & McDonald, M. A. (1995). Male student-athletes reported for sexual assault: A survey of campus police departments and judicial affairs offices. *Journal of Sport & Social Issues, 19*(2), 126–140.

Crosset, T. W., Ptacek, J., McDonald, M. A., & Benedict, J. R. (1996). Male student-athletes and violence against women: A survey of campus judicial affairs offices. *Violence Against Women, 2*(2), 163–179.

DeKeseredy, W., & Kelly, K. (1995). Sexual abuse in Canadian university and college dating relationships: The contribution of male peer support. *Journal of Family Violence, 10*, 41–53.

Ganim, S. (2014, May 2). Vanderbilt rape case evidence is missing, case should be tossed, defense says. *CNN*. Retrieved from www.cnn.com/2014/05/02/us/vanderbilt-football-rape-case/

Jackson, A., Veneziano, L., & Riggen, K. (2004). Sexual deviance among male college students: Prior deviance as an explanation. *Journal of Interpersonal Violence, 19*(1), 72–89.

Kreager, D. A. (2007). Unnecessary roughness? School sports, peer networks, and male adolescent violence. *American Sociological Review, 72*(5), 705–724.

Martin, P. Y., & Hummer, R. A. (1989). Fraternities and rape on campus. *Gender & Society, 3*(4), 457–473.

Moynihan, M. M., Banyard, V. L., Arnold, J. S., Eckstein, R. P., & Stapleton, J. G. (2010). Engaging intercollegiate athletes in preventing and intervening in sexual and intimate partner violence. *Journal of American College Health, 59*(3), 197–204.

Muehlenhard, C. L., & Linton, M. A. (1987). Date rape and sexual aggression in dating situations: Incidence and risk factors. *Journal of Counseling Psychology, 34*(2), 186–196.

Murnen, S. K., & Kohlman, M. H. (2007). Athletic participation, fraternity membership, and sexual aggression among college men: A meta-analytic review. *Sex Roles, 57*(1–2), 145–157.

Sanday, P. R. (1981). The socio-cultural context of rape: A cross-cultural study. *Journal of Social Issues, 37*(4), 5–27.

Sanday, P. R. (1990). *Fraternity gang rape: Sex, brotherhood, and privilege on campus.* New York: New York University Press.

PART III

Federal Policy and Institutional Compliance

6

LOOKING BEYOND THE NUMBERS

Understanding the Jeanne Clery Act and Sexual Violence

Alison Kiss and Kiersten N. Feeney White

The prevalence of sexual violence at institutions of higher education has remained consistent over the past two decades (Fisher, Cullen, & Turner, 2000; Sloan & Fisher, 2011). The empirical evidence consistently reveals a high frequency of sexual victimization in college, primarily of women perpetrated by men (Sloan & Fisher, 2011). The tradition of colleges and universities underreporting crime was the focus of a social movement in the 1980s and 1990s, which resulted in the passage of many federal laws, most notably the Jeanne Clery Disclosure of Campus Security Policy and Campus Crime Statistics Act (Clery Act). Further, the higher education community and its response to sexual violence has been under added scrutiny since the issuance of the 2011 Dear Colleague Letter addressing Title IX of the Education Amendments of 1972 (Title IX), the passage of the Violence Against Women Act (VAWA) amendments to the Clery Act, and a network of student survivors deemed the Know Your IX[1] mobilized to file complaints against colleges and universities for violating the Clery Act and Title IX (Perez-Pena, 2013). The notable difference with current student activism is that the students are not remaining anonymous; they are giving "Jane Doe" a name and attaching their identities as survivors to the issue of campus sexual assault. As a result of increased student activism, in January 2014 President Barack Obama convened a Task Force to Protect Students from Sexual Assault. This task force released a preliminary report in April 2014 identifying key elements of the prevalence of sexual violence, including intersections with federal laws such as Title IX and the Clery Act (White House Task Force, 2014). The increased focus on sexual violence from the federal government is just one reason for the need for institutional leadership to play a key role in establishing safe campuses. Additionally, technical compliance with the Clery Act and Title IX has been at the forefront of campus officials' efforts related to sexual violence.

Nonetheless, it is critical for institutional leaders to adopt an ethical commitment to campus safety. White (2014) defined ethical commitment utilizing Nel Noddings's (1986, 1988, 1992, 1994, 1995) "ethic of caring" theory. This commitment is demonstrated by accomplishing the "primary aim of moral education [which is] producing people who will engage successfully in caring relations . . . through modeling, dialogue, practice, and confirmation" (Noddings, 2010, p. 394). Campus officials' caring, in various capacities along the issue of sexual violence, is fundamental to education and, ultimately, the advancement of a democratic society (Noddings, 1986, 1988, 1992, 1994, 1995; Pinar, Reynolds, Slattery, & Taubman, 2004). Education is the chief vehicle to establishing a just society that embraces moral principles and combats social problems such as violence (Noddings, 1995).

Although technical compliance is critical to success with the Clery Act, "the point of the regulations is not to see if you comply, it's to keep people safe on campus" (Moore, 2013). Therefore, it may seem evident that providing clarity on the technical and ethical commitment to the Clery Act is paramount. Furthermore, ethical compliance is not reinforced through the Education Department's program reviews, although there is an expectation that campus safety is considered through a holistic lens (Duncan, 2011a). Campus officials' support and commitment to the spirit of the law is important because of their responsibility to uphold the mission of the Clery Act, the Education Department's focus on going above and beyond the technical aspects of the Clery Act, and the need for campus community members to be cared for through campus safety efforts that symbolize technical compliance and ethical commitment.

This chapter examines the elements of the Clery Act (20 U.S.C. 1092[f]) and its impact on sexual violence prevention, response, and policy. The topics discussed in this chapter include the elements of the Clery Act (including the Campus Sexual Assault Victims' Bill of Rights and the VAWA amendments to the Clery Act) and its intersection with Title IX. Many campus administrators define Clery requirements as simply collecting and publishing crime statistics (White, 2014). While this is one element of the law, there are numerous other elements focused on policy development, prevention education, and victim response. This chapter will also challenge readers to look beyond the numbers or statistics and develop an ethical commitment to compliance with the Clery Act.

Clery Act Background

On April 5, 1986, Jeanne Ann Clery, a freshman at Lehigh University, was brutally raped and murdered in her residence hall by another student whom she did not know. Jeanne's parents, Connie and Howard Clery, were devastated to learn of the murder of their daughter. In fact, the Clerys were quite prudent when selecting a college with Jeanne. At first, Jeanne chose to attend Tulane University in New Orleans, her two brothers' alma mater. However, shortly after her acceptance, the Clerys learned that a female student had been murdered off-campus and they decided to look for a "safer" campus. Eventually, the Clerys selected Lehigh University for Jeanne to attend. As Connie stated, "Jeanne fell in love with the campus" (Clery Center, 2011).

Connie and Howard's anger and frustration extended beyond the trial of Joseph Henry when they learned of lapses with Lehigh University's security protocols. Some examples included no regulation on entrance into buildings, no policies regarding alerting the campus community about crime, and no systematic efforts to educate students about safety on campus. In fact, there was nothing governing campus crime response and prevention. They brought a lawsuit against Lehigh University for negligence and settled for an undisclosed amount. They used the award along with personal funds to found the national nonprofit organization Security on Campus, Inc., in 1987, renamed the Clery Center for Security on Campus in 2012. They started to lobby at the state level and then federal level to pass legislation requiring colleges and universities to publish their crime statistics, so that current and prospective families would have a sense of reported crimes on campus. The Clery Act was amended several times, and two significant revisions centered on sexual violence: the Campus Sexual Assault Victims' Bill of Rights and the VAWA amendments to the Clery Act.

Campus Sexual Assault Victims' Bill of Rights

In 1992, Congress enacted the Campus Sexual Assault Victims' Bill of Rights as part of the Higher Education Amendments of 1992 (Public Law:102–325, section 486 (c)), which President George Bush signed into law in July of 1992. This law was originally introduced in May 1991 by Congressman Jim Ramstad (R-MN) and has been referred to as the Ramstad Act. The Campus Sexual Assault Victims' Bill of Rights articulates policies, procedures, and services for all victims of sexual assault at postsecondary educational institutions (that participate in federal student aid programs). It is designed to ensure that victims and offenders are afforded the same rights throughout the reporting and disciplinary process. This law affords certain basic rights to students in cases of sexual assault:

- The accuser and accused must have the same opportunity to have others present at campus disciplinary hearings.
- The institution shall inform both parties of the outcome of any disciplinary proceeding.
- The institution shall inform survivors of their options to notify law enforcement and assist them in doing so, if requested.
- The institution shall notify all survivors of counseling services.
- The institution shall notify survivors of options for changing academic and living situations.

VAWA Amendments to the Clery Act

The Clery Center for Security on Campus, in partnership with multiple non-profit, victim service organizations, advocated for the VAWA amendments to the Clery Act, informally known as the Campus Sexual Violence Elimination Act (SaVE Act) to amend the Clery Act to include dating violence, domestic violence, and stalking in the legislation. The bipartisan amendments were signed into law in March 2013 and will help colleges and universities to educate, to respond to, and to prevent multiple forms of sexual violence. Amendments to the Clery Act are subject to the negotiated rulemaking, a process where multiple stakeholders provide insight to determine consensus on final regulations written but the U.S. Department of Education (ED). The negotiated rulemaking panel included representation from public and private institutions, 2-year institutions, victim advocacy organizations, and higher education associations. The panel reached consensus on April 1, 2014, and the final regulations are open for public comment and are expected by November 1, 2014. These updates will modernize the 1992 Campus Sexual Assault Victims Bill of Rights and through their implementation could contribute to better prevention and response on college and university campuses.

Effectiveness of the Clery Act

The ED has been increasing their Clery Act evaluative reviews of institutions in recent years:

> A review may be initiated when a complaint is received, a media event raises certain concerns, the school's independent audit identifies serious non-compliance, or through a review selection process that may also coincide with state reviews performed by the FBI's Criminal Justice Information Service Audit Unit.
>
> *(U.S. Department of Education, Office of Federal Student Aid, 2012)*

As of April 2012, the ED, which is responsible for enforcing the Clery Act, reviewed 55 institutions for noncompliance with the law (U.S. Department of Education, Office of Federal Student Aid, 2012). From 1997 to 2008, the ED reviewed 25 institutions for Clery Act noncompliance. Since then, random audits have increased; from 2009 to April 2012, 30 institutions were reviewed, indicating a stronger governmental focus on compliance and enforcement (U.S. Department of Education, Office of Federal Student Aid, 2012).

If an institution of higher education violates the Clery Act, the ED has the ability to sanction a fine up to $35,000 (U.S. Department of Education, Office of Postsecondary Education, 2011, p. 9). On October 2, 2012, the penalty was increased from $27,500 to adjust for inflation ("Clery Act fines increase," 2012). Some of the institutions found in technical violation of the Clery Act by the ED were sanctioned for their noncompliance in relation to their sexual assault policies and procedures (U.S. Department of Education, Office of Federal Student Aid, 2012). For example, in 2005, Miami University of Ohio was fined $27,500 for not complying with the Campus Sexual Assault Victims' Bill of Rights, specifically for violating notification requirements to the respondent and complainant in cases of alleged sexual offenses (U.S. Department of Education, Office of Federal Student Aid, 2012). Of the 55 findings issued by the ED from June 1997 to April 2012, 12 resulted in fines. Of those, six were negotiated through settlement agreements and four were appealed (U.S. Department of Education, Office of Federal Student Aid, 2012).

At a Clery Center Collaborative meeting in Hershey, Pennsylvania, in June 2013, James L. Moore, III, Compliance Manager of Clery Act Compliance Division from the ED, shared the top ten Clery Act violations: (1) failure to disclose crimes based on Clery Act geography; (2) improper classification and disclosure of crimes; (3) lack of or inadequate policy statements; (4) failure to publish and distribute the ASR as a comprehensive document; (5) inadequate systems for collecting statistics from required sources (i.e., Campus Security Authorities); (6) incorrect reporting of arrest and disciplinary referrals of drug, liquor, and weapons violations; (7) inaccurate reporting of crime statistics to Office of Postsecondary Education; (8) deficient crime log; (9) inaccurate reporting of hate crimes; and (10) failure to develop, implement, and adhere to established policy. Despite limited monetary damages, reputational damage for noncompliance is significant (Tsikoudakis, 2012). Various factors that influence the success of a higher education institution may be impacted. "When a college's reputation is damaged, it can adversely affect student recruitment, alumni donations, and even federal funding" (Tsikoudakis, 2012, para. 2).

Perceptions of the effectiveness of the Clery Act in prevention of crime and raising awareness vary (Cantalupo, 2009; Gregory & Janosik, 2002; Jennings, Gover, & Pudrzynskas, 2007). Studies showed that 44% of campus law enforcement believe the Clery Act improves the quality of law enforcement programs, 70% of senior student affairs officers (i.e., vice presidents of student life) believe that programs mandated by the Clery Act help students to protect themselves (Gregory & Janosik, 2002; Janosik & Gregory 2009). White (2014) recommended an area for future research to assess the efficacy of the Clery Act in relation to campus safety:

> For example, do Clery Act-reportable crimes listed within the required statistics provide an accurate representation of the transparency of crimes for campus community members? How effective are crime prevention and security awareness programs? Are Clery Act-required emergency notifications and timely warnings perceived to be comprehensive of what campus community members should be aware of? In other words, do the technical requirements of the law fulfill the intended mission of the Clery Act?
>
> *(pp. 233–234)*

Others believe that the Clery Act has changed the scope of campus safety. Terry Hartle, Senior Vice President at the American Council on Education, commented that the Clery Act has forced universities (and colleges) to significantly expand and professionalize their campus security operations, and said the ED has not hesitated to use the Clery Act as a "blunt instrument" against institutions. He further stated, "I think the Clery Act has resulted in every institution in higher education taking campus security far more seriously than was the case twenty years ago" (Hefling, 2011). The scope of today's environment includes positions on colleges and universities dedicated to comprehensive prevention, advocacy, Clery Act compliance, and coordination of Title IX efforts. This approach represents not only technical but ethical commitment to federal law.

Intersections of the Clery Act and Title IX

Title IX promotes equal opportunity by stating that no person shall be discriminated against on the basis of sex in any educational program or activity receiving federal financial assistance. Title IX intersects with the Clery Act, especially as related to sexual assault. In April 2011, the ED Office for Civil Rights (OCR) sent college and university presidents a "Dear Colleague" letter outlining their interpretation of Title IX and its applicability to sexual violence, not only sexual harassment.[2] Since the issuance of the "Dear Colleague" letter, colleges and universities have revised policies, and a growing number of students have become aware of their rights under Title IX and filed complaints, coupled with Clery Act complaints, arguing that their institutions have violated Title IX (Perez-Pena, 2013). In April 2014, after receiving pressure from student activists, OCR released a list of 55 institutions of higher education currently under investigation for possible violation of Title IX. From 2012–2014, students across the country filed Title IX and Clery Act complaints and appeared in national media outlets to put their face to the issue of sexual violence. These students empowered one another to report their institutions for noncompliance and provided a face to the issue of campus sexual violence. More than ever, there is a significant need for institutional leaders to comply with federal regulations focused on sexual violence.

Institutional Leadership and Compliance With the Clery Act and Title IX

Janosik and Gregory (2009) emphasized that efforts by national higher education student affairs organizations have been more reactive than proactive in response and prevention of campus crime. Institutions of higher education struggle with compliance and often one person is tasked with the responsibility for compiling data and creating prevention programs. In April 2014, the White House Task Force on Sexual Violence provided sample language regarding the development of policy around reporting, examining climate, and prevention (White House Task Force, 2014). Extant literature found that institutions do not report crime data in a manner fully consistent with federal law and that college and university administrators need more guidance to comply properly (Karjane, Fisher, & Cullen, 2002; U.S. Department of Justice, 2005; White, 2014). Lack of compliance is often correlated to a lack of understanding of elements of the Clery Act (Karjane et al., 2002; Gregory & Janosik, 2003; White, 2014).

Institutional Leadership, Response to Crime, and Culture

A college or university president is tasked with governance over multiple constituencies. Leadership training is a staple in most companies and the "baseline in developing military officers" but is all but absent in universities (Portney, 2011). The job of a college or university president is arguably more complex than that of a business manager because of the constituencies that they serve (Portney, 2011). An engaged college or university president is an advocate, a model citizen, and understands the economic development of an institution through budget analysis and fundraising (Brand, 2002). The role of a college president requires myriad experience. Often the president is primarily concerned with fundraising due to pressure from the Board of Trustees. Most college and university presidents have made their path through an academic hierarchy either as a senior administrator from academic affairs or as a tenured faculty member (Risacher, 2004). Beyond a concern with fundraising, presidents also have concern for facilities, assessment, academics, diversity, and the overall well-being of students. Less than 10% of former student affairs deans or officers go on to be campus presidents. However, in a study examining senior student affairs officers and their scores using the Fisher/ Track Effective Leadership Scale, senior student affairs officers demonstrated the same characteristics as current presidents in management, social reference, confidence, and image (Risacher, 2004). Leaders at colleges and university are obligated to empower administrators to respond to violence on campus and empower them to build systems to prevent and respond.

Institutional Leadership and Response to Crime

Numerous media and professional sources suggest that campuses continue to underreport crime in spite of the Clery Act because of jurisdictional confusion, organizational inefficiency, and concern with student (offender) confidentiality (Wilcox, Jordan, & Pritchard, 2007). In a study of senior student affairs officers, 99% of the respondents self-reported that they are candid about campus crime and 3% reported that there was an attempt to hide campus crime (Janosik & Gregory, 2009). To contrast this finding, Janosik and Plummer (2005) found that 16% of campus victim advocates expressed a belief that campus senior administrators attempted to hide crime on campus, specifically sexual assault and rape.

There are few studies investigating the effectiveness of compliance with the Clery Act. Findings in multiple studies highlight confusion with the reporting and statistical gathering component of the law. The legislation includes specific language regarding geography when counting and coding crime statistics with which many respondents in multiple studies express frustration (Cantalupo, 2009; Gregory & Janosik, 2002, 2003, 2009). However, data suggest that prevention education and awareness programs contribute to student safety. In one study, 51% of students state that they are more likely to report crime as a result of the legislation (Janosik, 2002). Law enforcement on campuses (members of the International Association of Campus Law Enforcement Administrators) note that prevention programs increase student confidence in their departments and departmental response to crime (Gregory & Janosik, 2002).

Institutional Leadership and Culture

A campus sexual assault awareness, prevention, and response program needs buy-in not only from students and administrators but also support from leadership within the institution. There is a recognized lack of awareness regarding the roles of administration in the process (Cantalupo, 2011). Furthermore, specific administrators need to understand their roles within an institution. For example, healthcare staff need to know the process of their institutional facility or county in the event of a report of rape. College and university presidents need to understand their role in the process, as many times a disciplinary appeal will reach the level of the president (Fossey & Smith, 1996). The rate of campus peer sexual assault remains high and the culture of nonreporting by victims leads to a perpetual cycle (Cantalupo, 2011). Campus sexual assault advocates, prevention educators, health educators, and staff charged with responding to and preventing sexual violence need support from leadership financially, as well as a demonstrated ethical commitment to handling incidents of sexual violence. A consistent concern for administration is that an institution of higher education that provides a variety of education geared toward students, staff, and community change will experience an increase of reports of sexual assault (Cantalupo, 2011). This is a common challenge for campus sexual assault programs as it is difficult to assess programs since one cannot measure a decrease due to the historic underreporting of violence against women (Kress et al., 2006). Recipients of the U.S. Department of Justice Office on Violence Against Women Campus Program grants are informed by a program director with the federal government that when they receive funds to create and sustain a prevention and response program for violence against women that their reported numbers will increase (M. Charles, personal communication, July 30, 2012). The federal government understands that reports of sexual violence will increase when a prevention program is proactive and comprehensive. Leadership at institutions of higher education need to understand this phenomenon and use it as an opportunity to educate parents, students, donors, alumni, and other stakeholders.

There is a significant need for increased training of multiple constituencies within an institution. Higher education can be siloed by department: student affairs, athletics, academics, etc. In order to embrace a broader social change around the culture of sexual assault on campuses, administrators must understand the dynamics and embrace survivors (Edwards, 2009; Palmer, McMahon, Rounsaville, & Ball, 2010; Rothman & Silverman, 2007). Despite the requirements of the Clery Act specific to sexual assault education and the guidance provided by Title IX, research has highlighted that fewer than 40% of higher education institutions require sexual assault training for campus public safety and law enforcement (Malveaux, 2004). Practitioners dedicated to sexual assault prevention and response should not only educate students as required by the letter of the law, they should also provide training for faculty and staff in the spirit of a law created after the tragic rape and murder of a student (Carmody, Ekhomu, & Payne, 2009).

Ethical Commitment to Compliance

A recent focus from the media and the U.S. government on the moral obligations associated with compliance has prompted higher education institutions to review their practices (Duncan, 2011a). Specific to the Clery Act, this moral obligation is found in reducing violence on campus. Following the highly publicized crimes of sexual abuse of minors committed by former Penn State assistant football coach Jerry Sandusky, some are questioning the technical *and* moral compliance with the Clery Act (Duncan, 2011a; Freeh Sporkin & Sullivan, LLP, 2012; Gifford, 2011; Kiss, 2011; Meehan, 2011).

Currently, the ED is reviewing Penn State's compliance with the Clery Act after public outcry implored stronger enforcement for the prevention of sexually violent crimes and overall safety on college campuses (Duncan, 2011a; Gifford, 2011; Kiss, 2011; Meehan, 2011). The recent focus on the Penn State scandal may positively influence campus officials' commitment to safety; moreover, the ED investigation at Penn State may alter former interpretations of compliance. U.S. Education Secretary Arne Duncan noted in a November 9, 2011, statement:

> If these allegations of sexual abuse are true then this is a horrible tragedy for those young boys. If it turns out that some people at the school knew of the abuse and did nothing or covered it up, that makes it even worse. Schools and school officials have a legal and moral responsibility to protect children and young people from violence and abuse.
>
> *(Duncan, 2011a, para. 3)*

Additionally, following their thorough investigation of Penn State's involvement and response to the Sandusky crimes, Freeh Sporkin and Sullivan, LLP (2012) made numerous recommendations emphasizing the need "to create an atmosphere of values and ethics-based decision making" (p. 131).

In light of this recent scandal at Penn State, key stakeholders have expressed their ethical interpretation of Clery Act compliance and outrage for the lack of morality by campus officials, even if they were somewhat compliant in a technical sense (Duncan, 2011a, 2011b; Meehan, 2011). An example of this is Duncan's (2011a) revulsion toward those who may have been put on notice but did not respond appropriately. These responses provide an evolving distinction between the legal requirements and the larger moral intentions of the law. The Penn State scandal currently serves as the exemplar for this assertion; complying with the Clery Act on a technical level is not enough (Duncan, 2011a, 2011b; Freeh Sporkin & Sullivan, LLP, 2012; Meehan, 2011). Yet, negative public perceptions as they relate to issues associated with serious crimes and violence do not need to be the motivating factor for the need for ethical practice; a safe campus where all can fulfill their potential is paramount. This sentiment is supported by many who work in the field of education. Alison Kiss, Executive Director of the Clery Center for Security on Campus, described her interpretation of the Clery Act and Title IX on November 23, 2011:

> Institutions must embrace both the letter and spirit of the Clery Act and Title IX laws to build safer campus communities that do not tolerate sexual violence. We all need to get off the sidelines, get in the game and end sexual violence.
>
> *(Kiss, 2011, para. 9)*

Markedly, when asked to reflect on college's and university's interpretations of the Clery Act, Connie Clery (personal communication, June 14, 2012) noted that she was "elated, and in some ways, it's hard to believe. But it's great to see the change in attitude, finally. Now, I'm hoping that will translate to spirit." More than before, key stakeholders are prominently describing their expectations that campus officials comply with the technical *and* ethical obligations of the Clery Act (Duncan, 2011a, 2011b; Kiss, 2011, 2012).

Ethic of Caring

White (2014) asserted that incidents of sexual violence magnify the need for campus officials to adopt an "ethic of caring" in relation to campus safety (Noddings, 1986, 1988, 1992, 1994, 1995). In consideration of Noddings' "ethic of caring" theory, there is a connection to caring, educational decision-making, and one's responsibility for morality, fidelity, and true concern for individuals. If campus officials neglect to adopt a higher level of caring and an ethical approach to campus safety, real change will not happen, campus crime and violent tragedies will endure, and the status quo will persist (White, 2014).

Care is basic in human life, and every person has a desire to be cared for (Noddings, 1992). In support of that premise, Noddings asserted that caring is undoubtedly connected to educational decision-making and declared that one's significant responsibility for morality and fidelity are linked to expressions of true concern for individuals. This theory supports educators' understanding and compassionate interactions with others, "The fundamental idea, of course, is that education is basically a relational enterprise and to do it well, teachers and students have to develop a relation of care and trust. That is absolutely fundamental" (N. Noddings, personal communication, June 8, 2012). Thus, infusing an "ethic of caring" concept into the mission of American education is of great consequence.

Ethic of Caring and Campus Safety

Campus safety is an ethical good and the meta-outcome (White, 2014). Noddings' "ethic of caring" framework articulates the importance of people caring for one another on a human level. Noddings (1995) asserts that the essence of caring in a learning environment bolsters the philosophy of education. To that end, those who play an active role in preventing crime in an educational setting demonstrate the care required to sustain a just society (Noddings, 1994, 1995).

The Clery Act is a technical vehicle for measuring compliance, but this law may be translated and interpreted by those who are responsible for campus safety on a higher, moral level (White, 2014). According to Noddings (personal communication, June 8, 2012): "It strikes me . . . that if the spirit, what you're calling the spirit of the Clery Act, which is compatible with care ethics, if that were embraced and followed, you probably wouldn't need the law." Elevating compliance into a moral arena equates with a greater level of care and concern for students and campus communities (White, 2014). A technical interpretation of the Clery Act may not suffice for meeting the intended purpose of the law (C. Clery, personal communication, June 14, 2012). Additionally, caring in education is deemed a fundamental concept to the mission of schools (N. Noddings, personal communication, June 8, 2012).

A recent qualitative case study focused on the influence of a Security on Campus, Inc. (now Clery Center for Security on Campus) Clery Act Training Seminar (CATS) on participants' ethical commitment to campus safety beyond compliance with the Clery Act at their respective institutions (White, 2014). Noddings' "ethic of caring" was utilized as a theoretical framework to assess enhanced commitment to campus safety. In this study, the researcher utilized several data sources, such as campus police/public safety personnel, noncampus police/public safety personnel, and documents at institutions of higher education and several themes were identified: understanding of the Clery Act; experience with CATS; commitment to the Clery Act/campus safety; involvement with Clery Act/campus safety efforts; and barriers and supports to success toward embracing the letter and spirit of the law (White, 2014).

After analyzing different perspectives, it was evident institutional commitment to campus safety and compliance with the Clery Act was more technical in nature (White, 2014). However, most CATS participants conveyed at least a small amount of an ethic of caring. Respondents often referenced the requirements of the law per *The Handbook for Campus Safety and Security Reporting* (U.S. Department of Education, Office of Postsecondary Education, 2011). Additionally, responses symbolizing an ethic of caring, and in particular, examples of modeling, dialogue, practice, and confirmation, were not as prevalent compared to technical answers; however, there was evidence of the beginnings of a deeper commitment to campus safety.

To aid in the comprehension of these themes, White (2014) developed a model (Table 6.1) based on the information collected depicting the advancement of an individual's development with embracing the letter and spirit of the Clery Act. Each of these facets of an individual's experience may be influenced by one's legal and/or moral position on the topic. The ideal outcome is to possess and perform with full technical compliance and ethical commitment to campus safety and the Clery Act, although participants in this study did not always achieve this ideal outcome.

Although each individual and institution presented different amounts of devotion to the letter and the spirit of the law, it was more likely that someone with thoughtful conviction, who attended a multi-dimensional training, retained a deeper commitment, implemented all-encompassing safety efforts, and was aware of supports and barriers to success was more sensitive to the technical and ethical dimensions of the Clery Act.

TABLE 6.1 Model for Technical Compliance and Ethical Commitment to the Clery Act

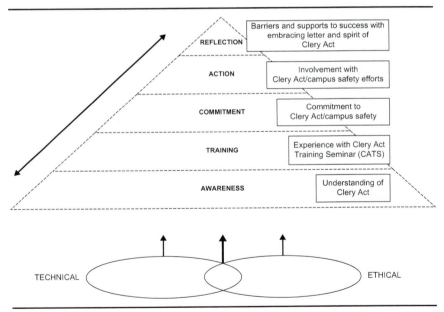

Source: White, K. N. (2014). The influence of "Clery Act Training Seminars" on participants' ethical commitment to campus safety beyond compliance in colleges and universities. Saint Joseph's University, Philadelphia, PA.

Recommendations for Greater Technical Compliance and Ethical Commitment to the Clery Act

White (2014) offered seven recommendations for enhancing institutional compliance with the Clery Act and building an ethic of caring to ensure greater campus safety. Many of these recommendations may also apply to other laws, such as Title IX.

Recommendation one. Campus officials and institutions should strive to make overt connections between strong campus safety efforts and ethical commitment to campus safety. Instead of correlating success with passing an audit from the ED, confirm that campus community members feel cared for and safer. This may motivate campus officials through validation of their efforts, and this realization may increase morale and reinforce one's commitment to the letter and spirit of the law.

Recommendation two. Individuals and institutions should concentrate on technical compliance with the Clery Act and ethical commitment to campus safety in tandem and not sequentially. In the same way, organizations should train with the same mindset, and the ED should measure compliance in both arenas. If this was done, proactive training, campus implementation, and governmental enforcement would align with the purpose and mission of the Clery Act, as noted by Connie Clery and the Clery Center for Security on Campus. During a conversation with Connie Clery (personal communication, June 14, 2012), White (2014) noted Connie Clery's desire to see institutional compliance efforts "translate to spirit."

Recommendation three. Institutions should partake in a hypothetical exercise that was inspired by Noddings' (personal communication, June 8, 2012) response to her ethic of caring framework being applied to the Clery Act when she spoke with Kiersten N. White (2014). Campus officials should brainstorm what they would do to keep campus community members safe if the Clery Act did not exist. This drill may expand the confined thinking of those who implemented Clery Act requirements because they are mandatory. Removing these technical limitations may improve campus safety efforts because campus officials would be forced to think about why they would execute certain initiatives, as opposed to merely following the law without genuine care or intent.

Recommendation four. The ED should mandate annual training for campus safety officials responsible for Clery Act compliance, which includes campus security authorities. From the study, it was evident even those who were trained were not fluent in the nuanced law, impeding their ability to fully succeed in a technical manner, let alone with a deeper, ethical commitment. As previously noted, trainings should be enhanced to include tips and techniques for embracing the spirit of the law.

Recommendation five. Trainings, campus protocols, programming, etc. should be intended for a collaborative team, just as the Clery Center for Security

On Campus designed for CATS. White's (2014) study illuminated a multi-disciplinary team as an asset to institutional commitment to campus safety, and one prominent advantage of a committed collaborative team surfaced, which was the diversity of: (a) knowledge—team members attended different trainings and understood assorted techniques and tips for better compliance; (b) expertise—team members offered varied input based on experience, professional backgrounds, etc.; (c) perspectives—team members framed their involvement through different philosophical lenses, such as victim-centered versus institutional community-centered; and (d) interest—team members relayed distinctive attractions to various elements of campus safety (e.g., research, programming, training, etc.). When such diverse individuals were pooled together for a common goal, a comprehensive approach to campus safety was very likely. This team approach should not only be represented at trainings, but team efforts should continue back on campuses after trainings and each member should play an active role.

Recommendation six. Influential decision-makers, such as the ED or institutional Board of Trustees, and public communicators, such as the media, should emphasize the positive outcomes of an institution's high technical and ethical commitment to the Clery Act, rather than sensationalize or focus on the negative outcomes of noncompliance. Situations like the Penn State scandal have had a chilling effect on the motivation of campus officials to go above and beyond. From this study, it was evident there was an intense desire to prioritize technical compliance with the Clery Act for fear of being reprimanded for noncompliance, as opposed to caring and doing what was right by implementing campus safety initiatives because they best protected the community, even if they were not required by law.

Recommendation seven. Individuals and institutions should play an active role in combatting some of the barriers to success when possible. For example, many participants demonstrated their commitment to caring; however, doing so required increased resources, such as time and money, that many institutions did not have. Rather than reacting to a requirement to fund initiatives or positions following an audit or complaint, institutions should proactively address the concerns of its members and provide adequate resources to comply on the technical and ethical stages. Other resolutions to noted barriers to success included additional training, greater transparency and awareness of the Clery Act on campuses, institutional prioritization of campus safety, and dedicated collaborative teams focused on campus safety efforts.

White (2014) believed that although not all of these recommendations may be practical and/or feasible, implementing a few may accelerate an institution's commitment to campus safety and, in turn, create an ethic of caring.

Concluding Thoughts

Dedicated institutional leadership and an ethical commitment to campus safety represent the makings of a college or university that exemplifies the true duty of responsibility. Institutional leadership in higher education cannot ignore campus sexual assault. In order for students and administrators to embrace prevention efforts and create a survivor-supportive environment, campus presidents must understand the law governing campus sexual assault policy. Furthermore, college presidents have a moral obligation to put forth their best effort to prevent and respond to campus sexual assault.

The research on sexual assault prevention and response shows a need for an institutionalized program. It is clear that short, one-time programs will not affect the attitudes of college students. The programs need to be inclusive, offer information on the definition of sexual assault and rape, and engage men and bystanders. This education should trickle from student populations to administrators, faculty, and law enforcement for comprehensive information on campus policy and the dynamics of sexual assault.

It is evident from prior literature and case studies that the responsibility of preventing and responding to campus sexual assault cannot fall on the shoulders of a lone solider in counseling, student affairs, or campus police. Literature also reveals that campus law enforcement, victim advocates, campus judicial affairs, and senior student affairs officers all report better collaboration on response to crime and sexual assault as a result of the Clery Act (Gregory & Janosik, 2002, 2003; Janosik & Gregory, 2009; Janosik and Plummer, 2005).

A model for achieving full technical compliance and ethical commitment to the law is provided (White, 2014). In short, those who are aware, trained, committed, active, and reflective about campus safety utilize modeling, dialogue, practice, and confirmation to produce safer havens for campus community members, ultimately leading to an ethic of caring.

The Clery Act has been amended four times and contains many provisions requiring institutions to comply, but it is clear that leadership must play a role in institutionalizing compliance. Furthermore, a college or university president is tasked with governance over multiple constituencies. Leadership training is a staple in almost every type of company and the very baseline in developing military officers but is all but absent in universities (Portney, 2011). The job of a college or university president is arguably more complex than that of a business manager because of the constituencies that they serve (Portney, 2011). Numerous media and professional sources have suggested that campuses continue to underreport crime in spite of the Clery Act because of jurisdictional confusion, organizational inefficiency, and concern with student (offender) confidentiality (Wilcox, Jordan, & Pritchard, 2007).

Many institutions have a program or person charged with the prevention and response of sexual assault. The challenges include engaging leadership in the mission of the office or program, educating the institution on reporting of crimes, and truly centralizing efforts in coordinating multiple departments to eliminate rape culture on campus and to end the culture of silence centered on campus sexual assault. This demonstrated technical and ethical commitment to the elements of the Clery Act is a model for developing safer campuses and improved proactive measures for eliminating sexual violence on campus.

Notes

1. Know Your IX was founded by a group of survivors and students activists to educate college and university students about their rights under Title IX (www.knowyourIX. org).
2. Sexual assault is recognized as an extreme form of sexual harassment.

References

Brand, M. (2002). The engaged president: Changing times, unchanging principles. *Presidency, 5*(3), 26–30.

Cantalupo, N. C. (2009). Campus violence: Understanding the extraordinary through the ordinary. *Journal of College & University Law, 35*(3), 613–690.

Cantalupo, N. C. (2011). *Burying our heads in the sand: Lack of knowledge, knowledge avoidance and persistent problem of campus peer sexual violence.* Georgetown Law: The Scholarly Commons, Research Paper No. 11–41, Washington, DC.

Carmody, D., Ekhomu, J., & Payne, B. K. (2009). Needs of sexual assault advocates in campus-based sexual assault centers. *College Student Journal, 43*(2), 507–513.

Clery Act fines increase to $35K per violation. (2012, October). *Campus Safety Magazine.* Retrieved from www.campussafetymagazine.com/

Clery Center. (2011, March 6). Clery Policy. Retrieved from http://clerycenter.org

Duncan, A. (2011a, November 9). U.S. Department of Education to investigate Penn State's handling of sexual misconduct allegations. Retrieved from www.ed.gov/

Duncan, A. (2011b, December 14). Column: End double standards in sex abuse cases. *USA Today.* Retrieved from www.usatoday.com

Edwards, K. E. (2009). Effectiveness of a social change approach to sexual assault prevention. *College Student Affairs Journal, 28*(1), 22–37.

Fisher, B. S., Cullen, F. T., & Turner, M. G. (2000, December). *The sexual victimization of college women* (NCJ 182369). Washington, DC: National Institute of Justice.

Fossey, R., & Smith, M. C. (1996). Responding to campus rape: A practical guide for college administrators. *New Directions for Higher Education, 1996*(95), 29–42.

Freeh Sporkin & Sullivan, LLP. (2012, July 12). *Report of the Special Investigative Counsel regarding the actions of the Pennsylvania State University related to the child sexual abuse committed by Gerald A. Sandusky.* Freeh Sporking & Sullivan, LLP.

Gifford, N. P. (2011, November 9). Penn State Clery Act review request. Retrieved from www.psu.edu/ur/2011/DoE_Letter_110911.pdf

Gregory, D. E., & Janosik, S. M. (2002). The Clery Act: How effective is it? Perceptions from the field—the current state of the research and recommendations for improvement. *Stetson Law Review, 32,* 7–59.

Gregory, D. E., & Janosik, S. M. (2003). The effect of the Clery Act on campus judicial practices. *Journal of College Student Development, 44*(6), 763–778.

Hefling, K. (2011, November 10). Ed. Dept. uses law to investigate campus crimes. *Associated Press.* Retrieved from www.boston.com/news/education/higher/articles/2011/11/10/ ed_dept_uses_law_to_investigate_campus_crimes/

Janosik, S. M. (2002). *Parents' views on the Jeanne Clery Campus Crime Act and campus safety.* Educational Policy Institute of Virginia Tech Policy Paper, Blacksburg, VA.

Janosik, S. M., & Gregory, D. E. (2009). The Clery Act, campus safety, and the perceptions of senior student affairs officers. *NASPA Journal, 46*(2), 208–227.

Janosik, S. M., & Plummer, E. (2005). The Clery Act, campus safety and the views of assault victim advocates. *College Student Affairs Journal, 25*(1), 116–130.

Jennings, W. G., Gover, A. R., & Pudrzynskas, D. (2007). Are institutions of higher learning safe? A descriptive study of campus safety issues and self-reported campus victimization among male and female college students. *Journal of Criminal Justice Education, 18*(2), 191–208.

Karjane, H. M., Fisher, B. S., & Cullen, F. T. (2002). Campus sexual assault: How America's institutions of higher education respond. Washington, DC: National Institute of Justice. Retrieved from www.ncjrs.gov/pdffiles1/nij/grants/196676.pdf

Kiss, A. (2011, November 23). Re: Campus safety rests on community engagement [Web log message]. Retrieved from www.educationnation.com

Kiss, A. (2012). *Welcome letter.* Security on Campus, Inc. Clery Act Training Seminar Manual, Saint Joseph's University, Philadelphia, PA.

Kress, V. E., Shepherd, J. B., Anderson, R. I., Petuch, A. J., Nolan, J. M., & Thiemeke, D. (2006). Evaluation of the impact of a coeducational sexual assault prevention program on college students' rape myth attitudes. *Journal of College Counseling, 9*(2), 148–157.

Malveaux, J. (2004). From Kobe Bryant to campus rape. *Black Issues in Higher Education, 21*(6), 30.

Meehan, P. (2011, November 8). Meehan calls for federal investigation into Sandusky matter. Press release. Retrieved from http://meehan.house.gov/

Moore, J. (2013, June). *Clery Act compliance update.* Paper session presented at the meeting of Clery Center Collaborative Program, Philadelphia, PA.

Noddings, N. (1986). Fidelity in teaching, teacher education, and research for teaching. *Harvard Educational Review, 56*(4), 496–511.

Noddings, N. (1988). An ethic of caring and its implications for instructional arrangements. *American Journal of Education, 96*(2), 215–230.

Noddings, N. (1992). *Challenge to care in schools: An administrative approach to education.* New York: Teachers College Press.

Noddings, N. (1994). The role of educators in combatting violence. *Religious Education, 89*(4), 568–571.

Noddings, N. (1995). A morally defensible mission for schools in the 21st century. *Phi Delta Kappan, 76*(5), 365–368.

Noddings, N. (2010). Moral education in an age of globalization. *Educational Philosophy and Theory, 42*(4), 390–396.

Palmer, R. S., McMahon, T. J., Rounsaville, B. J., & Ball, S. A. (2010). Coercive sexual experiences, protective behavioral strategies, alcohol expectancies and consumption among male and female college students. *Journal of Interpersonal Violence, 25*(9), 1563–1578.

Perez-Pena, R. (2013, March 19). College groups connect to fight sexual assault. *New York Times.* Retrieved from www.nytimes.com/2013/03/20/education/activists-at-colleges-network-to-fight-sexual-assault.html?pagewanted=all

Pinar, W., Reynolds, W., Slattery, P., & Taubman, P. (2004). *Understanding curriculum: An introduction to the study of historical and contemporary curriculum discourses.* New York: Peter Lang.

Portney, P. (2011, October 31). The leadership vacuum in higher education. *Washington Post.* Retrieved from www.washingtonpost.com

Risacher, J. (2004). The extent to which four-year college presidents who previously served as senior student affairs officers report having the characteristics of effective presidents. *NASPA Journal,* 41(3), 436–452.

Rothman, E., & Silverman, J. (2007). The effect of a college sexual assault prevention program on first-year students' victimization rates. *Journal of American College Health,* 55(5), 283–290.

Sloan, J. J., & Fisher, B. S. (2011). *The dark side of the ivory tower: Campus crime as a social problem.* New York: Cambridge University Press.

Tsikoudakis, M. (2012, January 1). Re: Penn State scandal sharpens focus on reputational risk [Web log message]. Retrieved from www.businessinsurance.com/

U.S. Department of Education, Office of Federal Student Aid. (2012). Data Center Clery Act reports. Retrieved from www.studentaid.ed.gov/about/data-center/school/clery-act

U.S. Department of Education, Office of Postsecondary Education. (2011). *The handbook for campus safety and security reporting.* Washington, DC: Author.

U.S. Department of Justice. (2005). *Sexual assault on campus: What colleges and universities are doing about it.* Washington, DC: Author.

White, K. N. (2014). *The influence of "Clery Act Training Seminars" on participants' ethical commitment to campus safety beyond compliance in colleges and universities* (Unpublished doctoral dissertation). Saint Joseph's University, Philadelphia, PA.

White House Task Force to Protect Students from Sexual Assault. (2014). *Not alone: The first report of the White House task force to protect students from sexual assault.* Washington, DC: Author.

Wilcox, P., Jordan, C. E., & Pritchard, A. J. (2007). A multidimensional examination of campus safety: Victimization, perceptions of danger, worry about crime, and precautionary behavior among college women in the post-Clery era. *Crime & Delinquency,* 53(2), 219–254.

7

COMPLYING WITH TITLE IX BY UNIFYING ALL CIVIL RIGHTS-BASED POLICIES AND PROCEDURES

Brett A. Sokolow, Saundra K. Schuster, W. Scott Lewis, and Daniel C. Swinton

Sexual harassment and sexual violence are not new issues facing college campuses, though heightened government regulation and the voices of victims across the country are enhancing institutional attention to these critical issues. Since Vice President Joe Biden and Department of Education Secretary Arne Duncan released, with great fanfare, the April 4, 2011, Dear Colleague Letter (Ali, 2011) pertaining to Title IX and sexual violence on college campuses, institutions have been scrambling to comply and to identify best practices to improve how sexual violence is addressed.

One of the most transformative approaches to addressing sexual violence that campuses have identified is to harness the effectiveness of a civil rights investigation model akin to how campuses address other forms of discrimination. This powerful and empowering approach is founded on principles of equity, promptness, impartiality, and fairness, with the institution in the role of fact-finder. As forms of sex/gender discrimination, sexual violence and sexual harassment are especially amenable to resolution using a civil rights model.

Until the 2011 Dear Colleague Letter, many campuses followed a quasi-judicial adjudicatory model created over decades from a belief that "fairness" and "equity" mandate a disciplinary system replete with legalisms, hearing boards, and court-like due process requirements. Yet colleges and universities are institutions of education, not courts of law, corporations, or government agencies. Accordingly, campus investigative and resolution processes should reflect the context of higher education as well as the civil-rights based nature of sexual violence and sexual harassment, which has led to more widespread adoption and consideration of the civil rights investigation model. Rather than relying on a hearing board/panel of three-to-seven faculty, students, or staff to investigate and render findings on alleged violations, a true civil rights investigation model utilizes a robust and thorough investigation by trained investigators (typically one or two), who then render a finding on the alleged violations. These investigators are the experts in the evidence and have met with and questioned all parties and witnesses, gathered all relevant evidence, and rendered a finding based on the evidence and information gleaned from the investigation. Many institutions already use a form of this model for employee discrimination complaints and many are finding that it can be more broadly applied to students and faculty, as well. Campuses have historically pursued discrete due process models by creating separate disciplinary processes for students, faculty, and staff. With the implementation of revised civil rights investigation models, campus administrators are realizing that they can unify policy and process to address not only Title IX-based complaints but also all forms of discrimination across the institution for all faculty, students, and staff using one policy and one process.

Sexual violence is among the most heinous, difficult, and complicated forms of discrimination for campuses to investigate and resolve, in no small part because it is both a form of discrimination prohibited by campus codes of conduct and a crime prohibited by law. Many of those looking at colleges and universities from the outside often wonder why campuses are involved in addressing crimes at all, and again Title IX provides the answer. Because sexual violence is an extreme form of sexual harassment (unwelcomed sexual advances), colleges and universities are obligated to resolve and remedy all reported sexual violence, irrespective of whatever actions may parallel the campus process within the criminal justice system.

Among the most difficult to investigate on a college campus are incidents of student on student nonconsensual sexual intercourse (what would be termed a rape in criminal codes) when alcohol or other drugs play a role. In such cases, emotions run very high, the influence of alcohol or other drugs leaves memories dulled, and there are typically no witnesses to the incident other than the complainant(s) and respondent(s). Investigations must examine not only the alleged incident itself but also the situation leading up to and immediately following the alleged incident, including the specifics of alcohol and other drug consumption.

There are often a litany of other issues to address in such complaints, including dozens of ancillary witnesses to interview, remedies to provide—both short- and long-term—no-contact orders, court orders, simultaneous police investigations, attorneys, victim advocacy and support systems, advisors for the complainant and the respondent, parental concerns, Clery Act timely warning notifications, Title IX requirements, Campus Sexual Violence Elimination Act (Campus SaVE) compliance requirements, coursework concerns, on-campus living arrangements, and Sexual Assault Nurse Examiner reports. The list could continue, but the point is that there are few, if any, more complex issues addressed by campus administrators. Overlaid by an array of overly complex institutional culture and political issues, institutional investigations and adjudicatory procedures are often drawn out and unnecessarily adversarial. Today, Title IX adds further pressure with an explicit 60-day resolution goal from the time that notice of sexual violence and/or sexual harassment is received. Title IX also adds a mandate to provide comprehensive training to all investigators, hearing officers, boards/panels, and appeals officers. Thus, the more separate, but overlapping, processes a campus has, the more it must expend limited resources on unnecessarily duplicative training. Additionally, cross-constituency complaints (e.g., student-on-faculty, student-on-administrator, faculty-on-staff) introduce differing and, at times, conflicting policies and procedures that can lead to confusion, frustration, and differential treatment based on the constituency group to which each party belongs.

These variables make a persuasive case for unifying, simplifying, and streamlining institutional policies and procedures. They make a case for creating one institution-wide policy and set of processes to address sexual violence complaints. In making that case, it is instructive to examine the nature, function, and history of civil rights protections in the United States.

Brief History of "Civil Rights" in the United States

The goal of protecting civil rights and remedying invidious discrimination supports the argument for a stand-alone, specific set of policies and procedures to address all alleged acts of discrimination.

While we have made significant strides, American society remains a society where individuals were and are granted certain privileges or advantages on the basis of core characteristics such as race, sex, religion, or national origin. The advantages can be implicit or overt, public or private, malicious or inadvertent. Yet, over the course of American history and through each branch of government, laws and regulations have ultimately determined that inequality on the basis of such core characteristics is unacceptable. Moreover, such inequity is, regardless of intent, illegal. Indeed, the 13th and 14th Amendments to the U.S. Constitution directly address the issues by prohibiting slavery and involuntary servitude (U.S. Const. amend. XIII), as well as prohibiting each state from "deny[ing] to any person within its jurisdiction the equal protection of the laws" (U.S. Const. amend. XIV). Congress then created specific avenues of legal redress to allow individuals to enforce constitutional and civil rights via the Civil Rights Act of 1871.

Nearly three quarters of a century later during the "Civil Rights Era," a flurry of court cases expanded civil rights and protections by making various forms of discrimination unlawful. Indeed, the U.S. Supreme Court declared in *Brown v. Board of Education* (1954) that school segregation on the basis of race was illegal. A decade later, Congress passed the landmark Civil Rights Act of 1964, which addressed a litany of discriminatory practices including voting (Title I), public accommodations (Title II), public facilities (Title III), federally assisted programs (Title VI), and employment (Title VII). The last two are very familiar to most colleges and universities, with Title VII targeting equity in employment on the basis of race, color, sex, religion, and national origin. Continuing on the same course,

Congress passed the Voting Rights Act of 1965 prohibiting racial discrimination in voting.

Congress then passed another landmark piece of legislation, Title IX of the Education Amendments of 1972, targeting discrimination on the basis of sex in the educational environment. Title IX declares, "No person in the United States shall, on the basis of sex, be excluded from participation in, be denied the benefits of, or be subjected to discrimination under any educational program or activity receiving federal financial assistance" (20 U.S.C. § 1681). Title IX applies to all educational institutions that receive federal financial assistance, both K–12 as well as higher education. It is also critical to note that sexual assault and rape are extreme forms of sex-based discrimination and, therefore, fall under Title IX's purview and must be addressed by educational institutions in a manner as proscribed by the government. Subsequent prominent civil rights legislation that has significantly impacted on higher education has included Section 504 of the Rehabilitation Act of 1973 and the Americans with Disabilities Act of 1990.

Viewed in its historical context and alongside a number of similarly intended civil rights legislation, one wonders why discrimination on the basis of sex under Title IX should be addressed differently than other civil rights-based discrimination? *Dixon v. Alabama* (1961) provides some context. In 1960, six African American students were summarily expelled from Alabama State College after participating in a "sit-in" at a lunch counter in the Montgomery County Courthouse. The college provided these students no notice of the allegations, no opportunity to address the allegations; they were simply told they were expelled. The Fifth Circuit Court of Appeals determined that these six men were denied even minimal due process and invalidated the expulsions. The historical legacy of *Dixon v. Alabama* expanded the civil rights of accused students by ushering in the court-based due process era for campus discipline, but many campuses continue to use a model designed to comply with *Dixon* without reference to the comprehensive set of victim's rights enacted with Title IX.

In the aftermath of recent prominent Title IX guidance from the Department of Education's Office for Civil Rights, a number of institutions are reconsidering the fundamental question of how best to reconcile the procedural conflicts presented by ensuring due process for the accused and according civil rights protections for victims. For an increasing number, the answer is a civil rights investigation model.

Ultimately, sex and gender need strong protections, but institutions can and should strive to provide similar, high level protection and enforcement for all alleged civil rights-based violations. Discrimination on the basis of sex, race, religion, national origin, and disability have more in common with each other than not and a number of institutions are finding that complaints, investigations, and resolution processes can and should be similar, if not the same, for each form of discrimination.

Different Processes for Discrimination Complaints Than Those Used to Address Title IX-Related Complaints

Institutions have come by their scattered policies and procedures in organic, often reactionary fashion—creating new policies and procedures for specific constituencies based on lawsuits and court decisions, new or amended laws, regulations, and guidance, as well as reaction to specific cases or instances. Such influences and requirements have, at varying times, focused only on a specific constituency (e.g., tenured faculty, students, collective bargaining agreements), creating a patchwork of policies and procedures across the institution.

Additionally, the policies and processes for each constituency have matured at different times and relied on different laws and court cases, leaving institutions with myriad policies and procedures that look like Forrest Gump's box of chocolates. These varied approaches, however, typically have the same intent: ensuring that institutions appropriately, promptly, thoroughly, and impartially address discrimination in its many forms.

As the Department of Education and the Department of Justice heighten their regulatory and compliance activities, institutions have a window of opportunity to unify their civil rights-based policies and complaint resolution procedures; the governmental microscope provides an impetus for needed, if difficult, change. It also provides us with a way to explain the necessity for change to campus stakeholders who find the idea of change to be uncomfortable or threatening.

Any effort to merge or combine this patchwork of policies and procedures should first examine how and why these differing policies and procedures came to be. As with the historical civil rights analysis previously provided in this chapter, an examination of the historical context of college and university internal policy and procedure development can help us to understand why the underlying requirements and intentions pertaining to civil rights violations are better addressed under a more uniform approach.

Higher education in America began with two constituencies—faculty and students. Faculty wore many hats: teacher, researcher, human resources, admissions, registrar, hall advisor, and disciplinarian. Colleges and universities were fairly small, educating select, typically wealthy White male students who studied law, medicine, or theology from White male faculty members. Misbehavior by faculty or students was dealt with harshly and at the sole discretion of one or two individuals. The concept of due process was virtually nonexistent, leading at times to very subjective, arbitrary decisions based often on personalities and, at times, discrimination.

As the campus mission, context, and membership expanded, laws, regulations, court cases, and institutional policies and procedures have developed to help ensure fairness for all involved. Yet, these varied inputs have created a multitude of concomitant policies and procedures differing on the basis of the constituency for

TABLE 7.1 Types of Employees and Students at Colleges and Universities

Employees	*Students*
Administrators	• Undergraduate
• Academic	• Graduate
• Human Resources	• Professional (Medical, Dental, Law, etc.)
• Student Affairs	• Full-time
• Athletics	• Part-time
• Medical	• On-campus (residential)
	• Off-campus
Faculty	• Extension
• Tenured	• Dual Enrollment
• Tenure-track	• Visiting
• Non-tenure-track	• Traditional
• Adjunct	• Non-traditional
• Research	• English as a Second Language
• Medical	• International Students
	• Students with Disabilities
Staff	
• Full-time	
• Part-time	
• At-will	
• Student Worker	
• Paraprofessional staff	
• TAs and/or Graduate Assistant	
• Agent and/or Third Party	

which they are intended. Indeed, college and university campuses are now complex, often loosely coupled organizations that have grown and developed in varied silos such as colleges or schools, departments, divisions, unions, and affinity groups.

In the most simplified sense, colleges and universities still have two main constituencies: employees and students. In reality, institutions have dozens of constituencies, all of which are sub-categories of these two main groupings, many of which have differing policies and procedures pertaining to civil rights-based violations (see Table 7.1).

When looking at the varied box of chocolates, it's helpful to remember that institutions have created or provided differing rights, responsibilities, policies, and procedures for each or some combination of these constituency groups. For example, many institutions define "sexual harassment" differently for students than for faculty and/or staff. Student policies are often very detailed in prohibiting various forms of sexual violence, yet staff policies almost ignore it altogether. Accordingly, certain types of conduct may or may not be a violation, depending on which policies apply. A general example of differing constituency-based institutional policies and procedures can be seen in Table 7.2. This example provides 10 different constituency-based policy and procedural groupings.

TABLE 7.2 Groupings of Constituency-Based Policies and Procedures

Faculty	Staff & Administration	Students
• Tenured • Tenure-track • Non-tenure-track (full and part-time)	• Full-time • Part-time • Unionized • Third-party	• Undergraduate students • Graduate students • Professional school students

There is almost certainly overlap, similarity, and confusion when so many groupings exist; indeed, confusion and overlap can even persist when there are only two or three sets of policies and procedures. For many institutions (and their constituents), this array of policies and procedures creates not just confusion and overlap but, one could argue, inequity for the parties involved.

For example: A tenured faculty member accused of sexual violence faces an investigative and resolution process that is likely to be complex, multi-layered, steeped in court-like due process rights and which confers multiple levels of appeal. A staff member accused of identical conduct often faces very different investigative and resolution processes—one more akin to a traditional civil rights investigation process, with an administrative finding and rarely a hearing or appeal. A student who is accused of the same conduct likely faces an investigative and resolution process with a decision being rendered by a hearing panel composed of some combination of students, faculty, and staff. The investigative processes differ in each and the decision-making process and the decision-makers differ in each even though the conduct is identical. The decision-makers in each process are trained differently, as well. More troubling than the differences for the accused, however, are the differences for the accuser (typically the victim).

As discussed in the following, based on the current structuring of many college and university processes addressing sexual violence, a sexual assault victim's rights are dependent upon the identity of their attacker. Accordingly, victims of power-based personal violence are beholden to their attacker's policies and procedures when seeking redress. This only further disempowers victims and sends the overt message that the accused's rights trump those of the accuser. This is fundamentally inequitable. It also bespeaks one of the major benefits of unifying policies and procedures to address all forms of sexual harassment and sexual violence across the institution: policy and procedural equity regardless of the identity of the parties.

A related wrinkle institutions face with varying constituency-based (as opposed to institution-wide) policies and procedures are cross-constituency complaints. Cross-constituency complaints are those where the complainant and the respondent belong to different constituency groups (see Table 7.3).

TABLE 7.3 Sample Cross-Constituency Complaint Groupings

Complainant	Respondent
Student	Faculty, Staff/Administrator, Student
Faculty	Faculty, Staff/Administrator, Student
Staff/Administrator	Faculty, Staff/Administrator, Student

In such situations, the complainant is again beholden to the policies and procedures in place for the respondent's constituency group, which have not been intentionally designed to accommodate cross-constituency complaints, and for which specific training is rarely provided. The authors have seen situations where a student has sexually assaulted a faculty member and the faculty member sought redress through their typical channels—their department chair and dean, only to be informed that the only redress was through the dean of student's office. The faculty member then participated in a student conduct hearing, which was overseen and chaired by a young student affairs professional. The faculty member then felt humiliated presenting the details of the assault to a hearing panel composed of students and faculty.

A more frequently occurring situation involves a student complainant and a faculty respondent. It is quite common for a student who is sexually assaulted by a faculty member to report the incident to someone in the office of the dean of students. That report triggers an investigation in a realm that is often specifically designed for faculty and, therefore, is rather foreign to students. While the principles of court-like due process often apply for student and staff processes and sometimes involve attorneys, faculty resolution processes are typically more complex, steeped in an abundance of due process, focused on the rights of the respondent, and are more likely to involve attorneys as well. The student-complainant is often intimidated, overwhelmed, and feels disempowered. They typically face panels populated only by faculty, the constituency of the person they are accusing. Additionally, the multiple levels of appeal available in many faculty processes extend the process and typically do not provide the same rights of appeal to the complainant, though the Office of Civil Rights has indicated that equitable appeal rights are now required to comply with Title IX.

Interestingly, if the student had been the recipient of the same unwelcomed behavior at the hands of a fellow student, the aftermath of the complainant's report would look, and likely feel, much, much different. The scope and nature of prohibited conduct also may differ, depending on how the institution defines and delineates prohibited conduct. The same could be said of the situation where the faculty member is the complainant and the student is the respondent. Typically, for example, an accused faculty member would face a complaint of sexual harassment, whereas an accused student would face a complaint of sexual misconduct.

An Example

A recent joint investigation report by the Department of Education and the Department of Justice into alleged sex discrimination by the University of Montana, Missoula, highlighted the problems wrought by an array of sexual harassment policies and procedures. The joint investigation report noted, "the University has eight policies and procedures that explicitly or implicitly cover sexual harassment and sexual assault, their sheer number and the lack of clear cross references among them leaves unclear which should be used to report sexual harassment or sexual assault and when circumstances support using one policy or procedure over another" (Bhargava & Jackson, 2013). The report continued, "the University has three policies explicitly prohibiting sexual harassment or sexual assault" and "to add to the confusion about how to report sexual harassment and sexual assault, the University has four other policies and procedures that cover sex discrimination." Many institutions face similar problems.

The question then becomes: Why are they different? Why do many institutions define sexual harassment differently for different constituencies? Further, if the behavior is the same, why does "fairness" of process depend on the identity of the accused, rather than on the nature of the alleged violation? Civil rights violations are more universal than such fragmentation suggests and lend themselves readily to one umbrella policy and one process to address all civil rights based complaints.

Unifying Policy

Often "policies and procedures" get lumped together as if they are one and the same. Some campuses have intentionally blurred this line because policies often cannot be changed without high-level approval from the governed constituency itself, whereas procedures can often be shifted by divisional or departmental fiat without a lengthy approval via shared governance. By incorporating policy changes into procedural sections, administrators have found a clever way to avoid the black hole that many campus policy change processes resemble. But, the result is blurring of what should be distinct. A policy sets out a rule or expectation. A procedure describes how failing to meet that rule or expectation should be addressed. Shifting toward a more unified set of policies and procedures requires recognition that policies are, in fact, quite separate from procedures and must be addressed accordingly. Further, it is often more straightforward to tackle a unification of policy than of procedure because a unified set of policies and definitions is a rather logical approach for an institution to take.

Simply stated, sexual harassment is sexual harassment, regardless of whether the recipient of the unwelcomed behavior is a student, a faculty member, a staff member, or a visitor. Certain forms of sexual harassment may be more common in certain constituent groups (e.g., nonconsensual sexual intercourse is more common on a residential campus between students than it is between staff or faculty members), but relative frequency of conduct does not and should not alter what is and what is not acceptable behavior. Either a member of the community has had their civil rights infringed or they have not. Discrimination in any form—whether on the basis of sex, religion, race, ethnicity, national origin, or disability—deserves more uniform protection. Indeed, an approach utilizing unified policies and definitions supports the notion that the definitions of sexual harassment should not differ between these constituent groups, a practice that may leave public universities vulnerable to equal protection claims, in addition to the Title IX claims that can impact all institutions. A unified approach also provides greater clarity for constituents and visitors to know what is and what is not acceptable behavior. For institutions wondering how and where to start, unifying policies and their accompanying definitions is an excellent place. Unifying procedures often proves more challenging.

Unifying Procedures

While challenging, bringing greater uniformity to procedures does not require institutions to re-create the wheel, though it does require a shift in thinking—one that highlights the civil rights-based nature of sexual harassment. Indeed, institutions address Title VII-based discrimination issues between employees (race, sex, religion, and national origin) with a uniform approach that works, for the most part, well and efficiently. Given that Title VII already addresses sex discrimination by employees, addressing Title IX complaints (some of which are the same incidents) with the same process makes sense.[1]

Accordingly, most institutions already use some derivative of a civil rights investigation model—a set of procedures specifically targeted to address civil rights-based violations—for employee discrimination complaints. A typical process has the following basic components:

- Notice of complaint
- Preliminary investigation (to determine validity of complaint on its face)
- Full Investigation (wherein parties are allowed to provide evidence and a list of witnesses)
- Analyzing evidence and information gathering
- Finding by Investigator(s)/Administrator(s)
- Sanction (if applicable)
- Appeal

Unless an employee is employed at-will, this process is commonplace for many colleges and universities and is typically run by the Equal Opportunity and Diversity Offices or Human Resources. It works well in that it serves as a fair, equitable, and prompt resolution of the complaint. Colleges and universities resolve most of their employee civil rights-based complaints using a similar process because it allows for a full and thorough investigation, a weighing of the evidence presented, and a decision by the person(s) most familiar with the evidence.

Why, then, do colleges and universities simultaneously create complex and dif-ferential processes when dealing with students and/or faculty? If the civil rights investigation process is fair and appropriate to address civil rights violations involving a segment of employees of the institution, logic does not favor the use of differential procedures based solely on the identity of the parties involved. The determinant should be the nature of the violation, not the identity of the parties involved. While necessitating a shift in thinking and in politics for many schools, operationalizing such a change is aided by the fact that many schools already utilize a civil rights investigation model to address allegations of discrimination. Indeed, rethinking needs to extend to grievance processes by which employees (and sometimes students) may grieve institutional imposition of discipline, because these processes function as super-appeals and present problems of inequitable process (the accused grieves the institutional action without involvement of the victim) and of timing inequity, as most grievance processes cannot be completed within the 60-day goal set out by the U.S. Department of Education's Office for Civil Rights.

Interestingly, as a result of the student-specific focus of the 2011 Dear Col-league Letter, many colleges and universities rushed to update their student-based policies and procedures but have neglected those pertaining to faculty and/or staff or are constrained from making the necessary changes by other influences, such as collective bargaining agreements.[2] For many institutions, then, unifying policies and procedures will require some borrowing from both student as well as employment-based practices.

Accompanying Non-Civil Rights-Based Violations

Compounding the issue of addressing civil rights-based complaints, particularly Title IX issues, are the collateral non-civil rights-based violations that occur in tandem with the alleged discriminatory acts. Common violations in Title IX complaints deal with alcohol or other drug abuse, threats of violence, physical violence, and stalking. Such collateral issues can also be addressed utilizing a civil rights investigation model, though it appears that the Department of Education wants to ensure that institutions are fully addressing the civil rights-based viola-tion, rather than allowing it to be subsumed by the other violations (Ali, 2011, p. 15). In a civil rights investigation model, the investigator(s) would investigate collateral misconduct along with the alleged discrimination, gather available evi-dence, interview relevant witnesses and render findings on the related issues, just as they would for the alleged civil rights violation. Such a process remains fair, prompt, impartial, and thorough.

Conclusion

Institutions should give consideration to shifting their civil rights-based complaint resolution processes for Title IX from constituency-based to violation-based. This paradigm shift recognizes in Title IX both the nature of civil rights-based complaints as well as value in harnessing a process long-honed by Title VII-based complaints. Over the years many institutions have developed fragmented and differential policies and procedures based on the identity of the accused. This approach often creates policies and procedures that resolve identical conduct differently, based solely on the fact that the harasser belongs to a specific constituency. Further, this situation leaves victims at the mercy of the policies and procedures applicable to their harasser. Constituency-based policies, by their disparate nature, therefore, have a greater likelihood of producing inequitable outcomes—an approach that is anathema to Title IX compliance. Complications arise in the face of cross-constituency complaints or when the accused belongs to more than one constituency. An institution-wide set of policies and procedures is likely to mitigate many of these risks and problems and help ensure that institutions are not only complying with Title IX but also upholding it.

Notes

1. It should be noted that Title IX also applies in employment contexts even though Title VII addresses the same behavior. The U.S. Supreme Court settled the issue of Title IX's applicability to employees in *North Haven Board of Education v. Bell*, stating "employment discrimination comes within Title IX's prohibition" and that Title IX's "broad directive that no person may be discriminated against on the basis of gender . . . includes employees as well as students" (465 U.S. 512 (1982)).
2. Collective bargaining agreements create a unique hurdle that is not the focus of this chapter, but even they do not change the obligation institutions have to bring their policies and procedures across the institution into compliance with Title IX.

References

Ali, R. (2011, April 4). Assistant Secretary for Civil Rights, U.S. Department of Education, Office of Civil Rights. Dear Colleague Letter: Sexual Violence. Retrieved from http://www2.ed.gov/about/offices/list/ocr/letters/colleague-201304.pdf

Americans with Disabilities Act of 1990, 42 U.S.C. § 12101 et seq.

Bhargava, A., & Jackson, G. (2013, May 9). Letter of findings re: DOJ Case No. DJ 169–44–9, OCR Case No. 10126001. Washington, DC: U.S. Department of Education, Office for Civil Rights.

Brown v. Board of Education, 347 U.S. 483 (1954).

Civil Rights Act of 1871, 42 U.S.C. § 1983.

Civil Rights Act of 1964, Pub. L. No. 88–352, 78 Stat. 241.

Dixon v. Alabama State Board of Education, 294 F.2d 150 (5th Cir. 1961).

Section 504 of the Rehabilitation Act of 1973, 29 U.S.C. § 701.

Title IX of the Education Amendments of 1972. 20 U.S.C. § 1681.

U.S. Const. amend. XIII.

U.S. Const. amend. XIV.

Voting Rights Act of 1965, 42 U.S.C. §§ 1973–1973bb-1.

8

TITLE IX'S CIVIL RIGHTS APPROACH AND THE CRIMINAL JUSTICE SYSTEM

Enabling Separate but Coordinated Parallel Proceedings

Nancy Chi Cantalupo

As the topic of campus sexual violence[1] has received more and more attention by both national media and federal and state governments, the oft-repeated, immediate reaction of many lawmakers and media commentators is that sexual violence is a crime and, therefore, should be handled by the criminal justice system and those who run it: police, prosecutors, and criminal courts. For instance, in the week following the issuance of the first report of the White House Task Force to Protect Students from Sexual Assault, the editorial board of *USA Today*, after quoting the "1 in 5 college women will be sexually assaulted before they graduate" statistic, stated that, "A problem of that scale . . . requires treating rape as a crime, not as a violation of campus rules" ("College Rape Tribunals Fail Students," 2014). Similarly, when *Rolling Stone* published a story about the University of Virginia's handling of sexual assaults on campus, numerous state legislators announced intentions to propose bills that would require Virginia colleges and universities to refer all rape reports to the police (Ehrenfreund, 2014). Although the proposed federal legislation did not ultimately include such a provision, federal lawmakers' consideration of a similar mandatory referral requirement was at the backdrop of three roundtables on campus sexual assault that Senator Claire McCaskill held over the summer of 2014.[2]

This knee-jerk reaction to mandate that all campus sexual violence be dealt with primarily as a criminal matter presents serious problems for colleges' and universities' abilities to prevent and respond to sexual violence as an institutional matter. First, these schools' handling of campus sexual violence is subject to three federal legal regimes, including Title IX of the Education Amendments Act of 1972 (Title IX), the Jeanne Clery Disclosure of Campus Security Policy and Campus Crime Statistics Act (Clery Act), as amended by the Violence Against Women Reauthorization Act of 2013 (VAWA), and United States constitutional law precedents governing the administrative due process rights of students who are accused of perpetrating sexual violence. None of these three legal regimes is based in criminal law nor are they enforced by criminal courts. Rather, all are enforced by federal administrative agencies or by civil courts and require institutions of higher education (IHEs) to use very different institutional responses to sexual violence than those employed by the criminal justice system. Indeed, when IHEs seek to imitate criminal justice processes in responding to sexual violence against their students, they risk greater liability under Title IX, in particular.

Second, the media and legislature reactions to the epidemic of campus sexual violence assume that the criminal justice system has been effective at preventing and responding to sexual violence, when in fact the data suggests that it has been quite ineffective. Therefore, IHEs searching for effective practices to protect the rights of all their students have good reason to look elsewhere than the criminal justice system. In addition, even if the criminal justice system worked perfectly, it is simply not designed to fulfill the full range of needs that sexual violence victims have postviolence, needs which *can* be fulfilled under the mandates of Title IX and the Clery Act. Accordingly, even before IHEs focused on preventing and responding to sexual violence in response to increased federal government enforcement of Title IX and the Clery Act, many schools were already departing from or being advised by their insurers and attorneys to depart from criminal approaches in student conduct proceedings generally, including those involving sexual violence.

Accordingly, the first part of this chapter will explore in greater depth the dangers of conflating and confusing the criminal and Title IX/Clery-informed responses and prevention approaches, both for IHEs and their students. To avoid such negative consequences, the second part of this chapter discusses several proven methods for keeping criminal proceedings separate from administrative and civil proceedings but also coordinating such parallel proceedings in the instances where a victim wishes to pursue both options for redress. By doing so, the chapter demonstrates that both IHEs and lawmakers should look to civil rights and equality-based approaches for preventing and responding to sexual violence and should guard against having those approaches "criminalized" by an overreliance and overconfidence in criminal methods of addressing this violence.

The Negative Consequences of Conflating or Confusing Criminal Laws With Title IX, the Clery Act, and Administrative Due Process

Eliminating Sexual Violence Victims' Rights to Equal Educational Opportunity

The most serious consequence of conflating and confusing the criminal law with the three federal regimes that apply to sexual violence is the elimination of sexual violence victims' rights to equal educational opportunity. This consequence results from the substitution of the procedural rights given to alleged perpetrators and victims in the criminal system for the rights of alleged perpetrators and victims under civil rights statutes, including Title IX.

Title IX prohibits schools from engaging in sex discrimination that denies the victims of that discrimination rights to an equal education. Schools are considered to have engaged in sex discrimination when they tolerate sexual violence as a form of severe sexual harassment that creates a hostile environment for students.[3] Factors creating this hostile environment include the trauma caused by the violence itself and the exacerbation of that trauma by factors such as victims being required to encounter or risk encountering their assailants postviolence.

The trauma that results from sexual victimization makes it very difficult for victims to succeed in school at the same level as they did before the violence, especially in the immediate aftermath of the violence. Particularly if they are not addressed as soon after the victimization as possible, the negative health and educational consequences of sexual violence can have life-altering effects. The documented health consequences of sexual violence include increased risk of substance use, unhealthy weight control behaviors, sexual risk behaviors, pregnancy, and suicidality (Silverman, Raj, Mucci, & Hathaway, 2001). Common educational consequences include declines in educational performance, the need to take time off, declines in grades, dropping out of school, and transferring schools, all of which have potentially devastating life-long financial consequences (Loya, 2012). The cost of rape and sexual assault (excluding child sexual abuse) to the nation has been estimated at $127 billion annually (in 2012 dollars), the highest cost criminal victimization, some $34 billion more than the next highest cost criminal victimization (all crime-related deaths except drunk driving and arson) (Loya, 2012; Miller, Cohen, & Weirsema, 1996).

These traumatic effects are often exacerbated when victims are forced to encounter or to risk encountering their assailants repeatedly after being victimized. Many of the educational consequences listed above are at least partially caused by victims' efforts to avoid their assailants in shared classes and campus spaces, including by taking time off, not going to class, transferring or dropping out, all of which are linked to declines in educational performance and grades, which in turn can result in loss of scholarships and financial aid as well as tuition spent on classes the victims are not able to finish.

Therefore, under Title IX, although the initial violation of victims' rights are caused by their assailants, schools that tolerate those initial rights violations and do not seek to end such violations are themselves violating Title IX. The Office for Civil Rights (OCR) in the Department of Education has developed specific directives for how schools should address discriminatory violence that has already occurred and stop violence from reoccurring. One such directive requires schools to provide "prompt and equitable" grievance procedures to students who report being victimized. "Prompt and equitable" generally means that, although schools have some flexibility in how they construct their procedures, when those procedures give a right to the accused student, the student victim must also get that right and vice versa. In addition, such procedures must use a preponderance of the evidence standard of proof, the most appropriate standard of proof for a presumption-free proceeding that gives equal procedural rights to all parties because it requires just over 50% evidentiary weight in favor of one side or the other (Ali, 2011; Lhamon, 2014).

In contrast to the equal procedural rights provided to sexual violence victims under Title IX's civil rights approach, the criminal justice system structurally marginalizes all victims of crime, including sexual violence victims, from its procedures and affords them few if any procedural rights. Criminal cases are structured as contests between the defendant, represented by the defendant's counsel, and the community as a whole, represented by the state and, in the proceeding itself, by the prosecutor. The victim is not a party to the case, s/he is merely a "complaining witness" (Cantalupo, 2009, 2012).

Not having party status in a criminal proceeding leads to multiple inequities between the victim and the defendant, including unequal legal representation, unequal access to evidence, unequal privacy protections, unequal rights to be present in the courtroom, and an unequal standard of proof (Cantalupo, 2009). Because the prosecutor is not the victim's lawyer, the victim has no legal representative dedicated to protecting her/his rights and no control over the presentation of the victim's case by the prosecution (Cantalupo, 2009). The prosecutor is likewise restricted from protecting the victim's rights by rules such as the *Brady* rule, which require the prosecutor to disclose any exculpatory evidence (evidence that may support the defendant's innocence) but do not require the defendant to disclose evidence tending to prove the defendant's guilt (Cantalupo, 2009). Despite law reforms that have diminished these powers to a certain extent, defendants can still often demand disclosure of private information such as medical and counseling records that the victim wishes to keep private on the basis that these are exculpatory evidence relevant to the victim's credibility, a common target of attack by the defendant in the typical "word-on-word" sexual violence case with no third-party witnesses (Cantalupo, 2009). This inequality even extends to the victim's ability to be in the courtroom because the rule on witness sequestration bars the victim from being present in the courtroom other than when s/he is on the witness stand (Cantalupo, 2009, 2012).

Finally, the "beyond a reasonable doubt" standard of proof used in criminal cases is drastically unequal, requiring 98% or 99% likelihood that the victim's story is accurate and credible (Goldstein & Leonnig, 2007). Even the lesser standard of "clear and convincing evidence," commonly described as somewhere between "preponderance of the evidence" and "beyond a reasonable doubt," builds significant inequality into a proceeding, since it is a significantly higher standard than the closest-to-equal preponderance standard.[4] Moreover, while there are good reasons for the higher standards of proof in the criminal justice system, these reasons do not exist in a Title IX proceeding. The "beyond a reasonable doubt" and "clear and convincing evidence" standards provide necessary safeguards in systems where the potential penalties for convicted parties include significant jail time and for some offenses even death. Such coercive measures present powerful reasons to set a standard of proof that is most likely to avoid unjust convictions, even if it also risks many wrongful acquittals. Since schools do not have the coercive powers of the criminal system and no Title IX, Clery Act or administrative due process proceedings will result in incarceration or worse, these coercive factors cannot be a reason for abdicating a commitment to equality and civil rights principles.

For all of these reasons, it is downright dangerous to conflate civil rights and criminal justice approaches to sexual violence and allow criminal justice responses to dominate the public's collective imagination regarding how to address this violence. Doing so eliminates sexual violence victims' civil rights to equality, specifically student victims' rights to equal educational opportunity. Moreover, taking away victims' Title IX equality rights removes rights that directly address their educational needs and have the best hope of halting the devastating health, educational, and financial consequences that flow from sexual victimization. The criminal justice system is not structured to address these needs and, therefore, survivors are less likely to report to both criminal justice officials and to authority figures in criminal justice-imitative systems, a topic to which the next section will turn.

Chilling Victim Reporting

A second serious consequence of conflating the criminal justice system and the administrative/civil regimes of Title IX, the Clery Act, and the accused student administrative due process precedents is the likelihood that this conflation will chill victim reporting. This probability is of particular concern given the already extremely low victim reporting rates among sexual violence victims generally and student survivors especially (Fisher, Cullen, & Turner, 2000).

To understand why so few victims report sexual violence, it is helpful to start with Douglass Beloof's (1999) analysis that "[t]he individual victim of crime can maintain complete control over the process only by avoiding the criminal process altogether through non-reporting" (p. 307). Beloof includes the following reasons among the reasons why a victim might "[e]xercise the veto" on criminal systems: "the victim's desire to retain privacy; the victim's concern about participating in a system that may do [him/her] more harm than good; the inability of the system to effectively solve many crimes . . . the inconvenience to the victim; the victim's lack of participation, control, and influence in the process; or the victim's rejection of the model of retributive justice" (p. 307).

This list reiterates many of the reasons why student survivors say they do not report. For instance, in Beloof's category of "the victim's desire to retain privacy," college victims state that they don't report because they do not want family or others to know (Fisher, Cullen, & Turner, 2000) or to be embarrassed by publicity (Bohmer & Parrot, 1993; Warshaw, 1988). In addition, many student victims express concern about "the inability of the system to effectively solve many crimes" when they give reasons for not reporting such as not thinking a crime had been committed, not thinking what had happened was serious enough to involve law enforcement, and lack of proof (Beloof, 1999, p. 307). Finally, the top reason college victims give for not reporting is fear of hostile treatment or disbelief by legal and medical authorities (Bohmer & Parrot, 1993; Fisher, Cullen, & Turner, 2000; Warshaw, 1988). They also express a lack of faith in or fear of court proceedings or police ability to apprehend the perpetrator (Bohmer & Parrot, 1993), fear retribution from the perpetrator (Bohmer & Parrot, 1993), and believe that no one will believe them and nothing will happen to the perpetrator (Bohmer & Parrot, 1993; Fisher, Cullen, & Turner, 2000; Warshaw, 1988), all of which relate to "the victim's concern about participating in a system that may do [him/her] more harm than good" (Beloof, 1999).

These reasons for not reporting also demonstrate that, like most of the American public, college victims overall think about reporting sexual violence in terms of criminal justice system responses, not in terms of their rights to equal educational opportunity under Title IX. Therefore, consistent with Beloof's discussion of the crime victim's veto, college victims' general lack of reporting is a commentary showing their collective disbelief in the effectiveness of the criminal system to address their needs.

In making this commentary, college victims join a long history of survivors who have vetoed the criminal justice system's response to sexual violence and its victims. Table 8.1 summarizes Lonsway and Archambault's (2012) research, and shows that the vast majority of victims do not report to the criminal justice system, and the majority of those who do report do not receive the one form of redress that the criminal justice system is structured to provide: incarceration of the perpetrator.

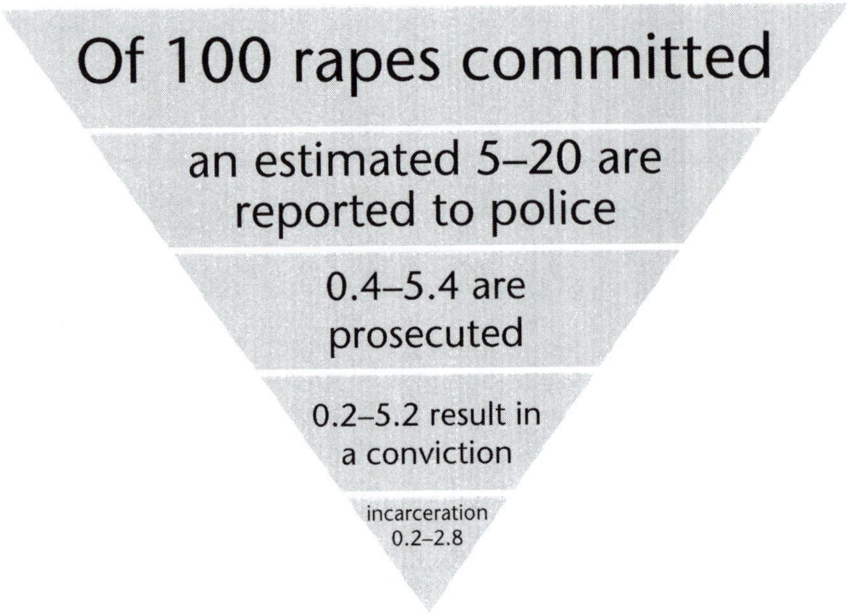

Of 100 rapes committed

an estimated 5–20 are reported to police

0.4–5.4 are prosecuted

0.2–5.2 result in a conviction

incarceration
0.2–2.8

FIGURE 8.1 Likelihood of Incarceration for Perpetrators of Sexual Violence

Source: K. A. Lonsway & J. Archambault (2012). The "justice gap" for sexual assault cases: Future directions for research and reform. *Violence Against Women, 18*(2), 145–168. © Violence Against Women. Reprinted by permission of SAGE.

Figure 8.1 also shows that college victims' fears regarding the reactions of law enforcement and the inability of the criminal justice system to "solve" sexual violence crimes and hold the perpetrators accountable are well justified. Although Lonsway and Archambault's research deals with a national population, not focused on college students, other evidence confirms that college students face the same, if not worse, barriers as all sexual violence survivors. For instance, a 2011 study conducted by the *Chicago Tribune* found that of 171 sex crimes *investigated* by police involving student victims at six Midwestern universities over a 5-year period, only 12 arrests (7%) were made and only four convictions (2.3%) resulted (Lighty, St. Clair, & Cohen, 2011). Because these percentages are not based on the total number of sex crimes that occurred, but only the ones that were both reported to and investigated by police, it appears that in Illinois and Indiana at least, the criminal justice system is failing student victims even more than it is failing sexual violence victims generally.

In addition, social science studies of the handling of sexual violence reports by criminal justice actors such as police and prosecutors reveal persistent stereotypes about the victims' credibility and the supposed prevalence of false reports. Police are frequently skeptical of reports of sexual violence that do not fit into stereotypes about "real rape"—i.e., "assaults that are committed by a stranger to the victim, involve a weapon, and result in physical injury of the victim" (Lonsway & Archambault, 2012, p. 152). When police rely exclusively on their own assessments of victims' credibility, they tend to conclude that many more victims are making false reports than in cases where an investigation produced actual "evidence that a crime did not occur" (Lisak, Gardinier, Nicksa, & Cote, 2010, p. 1319). These dynamics may be responsible for a significant decline in arrest rates for rape over the last 40 years, with approximately 50% of reported rapes resulting in arrests in the 1970s, while only 26% resulted in arrests in 2008, even as arrest rates for other violent crimes remained constant over the same period (Lonsway & Archambault, 2012, pp. 150–152). Scientists suggest that this drop in arrest rates is due to an increase in reports of sexual violence that do not fit the "real rape" stereotype (Lonsway & Archambault, 2012, pp. 156–157). Even when police and prosecutors do not believe such stereotypes themselves, they may still factor the stereotypes into their decisions about arrest and prosecution because they anticipate that juries will harbor them (Lonsway & Archambault, 2012, p. 159).

Again, evidence suggests that these phenomena are no different on college campuses. Anecdotal evidence from cases involving Florida State University and University of Oregon indicate that police and prosecutors dealing with college cases are hardly free from attitudes that stereotype victims. In the Florida State University case involving accusations against Jameis Winston, the most recent Heisman Trophy winner, the police's investigation was so slipshod that critical evidence was lost and the prosecutor determined he could not prosecute (Bogdanich, 2014). In the University of Oregon case involving three basketball players accused of gang-raping a freshman student, the prosecutor declined to prosecute due to the victim's past sexual history, failure to stop the violence, and lack of obvious incapacitation during the assault (Kingkade, 2014).

Moreover, police investigation techniques and the detrimental effects of trauma on victims' abilities to recall the details of their assault are a poor combination. Victims of trauma, including sexual trauma, "often are unable to remember what happened to them accurately" because "[t]he body may focus on the direct source of a threat rather than contextual details, such as the time and place, that could later complete the picture of an attack," and/or because trauma causes physical damage to the part of the brain that preserves memories (Ehrenfreund & Izadi, 2014). Accordingly, victim's memories are rarely organized in the "Who? What? When? Where? Why?" approach favored by traditional law enforcement investigation techniques and can "change with time as the mind works to organize its memories" (Ehrenfreund & Izadi, 2014). They, therefore, do not mesh well with investigation techniques that "make establishing the facts a priority and [that] look for discrepancies as an indicator that a subject might be untrustworthy" and that in some cases can even lead victims to develop or exacerbate victims' post-traumatic stress disorder (Ehrenfreund & Izadi, 2014).

All in all, this evidence shows that victims who exercise their veto on the criminal justice system have made a decision that the criminal system will "do them more harm than good." Such a decision is a rational, logical one not only because of the potential harm that has already been discussed but also because the criminal justice system does victims relatively little "good" in that it does not help them meet their many trauma-induced needs postviolence. Even if the criminal justice system succeeded in convicting and punishing sexual violence perpetrators significantly more than the current rate of 0.02–5.2%, it is simply not structured to assist the victim in the myriad areas of life that are disrupted by the violence, including her/his health, education, employment, housing, family responsibilities, and, if s/he is an immigrant, immigration status. Other than the limited compensation for which victims may qualify through state legislation and/or the federal Victims of Crime Act (U.S. Department of Justice, 1999), the criminal justice system provides minimal to no help to victims in avoiding or compensating for the $127 billion annual estimated cost that U.S. sexual violence victims collectively experience.

In contrast, through Title IX's administrative and court enforcement, as well as the Clery Act's administrative enforcement, student victims can get critical educational accommodations that can help them minimize the effects of sexual trauma on their educational trajectories. These include adjustments to academic coursework, living arrangements, stay-away orders, and other protective measures (Lhamon, 2014; U.S. Department of Education, 2014). OCR has also recently clarified that its "resolution agreements [with IHEs] to resolve investigations have included agreements to reimburse survivors for educational expenses where those remedies are required to eliminate a hostile environment or remedy the effects of sexual violence" (Lhamon, 2014).

Moreover, through Title IX private lawsuits, student victims can get access to monetary compensation, often compensation that far surpasses the minimal amounts available through crime victims compensation funds. The federal fund, for instance, states that "[m]aximum awards generally range from $10,000 to $25,000" (U.S. Department of Justice, 1999), whereas several of the publicly disclosed Title IX settlements have been in the six- and seven-figures, and a 2011 United Educators (a major insurer of IHEs) report indicates that the average amount paid out by IHEs in litigation filed by college victims during 2006–2010 by their schools for mishandling their cases was about $77,000 (Keehan, 2014).[5] While this amount includes legal fees, it still likely resulted in larger payments to victims than through crime victim compensation funds. Finally, a report by United Educators on similar claims filed during 2011–2013 shows that IHE costs nearly quadrupled to more than $280,000 per victim claim, significantly increasing the likelihood of high compensation payments to victims.[6]

All of this evidence suggests that conflating the criminal justice system and the administrative/civil systems of Title IX, the Clery Act, and the administrative due process cases will diminish victims' willingness to use the administrative/civil systems. In other words, it will cause them to veto the administrative/civil regimes just as most victims have vetoed the criminal system. This will have the practical effect of eliminating options that help victims stay in school and succeed in their educations, as well as help to compensate them for the trauma that they have experienced.

Interfering With Schools' Abilities to Adequately Address Student Misconduct and Implement Sound Educational Policy

Conflating the criminal justice system and the administrative/civil legal regimes will also eliminate options for schools and do so in a manner contrary to educational principles and policies that have been widely acknowledged as best practices by schools for at least 15 years, if not longer, and prior to the issuance of the current regimes of Department of Education guidance under Title IX and the Clery Act. During this time, schools and the representatives of schools have repeatedly articulated schools' obligations to treat all their students fairly, and schools have sought to achieve those principles in their policies on student misconduct. This commitment to fairness and equality has been supported by courts that have decided cases not only under Title IX but also under the U.S. Constitution's due process provisions.

Both before and after OCR issued its 2011 Dear Colleague Letter (DCL), school representatives clearly stated schools' commitment to fairness, equality, and evenhanded treatment of all college students. For instance, "Ada Meloy, the general counsel with the American Council on Education, which represents presidents of colleges and universities, said that . . . the issues 'can be very difficult on a campus because of the need to be careful and fair to both the accuser and the accused'" (Schoof, 2013). Likewise, long before the DCL, former general counsel for the American Council on Education Sheldon Steinbach noted repeatedly "if it involves two people on campus, the university has a responsibility to both the alleged victim and the alleged perpetrator" (Snyder & Woodall, 2006).

Also well before the DCL, higher education insurers and associations were encouraging schools to adopt "best practice" student conduct policies and procedures that implemented these fairness and equality principles. For instance, in a pamphlet published by United Educators and the National Association of College and University Attorneys (NACUA), attorney Edward N. Stoner (n.d.) promotes a "model student code" that explicitly rejects the criminal system as a model for student disciplinary systems. This pamphlet focuses preliminarily on three related points: 1) the goals behind student conduct policies, and 2) the differences between those goals and the purposes of the criminal system, which make 3) thinking about student discipline systems in terms of the criminal law inappropriate and counterproductive.

The NACUA/United Educators report characterizes the central goal of student disciplinary systems as helping "to create the best environment in which students can live and learn . . . [a]t the cornerstone [of which] is the obligation of students to treat all other members of the academic community with dignity and respect—including other students, faculty members, neighbors, and employees" (Stoner, n.d., p. 7). He reminds school administrators and lawyers that this goal means that "*student victims are just as important as the student who allegedly misbehaved*" (emphasis in original), a principle that "is critical" to resolving "[c]ases of student-on-student violence" (Stoner, n.d., pp. 7–8). In doing so, he points out that this principle of treating all students equally "creates a far different system than a criminal system in which the rights of a person facing jail time are superior to those of a crime victim" (Stoner, n.d., p. 7). Therefore, he advises that student disciplinary systems use the " 'more likely than not' standard used in civil situations" and avoid describing student disciplinary matters with language drawn from the criminal system (Stoner, n.d., p. 10).

Evidence suggests that schools in fact followed the advice of United Educators and NACUA regarding student disciplinary systems, again prior to the DCL. Two separate studies have been conducted on schools' choices of standards of proof for their student disciplinary proceedings (Anderson, 2004; Karjane, Fisher, & Cullen, 2002). In both surveys, while most schools did not specify their standard of proof, of those that did, the majority[7] used a preponderance standard. Only 3.3% of schools in the 2002 study used a "beyond a reasonable doubt" standard, and the 2004 study does not indicate that a single school used the criminal standard.

Court decisions in accused student administrative due process cases have clearly supported these policy choices. In *Goss v. Lopez* (1975), the U.S. Supreme Court considered a high school suspension and decided that the students were entitled to due process consisting of "*some* kind of notice and *some* kind of hearing" (p. 579, emphasis added). The *Lopez* Court also cited approvingly to *Dixon v. Alabama State Board of Education* (1961), where for cases involving expulsion the Fifth Circuit Court of Appeals required notice "of the specific charges," "the names of the witnesses [and] facts to which each witness testifies," and a hearing, "[t]he nature of [which] should vary depending upon the circumstances of the particular case" (pp. 158–159). Both courts have specified that these requirements fall short of "a full-dress judicial hearing, with the right to cross-examine witnesses," nor do they "require opportunit[ies] to secure counsel, to confront and cross-examine witnesses . . . or to call . . . witnesses to verify [the accused's] version of the incident" (p. 159).

For private IHEs, the requirements are even less onerous. While courts have reviewed private institutions for expelling or suspending students in an arbitrary and capricious manner,[8] most courts review private schools' disciplinary actions under "the well settled rule that the relations between a student and a private university are a matter of contract" (*Dixon v. Alabama State Board of Education*, 1961, p. 157). Therefore, private IHEs must do what they have promised students in the school's own policies and procedures, and courts will review disciplinary actions according to the terms of the contract.

Courts have consistently reiterated the distinction between disciplinary hearings and criminal proceedings and have upheld expulsions for a wide range of student behaviors, from smoking, drinking beer in the school parking lot and engaging in consensual sexual activity on school grounds, to participating in but withdrawing, prior to discovery, from a conspiracy to shoot several students and school officials,[9] to being found by two female students in a dormitory room with two other male students and the female students' roommate, who was inebriated, unconscious, and naked from the waist down.[10] Courts have explicitly rejected many assertions of criminal due process rights by students accused of sexual violence, including rights to an attorney, discovery, *voir dire*, appeal, and to know witnesses' identities and to cross-examine them.

As a result of this permissive legal standard, my research has discovered only a handful of cases where a court found a school to have violated the due process rights of a student accused of sexual violence and in only one case did the court require the institution to pay any damages.[11] When compared to the settlements made public in several Title IX cases, the top five of which have been in the six- and seven-figures (Cantalupo, 2012; Schlossberg, 2014), it is clear that schools also have liability-related reasons to make the policy choices that they have. That is, because schools risk losing much larger amounts of money from violating students' Title IX rights, they actually increase their own liability risks if they obligate themselves to criminal-justice-like procedures that the law does not require them to adopt and that make it harder to protect a student's Title IX rights. For these reasons, obligating schools to use criminal justice procedures could actually increase schools' liability risks through no fault of their own.

Despite all of this evidence that schools long ago decided—separately from enforcement of Title IX and the Clery Act and with the support of the courts—to treat all students equally, some recent cases have suggested that some schools may be tempted to use the criminal process to duck the school's responsibilities under Title IX and the Clery Act. In both the Florida State University and University of Oregon cases, the school did not conduct its own separate Title IX investigation (Bogdanich, 2014; Kingkade, 2014), and in a third case involving two Dartmouth College students, numerous articles about the criminal rape trial do not mention any attempt on Dartmouth College's part to conduct a Title IX investigation (Dries, 2014; Schwartz, 2014; Staff Report, 2014). When this happens, conflation of the criminal justice response with the school's obligations under these administrative/civil legal regimes facilitates excuses for why that school cannot (in actuality, *will* not) respond internally and protect the student victims' Title IX and Clery Act rights. In addition, this conflation creates a tendency for many—schools and others—to forget that the standard of proof and the due process requirements for schools governed by these administrative/civil legal regimes are different than those in the criminal process.

For all of these reasons—protecting our society's commitment to equality and civil rights, encouraging victims to report so they may access services and minimize the damage to their education that trauma can cause, and protecting widely adopted educational policies and best practices—IHEs and law and policymakers alike must vigilantly guard against conflation and confusion of the federal administrative/civil legal regimes that govern schools with the criminal justice system, which schools do not and cannot enforce. The following part turns to three very specific ways in which IHEs, as well as national and state governments, can and should keep these legal systems separate and avoid this confusion.

Parallel and Coordinated Administrative and Criminal Proceedings

All of the methods of keeping the criminal justice system clearly separate from Title IX, the Clery Act, and the accused student administrative due process case law require an acceptance of parallel proceedings. Such proceedings allow a school to protect a student's Title IX and Clery Act rights regardless of whether local, noncampus law enforcement is also investigating the case or the local prosecutor's office is considering prosecuting. Ideally, when a criminal case and a Title IX proceeding are happening at the same time, both processes should be coordinated so one does not interfere with or damage the other, as long as the victim is included in the coordination so that s/he is fully informed of the range of options available and has an opportunity to choose how to move forward in both proceedings or to drop one or both proceedings.

The current OCR guidance makes clear that parallel proceedings are possible under Title IX and that Title IX proceedings may not be delayed or not pursued due to an ongoing criminal case (Lhamon, 2014). In addition, similar parallel proceedings are typical in other legal areas where the same acts violate both the criminal code and a victim's rights under internal policies and/or civil rights statutes. For instance, it is common knowledge that entities such as employers or professional licensing boards need not wait to see what happens with a potential or even active criminal case before handling the case and assigning sanctions if necessary under their own internal policies and procedures. In addition, when in domestic violence cases there are both criminal and civil protection order proceedings occurring simultaneously, typically the counsel for both proceedings will try to coordinate the two cases. Therefore, arguments that have been advanced suggesting that it is unusual and unfair for such parallel proceedings to occur in campus sexual violence cases are not accurate.

Consistently separating criminal justice and administrative/civil processes into parallel proceedings allows each proceeding to fulfill its own purposes. As already discussed, Title IX's purpose is protecting students' equal educational opportunity, whereas the purpose of the criminal justice system is to separate criminal actors from society to protect the community as a whole, usually through incarceration. The Clery Act's original purpose was to inform consumers of higher education about the types and rates of crime on each college campus, although that purpose has expanded over the years to incorporate some of the same rights as those protected in a more comprehensive fashion by Title IX.

Allowing each of these legal regimes to fulfill their own purposes requires IHEs and those that regulate them to follow several more specific recommendations, all discussed in the following sections. First, institutions and lawmakers must use the most appropriate procedures for each legal regime's purposes. This means that rules based in procedural equality, such as the preponderance of the evidence standard, are the most appropriate standard for realizing both civil rights-based equality principles and educational best practices, and should be retained for Title IX and Clery Act proceedings. Second, understanding that victims are a large and diverse group who have many needs and goals that often lead them to pick and choose between the various processes available to them, IHEs should protect a diversity of options for survivors to use, as well as their ability to choose the option(s) best for them, and laws and public policies should support this approach. Third, where victims choose to pursue multiple options, resulting in parallel proceedings that may interfere with each other, institutions and governments should use coordination methods such as Sexual Assault Response Teams (SARTs), staff positions dedicated to serving victims and preventing this violence, and memorandums of understanding (MOUs) between institutional and community stakeholders, including police, prosecutors, and community-based victims' advocacy organizations.

Committing to Procedural Equality, Including the "Preponderance of the Evidence" Standard of Proof

Separating administrative/civil and criminal proceedings from each other and allowing each to fulfill its distinct purposes requires that investigations and resolution proceedings provide procedural equality to both student victims and accused students, including a "preponderance of the evidence" standard of proof. To allow any other standard of proof would essentially substitute concerns such as unjust incarceration, which are relevant only to the criminal system, for the equality and civil rights goals of Title IX. In addition, this would set Title IX proceedings apart from other administrative/civil proceedings without a meaningful justification for doing so.

As mentioned earlier, the preponderance standard comes closest to procedural equality for all student parties and this most effectively operationalizes the key civil rights assumption that the basic equality of all people precludes giving presumptions for or against any one person's account. Indeed, the preponderance standard communicates equality in that it does *not* suggest a general societal belief that one side or the other is more likely to lie or that this belief is so strong it needs to be systematically guarded against through the very design of our processes, including our choice of a standard of proof. Because campus sexual violence cases tend to be word-on-word cases that are decided largely based on the parties' credibility, using a standard of proof like "clear and convincing evidence" or "beyond a reasonable doubt" essentially signals that we, as a society, believe that those who report being sexually victimized are so *less* credible and so much *more* likely—*across the board*—to *lie* than the accused students are that we have to build our disbelief into the very *structure* of our process.

In addition, using a preponderance standard is consistent with legal approaches to other civil rights claims protecting equality, including under other statutes enforced by OCR and courts, other claims under Title IX itself, and claims under civil rights statutes outside of education, like Title VII of the Civil Rights Act of 1964, which prohibits sexual harassment in employment (Chaudhry & Kaufmann, 2012; Chmielewski, 2013). Adopting a different standard of proof separates sexual violence victims, the majority of whom are women and girls, from the other populations who are protected from discrimination based on race, disability, age, Boy Scout membership, etc. Such a separation would mean that we as a society are comfortable with giving one group of women and girls at least and arguably women and girls as a whole, never mind many men and boys who are gender-minorities, *un*equal treatment.

Moreover, as already mentioned, the preponderance standard is used in all of the regimes under which a school itself could be sued for mishandling a report of sexual violence, not only in cases brought by student survivors under Title IX, but also through claims brought by accused students themselves, when alleging violations of their administrative due process rights. It is also used in sexual violence civil tort cases under state laws and in civil protection order proceedings often used to protect victims of domestic violence. In those cases and many, many others, courts use the preponderance standard every day in matters that are deeply important to the parties involved and that can change the parties' lives forever, including orders to pay millions of dollars, to take children away from their parents, and in countless other ways.

Finally, requiring schools to use a different standard than a preponderance is unfair to schools. As discussed earlier, schools have demonstrated their preference for the preponderance standard and recognize it as a best practice. The administrative due process precedents emanating from the U.S. Supreme Court and lower courts clearly allow schools to follow these policy preferences and explicitly state that criminal law standards do not apply to accused student cases. In addition, when schools themselves are sued regarding their handling of sexual violence cases, they must defend claims that must only achieve a preponderance of the evidence themselves to require schools to pay damages up to millions of dollars. Furthermore, because of the greater liability schools face from Title IX lawsuits as opposed to accused students' administrative due process claims, schools' use of other evidence standards for their internal proceedings increases their risks for this potentially debilitating liability.

For all of these reasons, the preponderance standard should be retained as the standard by which schools conduct their administrative proceedings regarding sexual violence. To do otherwise is unfair to both survivors and schools and would communicate a particularly offensive and backward form of gender inequality.

Expanding Victims' Reporting Options and Respecting Their Autonomy to Choose the Best Option for Them

IHEs and regulators should also retain the aspects of the current administrative systems that support and expand victims' options to report under circumstances that they judge will best help them meet their many, diverse needs, including recovering their health and minimizing the damage of the violence to their education. Schools and lawmakers should avoid adding any requirements that diminish survivors' autonomy and control over their cases, understanding that adding such burdens will likely chill victim reporting by increasing the likelihood that victims will establish control by exercising their veto on the entire process. In general, institutions should seek to structure their administrative systems to encourage victims to report, understanding that the first and foremost goal for increasing reporting is helping victims to access services, because such access is critical to recovery from sexual violence and reporting is a prerequisite to such access. While increased reporting may have other goals such as providing data about the violence that can inform prevention efforts, reaching such a goal cannot place more burdens on survivors, who are already suffering.

One way IHEs can expand student survivors' options, access to services, and autonomy is by creating multiple reporting paths for student victims, and government regulators can and should support such structures via laws and policies. Such legal support has already been issued by OCR in its recently articulated guidance, as well as by best practices documents issued by the White House Task Force to Protect Students from Sexual Assault. Under this system, schools may designate some employees as confidential and some as nonconfidential, "responsible" employees. Only the confidential employees may take a report of sexual violence from a student and not pass that report to others at the institution, particularly the school's Title IX Coordinator (Lhamon, 2014).[12] This approach was generally supported by victim advocates and service providers, who work with the largest numbers and greatest diversity of sexual violence survivors. A similar structure has also worked well to empower sexual violence survivors in the military.

In addition, neither lawmakers nor IHEs should add requirements that have the effect of diminishing survivors' options and increasing the likelihood that they will not report in order to avoid that requirement. In light of the historical victim distrust of the criminal justice system discussed earlier, this means avoiding any requirement that links criminal justice proceedings with administrative/ civil proceedings without a survivors' informed, affirmative choice to seek that involvement and link. For instance, requiring school officials to refer reports of sexual violence to local law enforcement is likely to chill reporting by students who do not want to involve the criminal justice system in their cases. Even an opt-out provision (where a student victim could specify that s/he did not want his or her report to be referred, but without such a specification, the referral would be made automatically) would be insufficient for several reasons. First, a referred report would potentially allow many cases where the survivor did not take fully informed, affirmative action. Second, it would ask victims to make a critical decision in a moment of trauma when they are likely focused on more basic needs than whether they will seek justice through the criminal system (recall that the criminal justice system is not structured to help victims with most of their most immediate needs postviolence). Providing information sufficient for a truly informed decision by a survivor, especially in a moment of trauma, is susceptible to mishandling by schools, many of whose staff currently lack the broad-based, sophisticated understanding of sexual violence and the reactions to trauma that victims often experience. Finally, such a referral conflates criminal justice and administrative/civil processes in precisely the manner that the first 10 pages of this chapter was devoted to criticizing.

If the mandatory referral is designed in part to increase transparency regarding the sexual violence that is occurring on campuses, the better way to increase transparency is to mandate that all schools receiving federal funds conduct victimization surveys with their students, using the same survey designed by the

Department of Education or Department of Justice, administered at the same time and in the same interval with each school's students, and publishing the results in the school's campus crime report. Conducting these surveys separates information and data gathering from victim reporting and encourages all of us to think about reporting as facilitating access to services, not about proving that sexual violence exists or has a particular scope in society or on a specific campus.

Mandatory surveys also eliminate barriers to innovation, including innovative methods to increase reporting. They would eliminate barriers to innovation because schools currently have incentives, born out of public image concerns, to suppress reporting, which in turn suppresses innovation (institutions do not tend to create new ways to address problems they are trying to avoid acknowledging). Mandatory surveys would shift these incentives so that schools would not only not suppress victim reporting but would encourage it. When all schools administer the same survey at the same time and in the same interval, then publish the results of that survey to the public, all are on an equal footing. Because all indications suggest that at least initially most schools will have an incidence rate close to the national average, this survey is unlikely to raise one school significantly above the others in terms of its campus climate (Cantalupo, 2014). Therefore, there would no longer be a perverse public image incentive to suppress reporting in order to look safer than other schools. In contrast, since a large gap between incidence rates and reporting rates will look suspicious, schools will now have an incentive to bring the two numbers closer together by encouraging victim reporting and/or developing prevention programs that actually cause violent incidence rates to fall or both to occur simultaneously. These new incentives will support innovation, as schools seek to develop ever more effective practices for increasing reporting and preventing violence.

Coordinating Parallel Proceedings Where Necessary Through Use of CCRTs/SARTs, Full-Time Campus-Based Victims' Advocates, and MOUs

Another potential goal for the mandatory referral requirement rejected in the preceding is to encourage coordination between criminal justice and school officials. As with mandated surveys and the goal of collecting data on sexual violence, more effective methods exist for achieving such coordination. They include forming Coordinated Community Response Teams (CCRTs) and Sexual Assault Response Teams (SARTs), employing full-time victims' advocates on campus, and developing memorandums of understanding (MOUs) both with community-based victims' services organizations and with local law enforcement and prosecutors' offices. All of these methods allow for coordination of parallel criminal and administrative/civil proceedings without linking that coordination to victim reporting. In addition, they accomplish this coordination before any particular case is active and, therefore, are in a better position to develop coordination best practices.

It bears repeating that parallel civil and criminal proceedings are quite typical throughout the U.S. legal system. As already noted, there are many examples where employers and other entities may and will take administrative or civil actions to address violations of internal policies, civil rights laws, and other civil laws, regardless of whether police have investigated or prosecutors have decided to bring criminal charges arising from the same events. Therefore, there is no reason to suggest that schools cannot investigate and resolve reports of sexual violence against their students according to their Title IX and Clery Act obligations even when police are investigating or a prosecutor has decided to prosecute. However, from the survivor's and prosecution's perspective, coordination between these parallel proceedings will likely increase the effectiveness of both actions. From the accused student/defense perspective, parallel proceedings will require accused students and their counsel to develop a strategy for defending only one or both depending on such factors as the strength of the evidence, the relative importance to the accused student of achieving "not guilty" verdicts or "not-responsible" school disciplinary decisions, and myriad other factors.[13] Like the parallel proceedings themselves, the development of such strategies is typical in many areas of law where parallel proceedings can and do result.

As coordination methods, CCRTs/SARTs, full-time campus-based victim advocates, and MOUs are superior to mandatory referral because all will tend to establish coordination before any specific case becomes active. CCRTs/SARTs generally gather school employees and other campus stakeholders to develop a coordinated response to sexual and related forms of gender-based violence, giving schools an opportunity to involve local law enforcement and community-based victims' advocates in that coordinated response. If a school employs its own full-time dedicated victims' services and advocacy office, that office will inevitably play a similar coordination role, ideally in collaboration with a CCRT/SART. Victims' advocacy offices often act as the hub of a wheel full of different offices, facilitating victims' access to various services, such as health care, housing, counseling, academic affairs, campus police, student conduct/Title IX coordinator, financial aid, etc. This network of relationships also means that victims' advocates are often informally coordinating a *de facto* CCRT/SART.

Even if a school has a CCRT/SART and/or a dedicated advocacy office, forming MOUs with local law enforcement and community victims' services organizations can improve coordination even further. In addition, if the school is too small or has other characteristics that make it impractical to hire full-time victims' services staff or form a CCRT/SART, it can still enable coordination by forming these MOUs. The White House Task force has also suggested that schools develop such MOUs and has provided or is developing models for schools to use.

Conclusion

Conflating the criminal justice system with the administrative and civil law regimes of Title IX, the Clery Act, and the accused student administrative due process cases and/or not countering such conflation by others leads to several negative consequences for IHEs and student survivors of sexual violence. These include eliminating sexual violence victims' rights to equal educational opportunity, chilling victim reporting, and interfering with schools' abilities to adequately address student misconduct and implement sound educational policy. IHEs and lawmakers should instead be seeking to keep administrative/civil proceedings clearly separate from the criminal justice system, first by retaining a preponderance of the evidence standard of proof for Title IX and Clery-related administrative/civil proceedings. In addition, they should increase victims' options for reporting and support survivors' autonomy to make the best choices for meeting their diverse needs. Finally, schools and government officials must establish systems to coordinate IHE and criminal justice responses to sexual violence, especially when survivors decide to pursue parallel criminal and administrative/civil proceedings.

Notes

1. This chapter uses "sexual violence" instead of terms such as "sexual assault" or "rape" as a broad, descriptive term that is not a term of art and which includes a wide range of behaviors that may not fit certain legal or readers' definitions of "sexual assault" or "rape." The term, therefore, includes "sexual assault" or "rape," as well as other actions involving physical contact of a sexual nature.
2. This knowledge derives from the author's involvement in discussions with Senate staff drafting the bill.
3. *See* U.S. Department of Education, Office for Civil, Rights, *Revised Sexual Harassment Guidance: Harassment of Student by School Employees, Other Students, or Third Parties* 2, 6 (2001).
4. See Clear & Convincing Evidence, Legal Information Institute, www.law.cornell.edu/wex/clear_and_convincing_evidence.
5. The 2014 "Student Sexual Assault: Weathering the Perfect Storm" report produced by United Educators states that 72% of $36 million dollars was paid to 54% of 262 students who sued their schools in sexual assault cases from 2006–2010. The 54% was made up of accused students suing for due process violations, with the remainder being student victims. Therefore, 28% of $36 million dollars was paid to 131 student victims, equally just under $77,000 each.
6. This number is calculated based on $17 million spent by IHEs on just over 85 claims (28% of 305 total claims) by student "victims" or "perpetrators" (the terms used in United Educators' report). $14.3 million of the total costs involved "victim-driven litigation," and of the 85 claims, 58 (68% of the litigated claims) were filed by victims, 24 of which involved victim complaints to OCR (28% of the 85 total claims). Because OCR has only recently begun publishing resolution agreements that arrange for IHEs to pay compensation to victims, the amount spent by IHEs defending these 24 OCR complaints, $4.65 million (50% of $9.3 million spent in litigation defense costs) was subtracted from the total victim-driven litigation costs of $14.3 million and the 24 OCR complaint-related claims were subtracted from the 58 claims litigated by victims, leaving $9.65 million divided between 34 victim lawsuits or demand letters, an average cost of $283,824 per victim. United Educators, *Confronting Campus Sexual Assault: An Examination of Higher Education Claims* 2, 14, 16 (2015) (on file with author).
7. A total of 80% of just over 1,000 schools (Karjane, Fisher, & Cullen, 2002) and a majority of 64 schools (Anderson, 2004)
8. See, e.g., *Ahlum v. Administrators of Tulane Educ. Fund*, 617 So. 2d 96, 100 (La. Ct. App. 1993); *Rollins v. Cardinal Stritch Univ.*, 626 N.W.2d 464, 469 (Minn. Ct. App. 2001).

9. See *Remer v. Burlington Area Sch. Dist.*, 286 F.3d 1007 (7th Cir. 2002).
10. See *Coveney v. President & Trustees of Holy Cross Coll.*, 445 N.E.2d 136, 137 (Mass. 1983).
11. See *Fellheimer v. Middlebury Coll.*, 869 F. Supp. 238, 247 (D. Vt. 1994). See also *Marshall v. Maguire*, 102 Misc. 2d 697 (N.Y. Sup. Ct. 1980); *Doe v. University of the S.*, 2011 U.S. Dist. LEXIS 35166 (E.D. Tenn. 2011).
12. This confidentiality does not extend to reporting aggregate data for Clery Act purposes. Who reports aggregate data for the Clery Act is determined by the Clery Act's separate statutory provisions, regulations, and enforcement regime.
13. There are also ways to address concerns that might arise regarding accused students' criminal due process rights in the criminal proceeding, particularly regarding the way in which information gathered and disclosed through an administrative or civil proceeding might nullify the right of an accused student who is also a criminal defendant against self-incrimination. First, a statute can grant "use immunity" to evidence gathered in the administrative/civil proceeding. For instance, DC Code Section 16–1002, part of the subchapter setting out the rules for seeking a civil protection order in, for example, a case of domestic violence, states that, "Testimony of the respondent in any civil proceedings under this subchapter shall be inadmissible as evidence in a criminal trial or delinquency proceeding except in a prosecution for perjury or false statement." Second, even if the applicable statute does not provide use immunity, there are ways, in civil cases at least, to request, on a case-by-case basis, a stay of the civil case until the criminal case has concluded. Kimberly J. Winbush, *Pendency of Criminal Prosecution as Ground for Continuance or Postponement of Civil Action Involving Facts or Transactions upon which Prosecution Is Predicated—State Cases*, 37 A.L.R.6th 511.

References

Ali, R. (2011, April 4). Dear colleague letter. Washington, DC: United States Department of Education, Office for Civil Rights. Retrieved from http://www2.ed.gov/about/offices/list/ocr/letters/colleague-201104.html

Anderson, M. J. (2004). *The legacy of the prompt complaint requirement, corroboration requirement, and cautionary instructions on campus sexual assault*. Villanova University School of Law Working Paper Series, 20, 8–64, Villanova, PA.

Beloof, D. E. (1999). The third model of criminal process: The victim participation model. *Utah Law Review*, 289–332.

Bogdanich, W. (2014, April 16). A star player accused, and a flawed rape investigation. *New York Times*. Retrieved from www.nytimes.com/interactive/2014/04/16/sports/errors-in-inquiry-on-rape-allegations-against-fsu-jameis-winston.html

Bohmer, C., & Parrot, A. (1993). *Sexual assault on campus: The problem and the solution*. New York: Lexington Books.

Cantalupo, N. C. (2009). Campus violence: Understanding the extraordinary through the ordinary. *Journal of College and University Law, 35*, 613–690.

Cantalupo, N. C. (2012). "Decriminalizing" campus institutional responses to peer sexual violence. *Journal of College and University Law, 38*, 483–526.

Cantalupo, N. C. (2014). Institution-specific victimization surveys: Addressing legal & practical disincentives to gender-based violence reporting on college campuses. *Trauma, Violence & Abuse*.

Chaudhry, N., & Kaufmann, L.S. (2012). National Women's Law Center letter to Office of Civil Rights re: Dear Colleague Letter. *National Women's Law Center*. Retrieved from www.nwlc.org/resource/national-womens-law-center-writes-letter-support-department-educations-2011-dear-colleague-

Chmielewski, A. (2013). Defending the preponderance of the evidence standard in college adjudications of sexual assault. *Brigham Young University Education and Law Journal*, 143–174.

College rape tribunals fail students. (2014, May 6). *USA Today*. Retrieved from www.usatoday.com/story/opinion/2014/05/06/sexual-assault-college-rape-tribunal-editorials-debates/8786197/

Dixon v. Alabama State Board of Education, 294 F.2d 150 (5th Cir. 1961).

Dries, K. (2014, March 27). Dartmouth wants to make it clear they're taking sexual assault seriously. *Jezebel*. Retrieved from http://jezebel.com/dartmouth-wants-to-make-it-clear-theyre-taking-sexual-1553069458

Ehrenfreund, M. (2014). Virginia wants to force universities to report every rape to the police. That won't address U-Va.'s real problem. *Washington Post*. Retrieved from www.washingtonpost.com/blogs/wonkblog/wp/2014/12/03/virginia-wants-to-force-universities-to-report-every-rape-to-the-police-that-wont-address-uvas-real-problem/

Ehrenfreund, M., & Izadi, E. (2014, December 11). The scientific research shows reports of rape are often murky, but rarely false. *Washington Post*. Retrieved from www.washingtonpost.com/blogs/wonkblog/wp/2014/12/11/the-scientific-research-shows-reports-of-rape-are-often-murky-but-rarely-false/?hpid=z2

Fisher, B. S., Cullen, F. T., & Turner, M. G. (2000). *The sexual victimization of college women* (NCJ 182369). Washington, DC: U.S. Department of Justice, Office of Justice Programs.

Goldstein, A., & Leonnig, C. D. (2007, March 3). Libby jury seeks clarity on "reasonable doubt." *Washington Post*. Retrieved from www.washingtonpost.com/wp-dyn/content/article/2007/03/02/AR2007030200406.html

Goss v. Lopez, 419 U.S. 565 (1975).

Karjane, H. M., Fisher, B. S., & Cullen, F. T. (2002). *Campus sexual assault: How America's institutions of higher education respond*. Final report, NIJ Grant # 1999-WA-VX-0008. Newton, MA: Education Development Center.

Keehan, A. (2014). Student sexual assault: Weathering the perfect storm. United Educators. Retrieved from www.edurisksolutions.org/downloadasset.aspx?id=378

Kingkade, T. (2014, May 9). University of Oregon allowed 3 basketball players accused of gang rape to play March Madness. *Huffington Post*. Retrieved from www.huffingtonpost.com/2014/05/09/university-of-oregon-rape_n_5297928.html

Lhamon, C. E. (2014, April 29). Questions and answers on Title IX and sexual violence. United States Department of Education Office for Civil Rights. Retrieved from http://www2.ed.gov/about/offices/list/ocr/docs/qa-201404-title-ix.pdf

Lighty, T., St. Clair, S., & Cohen, J. S. (2011, June 16). Few arrests, convictions in campus sex assault cases. *Chicago Tribune*. Retrieved from http://articles.chicagotribune.com/2011–06–16/news/ct-met-campus-sexual-assaults-0617–20110616_1_convictions-arrests-assault-cases

Lisak, D., Gardinier, L., Nicksa, S. C., & Cote, A. M. (2010). False allegations of sexual assault: An analysis of ten years of reported cases. *Violence Against Women, 16*(12), 1318–1334.

Lonsway, K. A., & Archambault, J. (2012). The "justice gap" for sexual assault cases: Future directions for research and reform. *Violence Against Women, 18*(2), 145–168.

Loya, R. M. (2012). *Economic consequences of sexual violence: Implications for social policy and social change* (Doctoral dissertation proposal). Retrieved from http://heller.brandeis.edu/bulletin/bulletin-items/dissertations/pdfs/Loya%20Abstract.pdf

Miller, T. R., Cohen, M. A., & Wiersema, B. (1996). Victim costs and consequences: A new look. National Institute of Justice. Retrieved from www.ncjrs.gov/pdffiles/victcost.pdf

Schlossberg, T. (2014, July 18). UConn to pay $1.3 million to end suit on rape cases. *New York Times*. Retrieved from www.nytimes.com/2014/07/19/nyregion/uconn-to-pay-1–3-million-to-end-suit-on-rape-cases.html?_r=1

Schoof, R. (2013, August 26). Students press feds to get tough on campus sexual assault. *McClatchy DC*. Retrieved from www.mcclatchydc.com/2013/08/26/200180/students-press-feds-to-get-tough.html

Schwartz, F. (2014, March 28). Parker Gilbert '16 found not guilty of rape. *Dartmouth*. Retrieved from http://thedartmouth.com/2014/03/28/parker-gilbert-16-found-not-guilty-of-rape/

Silverman, J. G., Raj, A., Mucci, L. A., & Hathaway, J. E. (2001). Dating violence against adolescent girls and associated substance use, unhealthy weight control, sexual risk behavior, pregnancy, and suicidality. *Journal of the American Medical Association, 286*(5), 572–579.

Snyder, S., & Woodall, M. (2006, December 20). La Salle in trouble over two rape cases the U.S. says it did not report the alleged assaults in '03 and '04 as required by law. *Philadelphia Inquirer*. Retrieved from http://articles.philly.com/2006–12–20/news/25398509_1_connie-and-howard-clery-catherine-bath-campus-crimes

Staff Report. (2014, March 27). Jury clears former Dartmouth student in rape trial. *Valley News*. Retrieved from www.vnews.com/home/11335496–95/jury-clears-former-dartmouth-student-in-rape-trial

Stoner, E. N. (n.d.). Reviewing your student discipline policy: A project worth the investment. United Educators. Retrieved from www.edstoner.com/uploads/UE.pdf

Warshaw, R. (1988). *I never called it rape: The Ms. report on recognizing, fighting, and surviving date and acquaintance rape*. New York: Harper and Row.

U.S. Department of Education. (2014). Violence Against Women Act. *Federal Register, 79*(202), 62752–62790. Retrieved from www.gpo.gov/fdsys/pkg/FR-2014–10–20/pdf/2014–24284.pdf

U.S. Department of Justice. (1999). Victims of crime act crime victims fund. Retrieved from www.ncjrs.gov/ovc_archives/factsheets/cvfvca.htm

PART IV

The Possibilities of Programmatic Solutions

9

COMPREHENSIVE COLLEGE- OR UNIVERSITY-BASED SEXUAL VIOLENCE PREVENTION AND DIRECT SERVICES PROGRAM

A Framework

Traci Thomas-Card and Katie Eichele

Concern around sexual violence and intimate partner violence has shifted significantly in our nation (Fisher, Cullen, & Turner, 2000). Conversations have transformed from "Should we act on sexual assault reports?" to *"How* should we act on sexual assault reports?" Why this important shift? When one in four to five college women experience rape or attempted rape while in college and one in 71 men and nearly 50% of transgender people experience rape in their lifetime (Black et al., 2011; Krebs, Lindquist, Warner, Fisher, & Martin, 2007; Stotzer, 2009), students, parents, and the federal government have placed significant pressure on higher education and campus administrators to provide safer campuses, clear sexual violence policies, comprehensive response protocols, and support services for victim/survivors. Communities see the importance of supporting victim/survivors and holding perpetrators accountable. One way to do this is by having multiple avenues of support for survivors of sexual assault, especially when not every victim/survivor feels comfortable filing a police report—only about 5–12% do—and if they do report, the likelihood of their case being prosecuted through the criminal justice system is relatively low (Fisher et al., 2000).

As national media coverage intensifies, magnifying incidents of college sexual violence, social outrage increases when universities fail to effectively address these incidents. These inadequacies resulted in the enactment of federal legislation such as Title IX, the Jeanne Clery Disclosure of Campus Security Policy and Campus Crime Statistics Act (Clery Act), and the Campus SaVE Act. These laws not only outline appropriate college/university response and guidelines to track sexual violence incidents, but they also serve as tools to hold institutions accountable for "deliberate indifference" or inaction to sexual assault reports.

While some institutions of higher education have been successful in meeting these expectations by implementing effective change to their policies, support services, and prevention programs, not all institutions have the time or funding needed to do so. These campuses may benefit from guidance, particularly around direct service programs for victim/survivors, sexual violence education for students, faculty, and staff and the investigation and adjudication process for sexual assault reports.

This chapter identifies key components to consider in developing a comprehensive campus-based sexual violence program that provides direct services to victim/survivors and education to students, faculty, and staff. Recognizing there is no "one-size-fits-all" solution or model, the following information highlights critical components in developing an effective sexual violence prevention program where direct services and prevention efforts work in tandem and drive one another to create a safe campus culture and to address critical issues for higher education such as retention rates, institutional reputation, student success, legal implications, regulatory pressures, and state or federal aid.

We outline three pillars of a campus-based sexual violence program that would be helpful to large or small institutions that may have adequate-to-limited access to funding and resources. Those pillars include: 1) peer leadership/advocacy, 2) direct services, and 3) education programs. Last, we provide recommendations when creating on-campus and off-campus collaborations to address sexual violence.

Critical Legislative Summary

Three particular laws dominate national conversation when it comes to shaping campus sexual violence protocol. They are Title IX and the April 2011 Dear Colleague Letter, the Clery Act, and the Campus SaVE Act, which is part of the Violence Against Women Act (VAWA). We outline parts of these three laws that directly shape victim services to students.

Title IX

Title IX is a federal civil rights law that prohibits sex discrimination in education. It also expands to other educational opportunities, opening doors for girls and women to advance in the math and science fields, providing fair treatment to pregnant and student parents, and protecting students from bullying, sexual harassment, and sexual violence. Every school, college, or university that receives federal funding is required to have a trained Title IX coordinator responsible for enacting and enforcing Title IX regulations. Some of those regulations outlined by the U.S. Department of Education's Office for Civil Rights include (OCR, 2011):

1. "Once a school knows or reasonably should know of possible sexual violence, it must take immediate and appropriate action to investigate or determine what occurred.

2. "If sexual violence has occurred, a school must take prompt and effective steps to end the sexual violence, prevent its recurrence, and address its effects, regardless of a criminal investigation.
3. "A school must take steps to protect the complainant, including interim steps taken prior to the final outcome of the investigation.
4. "A school must provide a grievance procedure for students to file complaints of sexual violence. These procedures must include an equal opportunity for both parties to present witnesses and evidence and the same appeal rights.
5. "A school's grievance procedures must use the preponderance of the evidence standard to resolve complaints of sex discrimination.
6. "A school must notify both parties of the outcome of the complaint."

Therefore, campus-based sexual violence programs should be familiar with who the Title IX coordinator is and, working together, may serve as checks-and-balances to ensure Title IX regulations are met.

Clery Act

Since it was signed in 1990, the Jeanne Clery Act requires colleges and universities to disclose crime statistics on and near campus. A campus-based sexual violence program may participate in gathering general information related to sexual assault, domestic violence, dating violence, and stalking for the "public crime logs documenting the 'nature, date, time, and general location of each crime' and its disposition, if known" (Summary of Jeanne Clery Act, 2008). It's important that campus-based sexual assault agencies know their state's confidentiality statutes (if any) so not to violate confidentiality statues by providing a victim/survivor's personal or identifying information for the Clery statistics. "Sexual assault advocates across the country have varying levels of confidentiality. Some states protect communications between advocates and victims of sexual assault, meaning advocates cannot divulge information without a written, time-limited release of information from the victim" (Lonsway, Jones-Lockwood, & Archambault, 2013).

Campus SaVE Act

The Campus SaVE Act is the most recent law, part of the VAWA that was reauthorized in February 2013 (S.834–112rh Congress, 2013). According to Campus SaVE (2013), students or employees reporting victimization will be provided written rights to:

1. "Have campus authorities assist them if reporting a crime to law enforcement.
2. "Change academic, living, transportation, or working situations to avoid a hostile environment.
3. "Obtain or enforce a no contact order or restraining order.

4. "Have a clear description of the institution's disciplinary process and know the range of possible sanctions and outcome of any disciplinary proceedings.
5. "Receive contact information about counseling, health, mental health, victim advocacy, legal assistance, and other services available on-campus and in the community."

Campus-based programs assist victim/survivors and the institution by making sure student legal rights are met through the Campus SaVE act, Clery Act, and Title IX regulations. In compliance with these laws, advocacy agencies may also provide training or resources to students and employees on campus who may be the recipient of victim/survivor disclosures, reports, or who provide support. Having employees competent with information or referrals about where a victim/survivor or concerned person can get crisis counseling, victim advocacy, medical assistance, or seek legal advocacy will help victim/survivors feel cared for during an already difficult time.

Institutional Policy Development

Great responsibility is placed on colleges and universities to not only respond effectively to sexual violence reports but to also coordinate prevention efforts. However, without a working knowledge of the laws already mentioned, institutions would not have the proper criteria to create their own definitions and policies. What follows is a list of recommendations for administrators to consider as they shape or reexamine institutional policies.

1. Statement of Impact: This statement should outline the institution's values and commitment to end sexual violence and provide a safe community. It emphasizes the importance and priority sexual violence prevention has at the institution and should be created with the aid of student input.
2. Definitions: Definitions for sexual assault/misconduct, sexual harassment, relationship violence (domestic and dating), stalking, and consent serve as an important foundation from which an institution can operate. It is imperative to use simple language students and employees can both understand and to utilize the guidelines from the Clery Act and the Campus SaVE Act. The definitions should be easily accessible and distributed to both students and employees.
3. Victim Bill of Rights: As outlined in the Campus SaVE Act, all victim/survivors of sexual assault, domestic violence, dating violence, and stalking who come forward on-campus should be provided a written copy of their rights and resources available to them.
4. Faculty/Staff Expectations and Responsibilities: For faculty and staff (including student staff), expectations and responsibilities must be

outlined regarding their confidentiality responsibilities, reporting responsibilities, and the criteria for reporting and to whom. This may include student victim/survivors, staff/supervisor reporting procedures, departmental reporting to disciplinary offices, and any employees working with minors.

5. Crisis Intervention Referrals: Training or resources should be made available to students and employees on campus who may be the recipient of victim/survivor disclosures, reports, or who provide support. Having employees competent with information or referrals about where a victim/survivor or concerned person can get crisis counseling, victim advocacy, medical assistance, or seek legal advocacy will help a victim/survivor feel cared for during an already difficult time.

6. Reporting Process: Choosing to report a sexual assault is a big decision for a victim/survivor. Many factors influence whether one chooses to file a report or not and with whom to file that report. If alcohol or drugs are involved, having an amnesty policy for victim/survivors is essential to establish both with the college/university and also campus security. As much as possible, officials taking a report must monitor their language and questioning style, as a victim/survivor can easily feel like the interviewer is blaming the victim/survivor for the sexual assault. Acknowledging the nature of the questions and carefully monitoring tone, nonverbal communication, and restricting any judgmental comments beyond the line of questioning will help the victim/survivor feel more at ease through the questioning process. For officials who must interview victim/survivors, extensive training and materials are available, often through state sexual assault coalitions.

7. Due Process: The final policy to examine is the disciplinary hearing process. Most disciplinary procedures are geared toward fairness for the respondent. However, sexual assault cases are very severe and unique in that there is another party directly impacted by the violation and also the process may rely on the victim/survivor's testimony and cooperation to build the case. Legislators understood this unique situation and, therefore, built it into law that both the complainant and respondent have equal rights throughout that process, including the right to an advisor of their choice to be present through proceedings, the right to written outcomes at the same time, and the right to appeal the outcomes. They also should have a right to officials and hearing panel participants who are well-trained and understand the policies and issues around sexual violence. Those issues include how to weigh evidence, myths and facts around sexual assault, understanding of consent, and the impact of alcohol or drugs.

8. Prevention Program: In addition to refining policies, institutions are advised to outline prevention strategies and campaigns that focus both

on sexual assault awareness and bystander behavior designed to reach all students and employees on an on-going basis. Creating educational goals and outcomes as well as assessment methods will help guide institutional sexual assault prevention efforts.

Processes for Developing Strong Peer Advocates, Educators, and Student Leaders

In addition to establishing an institutional approach to assessing and addressing sexual violence on college campuses, student involvement is a critical factor to consider. It is the grassroots energy that students provide that creates and spreads social and cultural norms on campuses. Thus, campus administrators and students must work together to create the strategy and approach, otherwise students may not adopt programmatic and educational efforts if their input has not been incorporated. While sexual violence programming takes on a variety of models, peer-based models are gaining in popularity (AAUP, 2013). Wawrzynski (2011) notes:

> College and university administrators recognized the important effect that peers have on one another and as a result look to these students to play a pivotal role in enhancing students' undergraduate education. Peers serve in a variety of leadership and mentoring capacities . . . and present numerous programs to enhance the development of college and university students.
>
> *(para. 4)*

This section provides recommendations that higher education institutions might consider in developing a peer-based model for sexual violence support and prevention.

To establish a strong peer-based program, focused recruiting techniques such as applications and pretraining interviews should be used. Once selected, volunteers must undergo comprehensive and ongoing training. Peer volunteers can take on a variety of roles within a sexual violence center, including but not limited to, advocacy, peer education, special projects, and internships.

Before recruiting peer volunteers, it is necessary for professional staff to determine what purpose volunteers will serve in the organization, the ideal number of volunteers, and the capacity for training and supervising them, as well as the qualifications and expectations they have for incoming volunteers. Ideally, recruitment should start early and happen on an ongoing basis. Several options are available to recruit potential volunteers: sign-up sheets at tabling events, informational sessions that are open to the general public, and advertisements on the web and social media outlets, as well as intentional recruitment from students associated with partner offices.

Given the sensitive and sometimes traumatic nature of this work, sexual violence centers must be cautious in choosing volunteers. There are many methods to assess the readiness and responsibility of student volunteers who will serve as peer advocates and educators. For instance, applications, letters of recommendation, and pretraining interviews are options that may be used to assess incoming peer leaders (Figure 9.1). Once volunteers have an established role with a sexual violence center, we recommend regular in-service training and performance reviews to ensure a successful experience for the student volunteer as well as the sexual violence center and the people they serve.

Student volunteers can assume many different leadership roles within a sexual violence center; peer volunteers have the potential to work as office advocates, helpline advocates, violence prevention educators, and special project volunteers. Office advocates are students who assist with the day-to-day office duties, answer the helpline, and work with clients who take advantage of the walk-in services provided by the center. Helpline advocates are students who answer the 24-hour helpline after business hours, provide medical advocacy for victim/survivors who go to the hospital for evidentiary exams, and provide crisis counseling on the phone line as needed. Violence prevention educators are students who provide the educational programming for the sexual violence center. The student peer educators are responsible for presenting to audiences of their peers on a variety of topics,

In addition to an interview, volunteers complete an
application that asks the following questions:

1. In what capacity are you most interested in serving the program?
   ___Helpline Advocate ___Prevention Educator ___Special Projects Volunteer
2. How did you hear about this organization?
3. Why do you want to volunteer for this center?
4. If someone asked you "How can you best prevent sexual assault from happening?" What would you say?
5. Describe time where you served as an ally.
6. How would you respond to someone who tells you they were sexually assaulted?
7. What experiences do you have that may be helpful for this organization?
8. Sexual assault and relationship violence happen to all regardless of gender, origins or creed. How would you respond to a client you might not expect to serve?
9. As you have already read in the policies of this center, it states "*All volunteers must fulfill the requirements set forth in the Volunteer Job Description(s). These requirements include, but are not limited to: the ability to conduct oneself in a professional manner, a thorough and demonstrated understanding of violence against women as oppression, closure on any personal experience as a victim.* Because we are concerned about your well-being and the well-being of the people we serve, have you had any experience of sexual assault, relationship violence, or stalking that is not resolved and might keep you from being able to fulfill your volunteer experience with us?
   ___YES   ___NO
10. Is there anything else you would like us to know?

FIGURE 9.1 Volunteer Application Questions

Aurora Center for Advocacy & Education. (2012). Flow chart of services. Retrieved from www. umn.edu/aurora including, but not limited to: sexual assault, relationship violence, stalking, consent and coercion, healthy relationships, and bystander intervention. Special projects volunteers are students who frequently volunteer for tabling opportunities, creating a homecoming banner, making buttons, facilitating unique events, and so on.

In addition to volunteer opportunities, sexual violence centers may also provide student leaders with the opportunity to apply for internships. Interns are given positions that carry considerable amounts of responsibility and often serve as mentors to incoming as well as experienced volunteers. Internships may be offered as paid positions, or in some cases, opportunities worked out with departments who ask their graduate students to complete practicum such as counseling or social work fields. If a center decides to develop roles for interns, it is critical to develop learning outcomes as a way to assess the work accomplished by students in these roles.

Direct Services

For institutions that provide or are exploring victim service options, they can be campus-based or community-based through a partnership with a local advocacy agency. However students receive services, several types of advocacy are beneficial to victim/survivors per recommendations by the U.S. Department of Justice and outlined in the VAWA (S.47, 2013). Those areas include: crisis counseling, university/academic advocacy, legal advocacy, medical advocacy, and housing advocacy (see Figure 9.2) (Lonsway et al., 2013). This framework comes from the Office on Violence Against Women, which indicates that the *core* services a sexual assault agency should provide includes 24-hour crisis intervention, hospital and legal accompaniment, and information and referrals for other needs (National Sexual Violence Resource Center [NSVRC], 2012). Comprehensive services, which is the ultimate goal, provides the core services and expands further "to address the physical, social, emotional, and spiritual needs of sexual assault victim/survivors and their allies" (NSVRC, 2012).

When students are sexually assaulted, their first priority generally isn't to report the incident or to get counseling but rather to maintain their academics and proceed with their "normal" life and behaviors (Fanflik, 2007). Over time, due to stress, they often drop academic courses, withdraw from school, or transfer if not given appropriate support or feel safe on campus (AAUP, 2013). Beyond the academic impact, victim/survivors may experience long-term outcomes such as social withdrawal, depression, substance abuse, self-harm, eating disorders, post-traumatic stress, disassociation, and suicide (Kirkland, 1994). Thus, it is essential for colleges/universities to have victim services available staffed by those who have a professional responsibility to maintain client confidentiality. These services give a student access to safe, confidential environments to talk to someone with no obligations to report and where emotional support, referrals, and information is provided, as well as the rights and options available per the student's needs

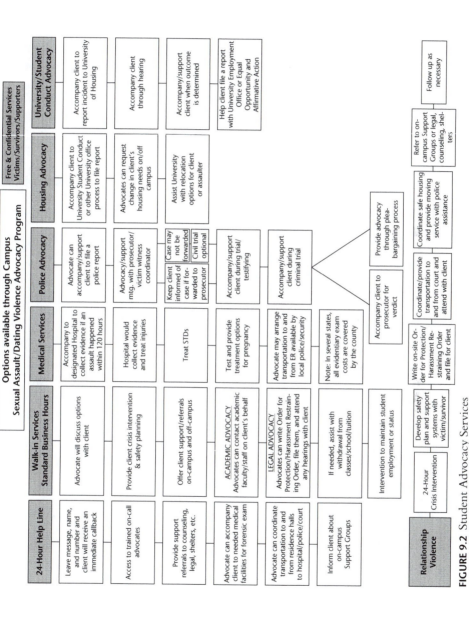

FIGURE 9.2 Student Advocacy Services

Aurora Center for Advocacy & Education. (2012). Volunteer Information & Application packet. Retrieved from www.umn.edu/aurora

and circumstances. Those options may include reporting to the police or campus authorities, a change in housing, safety planning, suppressing personal information, or requesting accommodations from an advisor or employer—especially if the perpetrator is a member of the same student group.

Victim advocacy focuses on the priorities important to the victim/survivor. Power and control has been taken away from victim/survivors of sexual assault, thus it is important to allow the victim/survivor to make their own decisions, even if they might choose to do nothing at the time.

Sexual assault advocates, therefore, are trained crisis counselors (not licensed therapists or psychologists) who are knowledgeable about victim rights, health care options, the criminal justice system, policies, and other processes or resources on- or off-campus related to victim/survivor experiences. They receive extensive training (around 40 hours), typically through a sexual assault agency, and students, staff, and faculty can receive this training rooted in an anti-oppression and empowerment-based framework, where they receive culturally specific response strategies, trauma-informed care principles, and institutional/systems knowledge (NSCRV, 2012).

Advocates help navigate systems and answer questions about resources while tending to feelings, victim/survivor healing, and support. They know about basic policies or procedures at the institution, like how to withdraw from a class or arrange a campus security escort, and they know who to contact to make those arrangements. Campus advocates need to be familiar with the different departments and have contact with the various people whom students may disclose to. If utilizing a community-based advocacy program, that program should have a campus orientation of the different offices, policies, and procedures linked to sexual assault and establish a campus liaison with whom the advocate can contact regarding questions or guidance. Research has found that "having services for victims, written law enforcement response protocols, coordination between campus and community, and campus-wide publicity about past crimes" encourages victim/survivors to report to authorities (National Institute of Justice, 2005).

Advocates present campus options to victim/survivors and understand individuals may not want to make immediate decisions; therefore, advocates do not pressure victim/survivors to report or take a certain course of action. It's important to understand that advocates operate under different privacy laws than the Family Educational Rights and Privacy Act (FERPA) or the Health Insurance Portability and Accountability Act (HIPAA). Most states have statues that indicate sexual assault advocates cannot discuss information a victim/survivor discloses unless the victim/survivor gives written permission. Advocates cannot confirm or deny whether an individual is working with them—that includes the police, faculty and staff, family, friends, etc.

Having confidential sexual assault advocates readily available to serve your campus is seen as best practice; however, if an institution does not have access to such people on-campus or within the local community, one possible option is to partner with nearby campuses that have victim services and contract with them. Other resourceful ways to provide victim services may include working with the campus counseling or health centers to provide confidential professionals who are knowledgeable about sexual assault and can assist students.

Crisis Counseling

Most sexual assault agencies are required to have a *24-hour crisis line* that operates 7 days a week, 365 days a year (VAWA, 2013). This service enables victim/survivors to access an advocate whenever needed. There are many ways to establish a 24-hour crisis line; for instance, through call centers, pager/alert systems, or other phone networking set ups. Additionally, *walk-in crisis counseling* helps survivors and their support people who choose to talk with someone in person and prefer business office hours to drop in with or without an appointment. Some sexual assault agencies will send an advocate directly to a residence hall, health center, counseling office, university office, or a general public, confidential space to meet with a victim/survivor if that victim/survivor does not feel comfortable going to the sexual assault agency or if their support person invites the advocate.

Victim/survivors may have needs that a sexual assault agency cannot meet on a short-term basis, such as long-term therapy. Many agencies, therefore, have a comprehensive list of *referrals to licensed therapists, counselors, or psychiatrists* that are on- or off-campus and can assist the victim/survivor in finding what they need. Last, many agencies provide in-house *support or self-help groups.* Support groups or peer support allows victim/survivors to hear and share survivor stories and work together toward recovery to achieve maximum benefits (Solomon, 2004). Some support groups might be facilitated through campus counseling, the health center, or a women's center. Others might refer victim/survivors to a local agency that provides support groups. No matter the size of an institution or the resources available, collaboration between departments and organizations can increase the types of services offered and still be cost-effective in addressing campus sexual violence prevention and response.

University/Academic Advocacy

University and academic advocacy is unique to colleges and universities and not something many community-based sexual assault agencies are familiar with nor do students know how to navigate while under duress. From the outside, campuses are a series of complex systems, paper work, and phone calls. According to System Justification Theory, those who are disenfranchised by the status quo may also be inhibited from denouncing and challenging the system for a variety of reasons, one which includes victim/survivor belief that the current system in place is reasonable and, based on the sensitive nature of their situation, they are hesitant to challenge the process (Blasi & Jost, 2006).

University advocacy requires an understanding of the many processes, offices and people that exist on a college campus and knowing where to go and who to go to. Some of those offices may include registration, the financial office, Greek life, housing, international student services, multicultural office, GLBT office, disability services, health and wellness services, academic programs, the graduate school, etc. Because there may be multiple offices and procedures a victim/survivor may have to access simultaneously, providing victim services specific to the student experience is beneficial for all students, staff, faculty, and parents involved. It also demonstrates that the university/college has a system and people in place to champion victim/survivors through the processes.

Academics are a priority for students. Academic advocacy involves finding out what victim/survivors need to successfully complete classes, assignments, exams, etc. and to contact professors on the victim/survivor's behalf (only with permission) to request accommodations. Accommodations can include extensions, extra time for taking exams, retaking exams that may have been administered only days after the assault, or having a private space in which to take exams. Often times, faculty are more receptive to these requests when they come from a third party professional who is willing to vouch for the student and knowledgeable about issues of sexual violence. It also alleviates awkward or uncomfortable conversations that could re-traumatize a victim/survivor if they aren't ready to disclose their experience directly to a faculty member.

Should a student decide to withdraw, financial advocacy helps students, especially if the sexual assault occurred after the university/college's tuition refund deadline. Students may need assistance when petitioning for a retroactive tuition refund. This process differs from school to school, but usually involves paperwork. Advocates can work with the financial office and the victim/survivor to make sure that the student has a clear understanding of potential financial consequences if there is any change in their student status, as well as what steps need to be taken to remedy financial hardship.

Student conduct/disciplinary advocacy is crucial to college campuses. Colleges and universities have standards of conduct for their students. Since sexual assault is considered to be the most underreported violent crime in America (Karjane, Fisher, & Cullen, 2005), having advocates available to explain the process, accompany victim/survivors to the student conduct office, provide victim/survivor support at any hearings, and serve as liaisons between offices and the victim/survivor can increase sexual assault reports to authorities (Lonsway et al., 2013). Additionally, advocates can provide critical feedback and input on disciplinary policies and procedures and provide training to investigators on how to work with victim/survivors.

University systems advocacy refers to the work advocates do on behalf of victim/survivors at the policy and protocol level. Many universities have made great strides to revise their sexual assault policies and procedures; however, there is still much work left to do to ensure victim/survivors encounter a supportive system when and if they report their assault to campus authorities.

Legal Advocacy

Legal advocates assist victim/survivors with the civil and/or criminal justice system and act as a liaison between the victim/survivor and criminal justice system professionals, including police and prosecuting attorneys, and can assist in writing and obtaining protective orders such as a harassment restraining order (Lonsway et al., 2013). Legal advocates should receive legal advocacy training through a victim services agency or the state sexual assault coalition (all states have them) since the criminal justice process is often confusing, intimidating, and complicated. Should victim/survivors choose to report, advocates can explain the process, support them during a police interview, expedite communication between the victim/survivor and criminal justice professionals, and see that the victim/survivor has information about their case. Advocates can also accompany the victim/survivor to court if their case is prosecuted; however, the legal advocates do not provide legal advice and they are not attorneys. Legal advocates provide information about the process so victim/survivors may make well-informed decisions.

Legal advocates may assist with both criminal and civil cases that a victim/survivor may be involved with. Depending on jurisdiction or the population served, advocates may also be involved with military or tribal courts. In most states, if a victim/survivor is assaulted by someone with whom they have had an intimate relationship, they can pursue a civil restraining order against the perpetrator. Some states also allow victim/survivors to request restraining orders against their perpetrators regardless of prior relationship (or lack thereof) between the two.

Advocating within the civil court system may include, but is not limited to, assisting with the preparation of paperwork for restraining orders, filing the orders in the appropriate county or jurisdiction, and accompanying the victim/survivor to court should a court hearing be either mandated by the courts or requested by a judge or the parties involved (Lonsway et al., 2013).

Criminal court legal advocacy helps victim/survivors understand and maneuver through the investigation and prosecution processes. Advocates can also assist victim/survivors who file for *crime victim reparations or restitution*. If a victim/survivor chooses to make a police report, they may be eligible for crime victim reparations. Although laws differ from state to state, often these funds can help defray the cost of medical bills, counseling services, lost wages, funerals, and child care. Victim/survivors can also apply for restitution to cover damage to property. Crime victim reparations are funded by the federal government, state, or county, and restitution is paid by the offender, if convicted. Advocates can aid victim/survivors in learning about these options and filling out the necessary paperwork.

If a campus doesn't provide legal advocacy, a campus ombudsman or police crime victim services program may be able to provide information about the legal process or provide a referral to the local sexual assault advocacy agency.

Medical Advocacy

Advocates may accompany victim/survivors or respond to hospital emergency departments for evidentiary exams (VAWA, 2013). Victim/survivors may want evidence of their assault collected for the purpose of prosecution. This option provides for the inclusion of a sexual assault response team (SART) member, a sexual assault nurse examiner (SANE), a specially trained medical professional who provides this service through the county; many hospitals also attend to health care needs such as treatment against STIs, pregnancy, and injuries for the victim/survivor in addition to the collection of evidence. Advocates are sometimes present during these exams, supporting and comforting the victim/survivor through the process and the trauma.

Some victim/survivors choose not to undergo an evidentiary exam or are not candidates for such an exam (if, for example, the assault occurred too long ago to collect evidence). These survivors may still need health care, and an advocate can help to locate such a medical clinic for care (perhaps on campus) and offer support and comfort to the victim/survivor. Advocates have also accompanied victim/survivors to follow-up exams or routine pelvic exams, which can be very traumatic for a victim/survivor to face alone. At a minimum, campus health practitioners and campus officials should be trained on what local medical options are available to victim/survivors.

Housing Advocacy

Most victim/survivors of sexual assault are attacked by someone they know and often in their own residence. Victim/survivors need to feel safe in their homes in order to work toward a healthy recovery. Advocates can assist victim/survivors to locate safe housing as well as to provide resources for the termination of a lease, to sublet, etc. If an institution has on-campus housing, a written protocol is helpful for the housing office to have in order to explain the process to the victim/survivor.

If the victim/survivor lives in a residence hall or other campus-sponsored housing, or even off-campus in the same apartment building or residence as their attacker, there are several reasons to arrange for safe, alternate housing. First, the assault may have occurred in the victim/survivor's place of residence. The victim/survivor may feel unsafe remaining there or the living quarters may serve as a constant reminder of their victimization. Second, the perpetrator may live in the same residence hall or apartment building, thus increasing the chance that the victim/survivor will see the perpetrator on a regular basis. Third, the "story" of the victim/survivor's assault may be circulating throughout their residence and this can increase the stress and discomfort the victim/survivor feels. The flow chart in Figure 9.2 is a visual representation of the types of victim services an on-campus sexual assault agency may provide.

Creating an Engaging Education Program

In addition to the emphasis on institutional policy and direct services regarding sexual violence, the Campus SaVE Act also requires higher education institutions to engage in proactive measures to provide comprehensive information on sexual violence to all students, staff, and faculty. Such efforts include: primary prevention and awareness education, bystander intervention training, and risk-reduction strategies, as well as ongoing prevention campaigns. The significance of creating and maintaining a solid education program to reduce the occurrence of sexual violence on college campuses must be emphasized. Increased educational awareness of sexual violence has long been touted as a method of prevention (AAUP, 2013; Banyard, Moynihan, & Crossman, 2009; Carmody, Ekhomu, & Payne, 2009; National Institute of Justice, 2005). Historically, prevention programming may have inadvertently been victim-blaming and often centered around the idea that males were perpetrators, as opposed to current best practices, which highlight the idea that all genders are affected by sexual violence and that bystander intervention programs are an effective means to rape prevention (Banyard, Moynihan, & Plante, 2007; Lee, Guy, & Perry, 2007). In a study on the effectiveness of peer-based sexual violence education on male college students, Stein (2007) found that "peer leaders may be able to correct misperceptions that men have about rape and rape prevention and communicate and promote pro-social behaviors" (p. 78). Foubert, Godin, and Tatum (2010) found similar results in their study on the effect of peer-based rape prevention programming. This section will discuss topics and methods for creating an engaging education program.

Developing Peer Educators

An engaging education program should include ongoing training for peer educators to develop both public speaking skills and curricular expertise. Training must be provided to teach students public speaking skills such as volume control, tone of voice, using direct eye contact, and awareness of as well as the ability to interpret body language. One strategy for helping students develop these skills is to ask peer educators to commit to quarterly in-service training as well as practice sessions prior to each presentation. Regular feedback is essential to ensure that peer educators are successful in their facilitation of the presentation material.

In addition to public speaking skills, peer educators in an engaging education program will have extensive knowledge on a variety of topics related to sexual violence. Subjects such as consent, coercion, bystander intervention, healthy relationships, sexual assault, relationship violence, stalking, alcohol and other drugs, healthy sexuality, the impact that violence has on the community from a public health perspective, policies, protocol, and mandated reporting are just some of the topics that may be covered by peer educators. Well-versed peer educators may also develop custom presentations developed around special topic areas such as violence within the LGBTQ and specific cultural or religious communities, hookup culture on the college campus, fraternity and sorority advisor trainings, etc. The wide array of subjects that higher education institutions are responsible for covering in their educational programming is vast.

Programming Considerations

Educational programming should be interactive and targeted to the audiences' needs. Depending on the goals and objectives of both the audience and presenters, programming can last anywhere from a half-hour presentation to a day-long workshop. Centers must exercise caution, however, in communicating about the effectiveness of shorter programming on making long-term changes to social norms regarding sexual violence. Bradley, Yeater, and O'Donohue (2009) note that although "the one-class-period mixed gender program may provide an introduction to sexual assault prevention and risk reduction, more intensive . . . intervention strategies may be needed to change college students' behavior over the long term" (p. 714). Finally, the digital age affords campus sexual violence centers with opportunities to educate like never before. It is important to consider the utilization of online modules/tools, social media, webinars, etc., to making education on sexual violence and bystander intervention as broad and accessible as possible. Exploring digital options for education may be particularly useful on campuses where staffing, time, and resources are limited.

Evaluation and assessment of the educational programming offered by a campus sexual violence center is imperative (Vladutiu, Martin, & Macy, 2011). Evaluation and assessment assists a center's ability to maintain and expand prevention/intervention education on a college campus, as well as to assess the effectiveness of any programming currently offered. There are many techniques that can be used to assess such programming; for instance, the use of pre- and posttests to determine growth in knowledge and changes in beliefs, the use of clicker-surveys to get real-time insight from audiences, and three- to six-month follow up surveys that allow a center to assess long-term impacts on the campus community. Stein (2007), for instance, argues that higher education institutions should conduct social norms research to assess the ongoing efforts in prevention, while Vladutiu et al. (2011) in their review of sexual assault prevention programming argue for a variety of methods to be used in assessment depending on what an institution is trying to assess (e.g., decrease in acceptance of rape myths, increase in number of students seeking direct services, etc.).

Building Relationships With On- and Off-Campus Partners

This section underscores the need for sexual violence centers to build relationships with both on- and off-campus partners. "Communities are vital in the development of violence preventions strategies" (NSVRC, 2005, p. 5). The importance of building relationships with both on- and off-campus partners cannot be emphasized heavily enough.

Campus Sexual Assault Response Teams and Protocols

Addressing sexual assault on college and university campuses cannot be done alone by any singular office or individual. Barry and Cell (2009) propose that

> supporting a comprehensive institutional approach to address sexual assault ensures that all members of a campus community have access to the education and employment they seek. A single campus constituency cannot eradicate sexual assault on its own. Sexual violence on campus affects everyone. The entire campus community must work collectively to create a safer environment in which all members can live, work, and learn. The impact of campus sexual assault can exact a tremendous toll on both the individuals involved and their institutions.
>
> *(p. xiii)*

The effort to support victim/survivors and to hold perpetrators accountable must be collaborative or the system will not work effectively. On-campus and off-campus community members have to work together in order to help victim/survivors, investigate reports, and eradicate sexual assault. Therefore, an institutional approach which includes a team of key stakeholders such as law enforcement/security, health care professionals, university investigators, mental health professionals, students affairs staff, etc., need to come together to examine policies, protocols, and training procedures. Outlining the policies, responsibilities, and actions of various offices or individuals in a written sexual assault response protocol will provide an operational framework for campuses to practice. Barry and Cell (2009) provide a comprehensive outline and considerations for forming such a team that could work with a victim services office.

Other On-Campus Partnerships

A comprehensive campus sexual violence center will most effectively serve students by establishing relationships with partner offices on-campus. Staff members in other areas of higher education are often primary responders to disclosures of sexual violence. In addition, staff and faculty members have the potential to be great sources of support for the campus sexual violence center. They have the potential to recommend potential volunteers, to request educational programming, and to work collaboratively with the center to ensure the safety and support of students.

It is imperative that a campus sexual violence program establish a relationship with and provide training to staff members who are likely to be first responders to disclosures of sexual violence. Police/safety officers, housing and residential life staff, student and employee conduct officers, equal opportunity and affirmative action staff, and student affairs staff are populations that often interact with victim/survivors in some way. It is equally important for a campus sexual violence center to build trust and establish relationships with both high profile and underrepresented populations on campus, as these students may face additional barriers to seeking support. For instance, athletes and members of Greek life would be considered high-profile populations, as their actions often garner media attention, both on a personal and an institutional level. Students of color, transfer students, students who identify as LGBTQ, and international students are populations that have historically been marginalized in higher education, which may prevent them from seeking the support of a sexual violence center. Encouraging student involvement from within these populations is one method of building trust so that victim/survivors feel safe in seeking services. In addition, intentionally establishing relationships with staff members from offices who work directly with these students can assist in opening lines of communication and increasing awareness about both direct and educational services. Such relationships can be established through individual relationship building, task forces, or participation in university and unit-wide committees. It isn't enough to simply establish such a relationship; it is imperative that campus sexual violence centers assess, maintain, and expand relationships with partner offices on an ongoing basis.

Off-Campus Partnerships

All states have a sexual assault coalition set up through the Department of Justice that can offer technical support and guidance to sexual violence programs. These coalitions often provide on-going training and education, develop and distribute educational materials, keep agencies updated on policy and legislative initiatives, and provide resources, referrals, and statewide networking. State sexual assault coalitions may also have information about how to build partnerships with your local police or campus security, health care systems, and criminal justice system to file restraining orders, or prosecutors, as well as other advocacy agencies within the area that may serve as a resource for your institution.

Conclusion

With the reauthorization of the VAWA and the implementation of the Campus SaVE Act, college and university campuses will soon be in the unparalleled position of implementing policies and providing support for victim/survivors, as well as training around sexual violence, for hundreds of thousands of students, staff, and faculty across the United States. This chapter identified key components to consider in developing a comprehensive, campus-based sexual violence program. It is essential for administrators of higher education institutions to understand key federal policies and the protocol development that must first be implemented to ensure the longevity of sexual violence response and prevention in higher education. This chapter highlighted the types of direct services an advocacy center might provide to victim/survivors and the components of an engaging education program to the campus community through a peer-based model, as well as emphasizing the importance of building relationships with both on- and off-campus partners. Recognizing that each institution will have unique student populations, varying sources of funding and staffing support and access to resources both on- and off-campus, colleges and universities may adapt the recommendations provided in this chapter to best fit their needs, which is essential to establishing a successful campus-based sexual violence center.

References

American Association of University Professors (AAUP). (2013). Campus sexual assault: Suggested policies and procedures. *Policy documents and reports* (10th ed.). Washington, DC: Author.

Aurora Center for Advocacy & Education. (2012). Flow chart of services. Retrieved from www.umn.edu/aurora

Banyard, V. L., Moynihan, M. M., & Crossman, M. T. (2009). Reducing sexual violence on campus: the role of student leaders as empowered bystanders. *Journal of College Student Development, 50*(4), 446–457.

Banyard, V. L., Moynihan, M. M., & Plante, E. G. (2007). Sexual violence prevention through bystander education: an experimental evaluation. *Journal of Community Psychology, 35*(4), 463–481.

Barry, D., & Cell, P. (2009). *Campus sexual assault response teams: Program development and operational management.* Kingston, NJ: Civic Research Institute.

Black, M., Basile, K., Breiding, M., Smith, S., Walters, M., Merrick, M., . . . Stevens, M. (2011). *The national intimate partner and sexual violence survey (NISVS): 2010 summary report.* Atlanta, GA: Centers for Disease Control and Prevention, National Center for Injury Prevention and Control.

Blasi, G., & Jost, J. (2006). System justification theory and research: Implication of law, legal advocacy, and social justice. *California Law Review, 94*, 1119–1168.

Bradley, A. R., Yeater, E. A., & O'Donohue, W. T. (2009). A program evaluation of a mixed-gender sexual assault prevention program. *Journal of Primary Prevention, 30*(6), 697–715.

Campus Sexual Violence Elimination (SaVE) Act, H.R. 2016, 112th Cong. (2013).

Carmody, D. C., Ekhomu, J., & Payne, B. K. (2009). Needs of sexual assault advocates in campus-based sexual assault centers. *College Student Journal, 43*(2), 507–513.

Fanflick, P. (2007). *Victim responses to sexual assault: Counterintuitive or simply adaptive?* Alexandria, VA: National District Attorneys Association, America Prosecutors Research Institute.

Fisher, B., Cullen, F., & Turner, M. (2000). *The sexual victimization of college women* (NCJ 180969). Washington, DC: U.S. Department of Justice, National Institute of Justice and Bureau of Justice Statistics.

Foubert, J. D., Godin, E., & Tatum, J. (2010). In their own words: Sophomore college men describe attitude and behavior changes resulting from a rape prevention program two years after their participation. *Journal of Interpersonal Violence, 25*, 2237–2257.

Karjane, H., Fisher, B., & Cullen, F. (2005). *Sexual assault on campus: What colleges and universities are doing about it* (NCJ 205521). Washington, DC: U.S. Department of Justice, National Institute of Justice.

Kirkland, C. (1994). *Academic impact of sexual assault.* George Mason University, Fairfax, VA.

Krebs, C., Lindquist, C., Warner, T., Fisher, B., & Martin, S. (2007). *The campus sexual assault study (CSA): Final report.* Washington, DC: National Institute of Justice.

Lee, D. S., Guy, L., & Perry, B. (2007). Sexual violence prevention. *Shifting the paradigm: Primary prevention of sexual violence.* Hanover, MD: American College Health Association.

Lonsway, K., Jones-Lockwood, A., & Archambault, J. (2013). *Breaking barriers: The role of community-based and system-based victim advocates.* Addy, WA: End Violence Against Women International.

National Institute of Justice. (2005). Sexual assault on campus: What colleges and universities are doing about it. U.S. Department of Justice, Office of Justice Programs. Retrieved from www.ncjrs.gov/pdffiles1/nij/205521.pdf

National Sexual Violence Resource Center. (2005). Sexual violence and the spectrum of prevention. Retrieved from www.nsvrc.org/sites/default/files/Factsheet_spectrum-of-prevention.pdf

National Sexual Violence Resource Center. (2012). Building comprehensive sexual assault services programs. Retrieved from www.nsvrc.org/sites/default/files/nsvrc_publications_article_sadi_building-comprehensive-sexual-assault-programs.pdf

Solomon, P. (2004). Peer support/peer provided services underlying processes, benefits, and critical ingredients. *Psychiatric Rehabilitation Journal, 27*(4), 392–401.

Stein, J. L. (2007). Peer educators and close friends as predictors of male college students' willingness to prevent rape. *Journal of College Student Development, 48*(1), 75–89.

Stotzer, R. (2009). Violence against transgender people: A review of United States data. *Aggression and Violent Behavior, 14*, 170–179.

Summary of the Jeanne Cleary Act. (2008). Clery Center for Security on Campus. Retrieved from http://clerycenter.org/summary-jeanne-clery-act

U.S. Department of Education, Office for Civil Rights. (2011). Dear colleague letter: Sexual violence background, summary, and fast facts. Retrieved from http://www2ed.gov/about/offices/list/ocr/docs/dcl-factsheet-201104.html

Violence Against Women Reauthorization Act (VAWA), S. 47, 112th Cong. (2013).

Vladutiu, C., Martin, S., & Macy, R. (2011). College-or university-based sexual assault prevention programs: a review of program outcomes, characteristics, and recommendations. *Trauma, Violence, & Abuse, 12*(2), 67–86.

Wawrzynski, M. (2011). Why utilize peer educators. *Peer Educator Effectiveness.* Retrieved from www.bacchusnetwork.org/advisor-peer-education-effectiveness.html

10

MANDATORY BYSTANDER INTERVENTION TRAINING

Is the SaVE Act Requirement the "Right" Program to Reduce Violence Among College Students?

Caitlin B. Henriksen, Kelsey L. Mattick, and Bonnie S. Fisher

It took almost 30 years after Kirkpatrick and Kanin's (1957) first single-campus estimates of attempted forced "male sex aggression" against college women for national estimates of sexual violence (e.g., completed and attempted rape, sexual coercion) against college students in the United States to be published. In their seminal study, the National Survey of Inter-Gender Relationships, Koss, Gidycz, and Wisniewski (1987) found that within one academic year, 6.5% of women experienced a completed rape, and 10.1% experienced an attempted rape; the percentage of males who experienced rape and attempted rape was 3.1% and 3.6%, respectively.

Their findings sparked researchers' interest in estimating the scope of different forms of sexual violence committed against college students, especially women. A decade later in the mid-1990s, the National College Women's Sexual Victimization study reported that nearly 16% of the sample of college women had experienced sexual victimization (e.g., sexual coercion, unwanted sexual touching) other than rape during the current academic term, with a substantial percentage having experienced recurring incidents (Fisher, Cullen, & Turner, 1999). More recently in early 2000, in their National Women's Study–Replication, Kilpatrick and colleagues (2007) shed light on the well-known link between alcohol and sexual victimization with their estimates of incapacitated or drug/alcohol-facilitated rape against college women. They reported that just over 5% of college women experienced rape in the last year, with 1.8% who experienced forcible rape and 3.6% who experienced drug-facilitated or incapacitated rape.

Scores of smaller scale studies (i.e., single campus) reaffirm the findings of these population-based national studies: sexual violence is a persistent problem among college students, especially women. Such a statement logically leads to a somewhat deceivingly simple question: What efforts have been undertaken both by the federal government—which oversees the educational activities of all 6,500 plus

Title IX postsecondary institutions—and other interested parties, such as university administrators and researchers from a range of disciplines, to prevent (and hopefully reduce) sexual violence committed against and by college students? Among the purposes of this chapter is to provide insight into this question. To this end, the first section provides a description of the evolution of the federal effort to combat sexual violence. These acts have led to the requirement that institutions of higher education provide prevention programs, in particular bystander intervention training, to their students. The next section critically reviews the research regarding prevention efforts, namely the evaluations of the effectiveness of bystander intervention training, focused on sexual violence among college students. Next, this emerging and nascent body of research is scrutinized. Questions are raised about what is still unknown about the effectiveness of these programs and what may possibly hinder understanding the effects of bystander efforts. The discussion then turns to the broader question of whether bystander intervention is the "right" primary prevention to effectively change college students' attitudes and reduce their sexual violence. Finally, the chapter provides closing thoughts about the promise of the findings to date and the importance of not only implementing but also evaluating the effectiveness of bystander intervention training on college campuses.

Evolution of Federal Legislation to Address Sexual Violence Among College Students

Title IX of the Educational Amendments of 1972 (Title IX) prohibits educational institutions, including colleges and universities, from discriminating based on sex in any federally funded education programs and activities (Lhamon, 2014). This means that Title IX prohibits sexual harassment as a form of sexual discrimination. The law extends to sexual violence perpetrated by a peer and is "generally considered a case of hostile environment sexual harassment that is so severe, pervasive and objectively offensive that it effectively bars the victim's access to an educational opportunity or benefit" (*Davis v. Monroe Country Board of Education*, 1999, p. 632, as cited in Cantalupo, 2013). Because of the severity of sexual violence, the Office for Civil Rights (2001, p. 6) states that even "a single or isolated incident of sexual harassment may, if sufficiently severe, create a hostile environment."

One landmark piece of legislation in the evolution of the federal government's response to campus sexual victimization came as a result of the efforts of the parents of a young woman, Jeanne Ann Clery, who was raped and murdered by a fellow student in her dormitory room in 1986. Her parents were troubled by the lack of information provided to students and families about crimes occurring on campuses. In response, they created the Clery Center for Security on Campus (formerly Security on Campus, Inc.) in 1987. Their advocacy secured passage of the Student Right-to-Know and Campus Security Act of 1990, and in 1998, this legislation was renamed in Jeanne's memory as the Jeanne Clery Disclosure of Campus Security Policy and Campus Crime Statistics Act. The Clery Act requires all Title IX postsecondary institutions, public and private alike, to publicly disclose an annual security report with crime statistics, including forcible and nonforcible sexual offenses (including rape), and security policies (Clery Center for Security on Campus, Inc., 2012; Fisher, Hartman, Cullen, & Turner, 2002).

Following this governmental response to campus sexual victimization, the Violence Against Women Act (VAWA) was enacted in 1994 to grant funds to postsecondary institutions to improve responses to and reduce crimes associated with domestic violence, dating violence, sexual assault, and stalking (National Task Force to End Sexual and Domestic Violence Against Women, 2013). Under VAWA, Congress also implemented the Grants to Reduce Sexual Assault, Domestic Violence, and Stalking on Campus Programs. The first of these grants was made in 1999, and between 2005 and 2011 totaled approximately $54 million. This money provided funding to strengthen schools' responses to victims of offenses included under VAWA. The 2013 reauthorization of VAWA ensured that campuses would continue to receive these grants to combat sexual violence. In April 2011, a Dear Colleague Letter issued by the U.S. Department of Education Office for Civil Rights reemphasized the purposes of Title IX (Ali, 2011). Among the purposes was to ensure that students receive an education free from sexual harassment and sexual violence. Further, it was recommended that schools provide preventive education programs during orientation for all new students, faculty, and staff (Ali, 2011).

The 2011 Dear Colleague letter issued by the Office for Civil Rights recommended that postsecondary schools provide education programs on sexual violence. As an amendment to the Clery Act and part of the VAWA reauthorization, President Obama signed the Campus Sexual Violence Elimination Act (SaVE Act) into law in 2013. The SaVE Act requires schools to provide these programs. Colleges must provide "primary prevention and awareness programs" for new students and employees, as well as ongoing prevention and awareness campaigns, including education on bystander intervention (Campus Sexual Violence Elimination Act, 2013, p. 5). This training is proposed to reduce rates of sexual violence and dating violence among college students.

The SaVE Act also requires domestic violence, dating violence, and stalking be reported in the annual security report; these are crime categories beyond those mandated by the Clery Act. College campuses must incorporate best practices for prevention and response to these crimes, while also providing prevention and awareness programs related to sexual misconduct and sexual violence, such as bystander intervention (Campus Sexual Violence Elimination Act, 2013).

In 2014, President Obama created the White House Task Force to Protect Students from Sexual Assault to address the well-established campus sexual assault statistics and campus culture that supported these criminal behaviors. The president's task force drafted guidelines to address these two related issues. First, the task force recommended that schools identify the extent of crime among all their students. Therefore, schools will be provided with instructions on how to design and implement a campus climate survey to better understand the scope of sexual assault on campus. The task force also offers schools better ways to respond to incidents of sexual assault, such as providing trained victim advocates to assist those who have been sexually assaulted. The task force also is encouraging increased efforts to enforce legislation regarding campus sexual assault and to make information on enforcement, prevalence of sexual assault, and other activities conducted by the Office for Civil Rights more available to the public. Further, the task force aims to provide administrators with a better understanding of strategies that have been documented to enhance awareness and prevention of sexual assault. Among these promising strategies noted by the task force is bystander intervention (White House Council on Women and Girls, 2014; White House Task Force to Protect Students From Sexual Assault, 2014). The task force refers to bystander intervention as "among the most promising prevention strategies" formed to protect students from sexual assault (White House Task Force to Protect Students From Sexual Assault, 2014, p. 9).

Bystander intervention has brought about a renewed approach to sexual assault prevention. Bystander intervention programs aim to change students' attitudes about acceptance of sexual assault and "teach both men and women to speak out against rape myths and to intervene if someone is at risk of being assaulted" (White House Task Force to Protect Students From Sexual Assault, 2014, p. 10). Bystander intervention recognizes that prevention efforts should not be limited to would-be victims and perpetrators. Rather the entire campus community— students, faculty, and staff—must be involved in changing their attitudes about sexual violence. Enabling bystanders to effectively intervene would then reduce the incidence of sexual violence among college students.

Bystander Intervention Among College Students

What Is Bystander Invention?

Imagine going to your first party as a first-year college undergraduate. You see a few new friends you know from your residence hall at the party, but you do not recognize by sight nor are you familiar with many of the other students there. Everyone is drinking alcohol and having a lively time chatting and dancing (except you are not drinking alcohol because you are underage). As the party is winding down and people are leaving, you notice a young woman who clearly had consumed too much alcohol. She is being held up by a young man who is leading her out of the party. You do not know either of these people even though they look like fellow college students. You can tell the woman is barely conscious by her body language; she is stumbling as she tries to walk, her eyes are half closed, and she is slurring her words. You are worried about her getting home safely without the young man taking advantage of her sexually given her state of mind and body. What do you do in this situation? Several questions swirl around in your head. Do you assume that the young man targeted her because she is intoxicated—either voluntarily, plied with alcohol intentionally, or surreptitiously drugged? Do you assume they came together as a romantic couple or as friends and the man is just making sure she gets home safely? Do you decide it is none of your business and walk away? Do you have someone distract the man and then ask the young women if she feels safe leaving the party with him? Do you volunteer to walk the woman home? If you chose one of the last two options, you are intervening as a bystander.

The idea of bystander intervention in a high-risk or emergency situation is not a new phenomenon. In the 1970s, Latané and Darley (1970) were among the first researchers to develop a model comprised of five steps necessary for a bystander to intervene in an emergency situation. First, the bystander must notice the event. Next, the bystander must identify the situation as one where an intervention is needed. Third, the bystander must take responsibility for intervening. Fourth, the bystander must decide how to help; that is, which action to take and when to initiate it. Fifth, the bystander must act to intervene.

As the example of the party highlights, it can be difficult to tell whether, when, and how to intervene. McMahon and Banyard (2012) have identified specific points at which a bystander could intervene to prevent sexual violence from occurring. First, a bystander could intervene before the assault takes place; this is an example of primary prevention. The second point of possible intervention is during the victimization; this is referred to as secondary prevention. This can be a difficult point of intervention, as many sexual assaults happen in private settings (e.g., a residence). The final intervention point is after the victimization has occurred; this is referred to as tertiary prevention. This type of intervention is usually accomplished in the context of someone disclosing to another person, whether a friend, family member, or an authority figure, such as the police, about the crime.

Furthermore, there is empirical evidence to suggest that individuals who experience sexual violence are at an elevated risk for a recurrent victimization (a second sexual victimization occurring). Specifically, Farrell and Bouloukos (2001) found that between 40–50% of sexual incidents were repeat incidents (i.e., at least the second sexual victimization experienced by the same victim within a short period of time; see also Fisher, Daigle & Cullen, 2010). Further, victims are more likely to disclose their experience to someone who is close to them (e.g., a friend or family member) as opposed to authorities (e.g., police, campus administrators) (Fisher et al., 2003). Therefore, the ability to intervene following an initial victimization may help to prevent a subsequent victimization, especially since research has shown that a subsequent sexual victimization incident is not only highly probable but also happens within a relatively short time period from the initial incident (Fisher et al., 2010).

What have researchers learned so far about bystander intervention? First, Latané and Darley (1970) identified five steps in intervening as a bystander. McMahon and Banyard (2012) described three distinct phases at which a bystander could intervene. However, not everyone who has the opportunity to intervene actually does take action. For example, Banyard, Moynihan, Walsh, Cohn, and Ward (2010) found that one in three female undergraduates and one in five male undergraduates had a friend disclose an unwanted sexual experience to them. However, responses to these disclosures differed greatly, with some individuals intervening to help their friend and others choosing not to intervene. Specific to the opportunity to intervene, Henriksen, Fisher, Williams, and Coker (2014) reported that for 11 out of 12 bystander behaviors, more than 50% of individuals had an opportunity to engage in each within the past year. However, percentages of actually engaging in bystander behaviors were as low as 6% for some behaviors.

One deceivingly simple question that arises is why some people decide to intervene while others do not. Based on Latané and Darley's model (1970), Burn (2009) identified five barriers to intervening in emergency situations. At the first step, noticing the event, the bystander could fail to notice the situation. This could be due to distractions in the environment or the bystander being focused on something else. The second step, identifying the situation as one that requires intervention, could be impeded by a failure to see the situation as high-risk. The bystander may simply be ignorant of warning signs to sexual assault, or, as in the original party situation, it may be unclear if there actually is a danger. At the third step, taking responsibility, the bystander fails to see intervention on behalf of the victim as his or her responsibility. The bystander may point to other people present and see intervention as someone else's responsibility or may see the victim as putting himself or herself at risk (i.e., through alcohol consumption). The fourth step, deciding how to help, can be inhibited by the bystander lacking the skills or knowledge to intervene. The bystander may just not know what to do in the situation. Finally, at the fifth step, acting to intervene, the bystander could still fail to intervene. This could be due to the bystander fearing responses of other individuals present. Bennett, Banyard and Garnhart (2014) found that the three biggest barriers to helping were failure to take responsibility, failure to intervene due to skill deficit, and failure to intervene due to audience inhibition. These barriers were significantly related to a decrease in helping behavior among strangers.

Research has shown that there are also individual characteristics that predict who is more likely to intervene than others. First, female college students are more likely to intervene in sexual violence situations than men (Banyard, Plante, & Moynihan 2005). Additionally, there is evidence to suggest that younger college students feel more confident in intervening in sexual violence and interpersonal violence (Banyard, 2008). Race may also be related to intervention, as McMahon, Postmus, Warrener, Martinez, and Spencer-Linzie (2013) found that White individuals tended to have more agreement with gender norms and more victim-blaming attitudes than African Americans. This may indicate that White college students are less likely to intervene in situations of sexual violence than African Americans.

Does Bystander Intervention Training Have Any Effect on College Students' Attitudes and Behaviors?

Researchers and practitioners alike have noted these barriers to intervention and have created college-based programs that will help reduce those barriers (Banyard, Plante, & Moynihan, 2005). These programs are known as bystander intervention training and are one of the programs required by the SaVE Act. These programs attempt to increase knowledge of sexual violence, change attitudes regarding rape and sexual assault, increase bystander behaviors, and ultimately decrease victimization and perpetration on college campuses. Changing students' acceptance of sexual and dating violence is a key component of bystander intervention training. Such training may reduce violent behaviors (and thereby victimization) by reducing students' violence acceptance and increasing their willingness and perceived self-efficacy to proactively intervene to prevent violence.

Several evaluations have shown promising outcomes for bystander intervention programs (Katz & Moore, 2013). Most of these evaluations have found that bystander intervention is effective in changing participants' attitudes about sexual violence. Bystander intervention programs also have been shown to increase participants' confidence in intervening (Banyard et al., 2009; Langhinrichsen-Rohling et al., 2011; Moynihan et al., 2010, 2011). For example, using a convenience sample of 139 student athletes on a single college campus, Moynihan et al. (2010) found that athletes who engaged in a bystander intervention training program felt more confident in intervening both at posttest and two months after receiving the intervention.

Rape myths are commonly held beliefs about rape and sexual assault. In most studies, the level of rape myth acceptance was decreased after participation in a bystander intervention program (Banyard et al., 2009; Foubert, 2000; Foubert & Marriott, 1997; Foubert & Newberry, 2006; Langhinrichsen-Rohling et al., 2011). Among fraternity members, Foubert and Newberry (2006) found that participating in a rape prevention program significantly reduced participants' acceptance of rape myths. Although these findings suggest students' level of rape myth acceptance levels decreased, there are other studies that refute this. Moynihan et al. (2010), in their study of college athletes, found no differences between the control group and the bystander-trained group with regard to rape myth acceptance at posttest. Supportive of Moynihan et al.'s findings, Gidycz, Orchowski, and Berkowitz (2011) found that the program had no effect on changing college men's rape myth beliefs.

Similarly, some programs have been effective in increasing actual bystander behaviors. Bringing in the Bystander is a bystander intervention program grounded in the community readiness to change model. The program targets recognition of inappropriate or dangerous behaviors and skill building. Facilitators act as role models throughout the session(s). The program focuses on community rape prevention by promoting the broader campus community to get involved.

Banyard, Moynihan, and Plante (2007) examined engagement in 38 different bystander behaviors during a 12-month study (including a pretest, posttest, two-month follow-up, four-month follow-up and 12-month follow-up) on a single campus using a convenience sample. The researchers found that Bringing in the Bystander was effective in increasing self-reported bystander behaviors. Additionally, the researchers found that knowledge and attitudes were strongly correlated to actual bystander behaviors. However, Moynihan and colleagues (2010) found no significant changes in behaviors among intercollegiate athletes who participated in Bringing in the Bystander.

Green Dot is another bystander intervention training program that has been evaluated and found to be effective in increasing bystander behaviors. Researchers have examined three different versions of the Green Dot intervention, each varying in intensity (Coker et al., 2011). The least intensive of these was a persuasive speech related to violence on campus and students' role in prevention. Next was an in-depth training known as Student Educating and Empowering to Develop Safety (SEEDS). The most intensive was students' engagement in the Violence Intervention and Prevention (VIP) program on campus. Individuals who had any form of the intervention reported higher engagement in bystander behaviors than those who received no intervention. SEEDS-trained individuals were more likely to engage in bystander behaviors than those who heard the speech alone, as were VIP-engaged individuals. There were no significant differences between SEEDS-trained and VIP-engaged individuals.

Considered collectively, these findings suggest that participation in bystander intervention training programs has positive effects on participants' attitudes. But there is still at least one outstanding unanswered question: Is bystander intervention training effective in decreasing victimization and perpetration? Unfortunately, there is not much research that has answered this question. What studies have been published, however, show promising results. Using a three-campus research design to evaluate the effectiveness of Green Dot training, Coker et al. (2014) found that male perpetration and victimization rates on a college campus with Green Dot were significantly lower than male perpetration and victimization rates on two other similar college campuses, which had no bystander intervention training. This study is a unique advancement, not only because it examined perpetration and victimization, but in that the study employed a random sampling design of a large number of students across three college campuses.

The research findings discussed indicate that bystander intervention training can be effective. First, it can change attitudes regarding rape myths and confidence in intervening among participants. In addition, these programs have been shown to change participants' behaviors. Finally, and perhaps most importantly, preliminary research indicates that bystander intervention training can reduce perpetration and victimization among college students. However, there are still some questions left unanswered by the research.

Unanswered Questions About the Bystander Intervention Among College Students

While these findings are promising, there are some unanswered questions when it comes to better understanding the effectiveness of bystander intervention training programs. There is some evidence to suggest that bystander intervention training works in the short-term, but few studies have examined the long-term effects of these programs on college students. How long can student participants retain the information they learned after completing one of these bystander intervention training programs? Are booster sessions necessary to sustain students' engagement in bystander behaviors? When should booster sessions be administered? Can a booster be administered online? There is not much published research that focuses on these questions. One exception is a study conducted by Banyard et al. (2007) that found that positive effects on college students' attitudes, such as a decrease in rape myth acceptance and increase in bystander efficacy, persisted at two months, four months, and even 12 months after the initial training. Differences in students' engagement in bystander behaviors, however, did not persist at 12 months. This study suffered from severe attrition by the 12-month follow-up (only 14% of the original sample completed the 12-month survey). While this study gives reason to be optimistic about the possible long-term effects of bystander intervention on college students' attitudes, more longitudinal research is needed to rigorously identify and estimate these effects.

Additionally, there are unanswered questions about the situations in which bystander intervention can be helpful in preventing sexual violence. First, there is an issue with the relationship between parties involved. Very few females are sexually assaulted by someone they have never met before (Krebs et al., 2009). Lindquist et al. (2013) found that 55.5% of forced sexual assault female victims knew their attackers well or very well. This finding was similar for 52.5% of incapacitated sexual assault victims. In most cases of both forced sexual assault and incapacitated sexual assault, the assailant was either a current or former significant other (38.4% and 20.7%, respectively) or a classmate (36.7% and 35.1%, respectively). This may cause confusion for bystanders who either do not know the relationship between parties or feel uncomfortable intervening in a situation where the parties have a close relationship. For example, when at that hypothetical party described, you did not know the relationship between the two people who were leaving the party together. The man could have been the intoxicated woman's boyfriend and he was helping her to get home safely and was not going to sexually assault her.

A second issue regarding the situation in which sexual violence occurs is where the victimization actually takes place. For bystander intervention to occur during a victimization (secondary prevention), there must, logically, be a bystander physically present either at the scene or nearly within earshot. This raises the question as to how many incidents of sexual violence can actually be prevented in this manner. If the victimization takes place at a public place (e.g., bar, park) or semi-public place (e.g., party), there may be some bystanders present. However, research shows that a majority of sexual victimizations, especially rape, occur in the privacy of the victim's or offender's living quarters or in an off-campus residence (Krebs et al., 2009). Other individuals in the building may hear the attack happening if one of the parties is vocal (e.g., screaming, yelling), but this may not be the case if the victim is passed out or asleep.

While research into the location of assaults is not as specific as would be preferred to answer this question, it does indicate that many sexual assaults occur in private. Hewitt and Beauregard (2014), for example, found that 64.8% of all sexual assaults occurred in private. Additionally Krebs et al. (2009) reported that of forced assaults, 74.7% that happen on campus and 72% that occur off campus take place in the victim's or the offender's residence. This percentage changes to 91% and 70.6%, respectively, for incapacitated sexual assaults. Lindquist et al. (2013) echoed these findings, with similar estimates indicating 82.1% of forced sexual assaults on campus and 80.6% off campus occurred in the victim's or offender's residence. Additionally, 85.5% of incapacitated sexual assaults on campus and 73.3% of incapacitated sexual assaults off campus occurred at one of those places. What is not known from this research is whether other people were in these residences during the assault.

This research indicates that it may be more effective to teach bystanders to intervene before a sexual violence incident. However, it remains relatively unknown where victims and offenders were prior to the assault. If there is indication of the potential for violence in a public or semi-public place, such as a bar, club, or party, it would be possible for bystanders to intervene. Consider if the victim and offender are not in a public setting prior to the assault, or if there is no indication of the potential for violence, then bystander intervention cannot be effective. Even if the participants in one of these programs are well trained, if they are not present as a bystander before, during, or after a victimization, their training cannot prevent the initial sexual victimization or even subsequent victimization, which research shows has a high probability of occurring among college women.

Is the SaVE Act Requirement the "Right" Program to Change Attitudes and Reduce Sexual Violence?

Given the preceding criticisms, it is understandable to conclude that one may think the federal government acted too hastily in their requirement of colleges and universities to implement bystander intervention training. Despite the strides researchers have made to understand how and why bystander training changes students' attitude and behaviors, their work still leaves many questions unanswered and is characterized by methodological shortcomings that may undermine the generalizability of the research findings. As previously summarized in this chapter, the current body of bystander intervention evaluations fall short in five major areas. First, many of these studies include small, nonrandom samples. Additionally, these samples are limited to only a few schools. There is also very little longitudinal research to determine if these programs have long-term effects. Fourth, there are only a small number of published studies that examined the effects of these programs on college students' victimization and perpetration rates. Finally, there is still much that remains unknown about the number of high-risk sexual violence situations that pose opportunities for bystanders to actually intervene.

Despite these criticisms, we are hopeful that the SaVE Act requirement is the "right" program to change college students' attitudes, and ultimately, reduce the risk of sexual violence among college students. Although the current research has methodological weaknesses, it also has very important strengths that should not be overlooked. First, despite the individual limitations of studies, the growing body of literature is overwhelmingly supportive of the bystander intervention model. Nonsupportive results tend not to be uniform across their outcomes. For example, although Gidycz et al. (2011) found that participation in a bystander intervention program did not alter rape myth acceptance, the program was effective in reducing association with sexually aggressive peers. Additionally, there is no published research indicating that individuals decreased their bystander behaviors after participating in a bystander intervention program. Hence, there does not appear to be any negative effects of bystander training.

Collectively, these findings are important because they indicate that the SaVE Act is on the "right" track to changing the campus culture that promotes sexual violence and, thereby, decrease victimization and perpetration rates among college students. The SaVE Act plays another very important role. This requirement shifts the burden of preventing sexual violence from individual responsibility to community responsibility. Although blame always lies on the perpetrator, it encourages others, namely college students, to get involved in actively preventing sexual violence. Given the grim statistics on sexual violence among college students, starting with Koss and colleagues (1987), the occurrence of sexual assault persists despite prevention approaches over four decades. The involvement of community responsibility through bystander intervention is a promising new approach to reducing sexual assault victimization and perpetration among college students.

Perhaps coupling bystander intervention training with other campus sexual violence prevention strategies can be part of a comprehensive, multi-pronged approach to changing college students' attitudes and behaviors (e.g., educating about alcohol abuse, addressing barriers to reporting, outreach to at-risk students, improving access to services, etc.). Such an integrated approach could be employed to create a coordinate campus-wide system of prevention and a seamless system of services to those who have experienced sexual violence. Understanding how bystander training can be coordinated with other campus prevention efforts is yet another avenue to further examine the effectiveness of its seemingly "right" positive impacts on college students to date.

Conclusion

In this chapter, we provided a brief description of the evolution of the federal legislation to address crime among college students, in particular sexual violence. We especially highlighted the prevention program requirements for all Title IX postsecondary institutions, namely bystander intervention training required by the SaVE Act. To understand what this type of training is and its theoretical underpinnings, we next described the bystander intervention approach and how it can be used as a mechanism to reduce opportunities of sexual violence. This was followed by a critical examination of the limited number of evaluations of bystander intervention programs published to date. Taken collectively, this small, but growing, body of research shows promising results for bystander intervention training; the research suggests that participating in this type of training changes college students' attitudes about sexual violence, increases their bystander behaviors, and ultimately reduces their victimization and perpetration. Bear in mind, it would be imprudent of us not to note that these promising findings rest on some weak empirical footings (e.g., single campus, nonprobability sample, relatively small sample size). That said, there are very few evaluations whose entire methods rest on strong empirical footings (e.g., pretest/posttest, multiple campuses, large probability sample).

In conclusion, is the SaVE Act requirement the "right" program to change college students' attitudes and reduce sexual violence? Our initial answer is yes. We can say that based on the evidence to date, the SaVE Act requirement is not the "wrong" approach to reducing sexual violence among college students. These evaluations of bystander intervention among college students are in their infancy stage. Despite the initial promising results, there are many unanswered questions, ones deserving of further scientific scrutiny about the effectiveness of these programs. Only then can it be known how and why these programs are effective in reducing sexual violence victimization and perpetration.

Nevertheless, the evaluators' efforts are to be applauded because without their work to date, the level of understanding of either the predictors or the outcomes would not have progressed. It is their dedicated efforts that will get us closer to learning more about both the facilitators and barriers to effective bystander intervention among college students. As a result of these efforts and findings, lessons have been learned and more questions have been generated for researchers and practitioners alike to answer.

The most compelling lesson that this growing body of bystander intervention training evaluations has taught us is that the science is always worth the wait. Hopefully, the enthusiasm of these promising results will not outpace the quantitative and qualitative evidence. As more and more postsecondary institutions implement bystander intervention training among their students, faculty, and staff, hopefully they also will be committed to documenting their implementation process and evaluating their effectiveness across a range of outcome measures. The logical next step in terms of the rigorous evaluation of bystander intervention programs implemented at Title IX postsecondary institutions is within reach, and the published studies to date have paved their way.

References

Ali, R. (2011, April 4). Assistant Secretary for Civil Rights, U.S. Department of Education, Office of Civil Rights. Dear Colleague Letter: Sexual Violence. Retrieved from http://www2.ed.gov/about/offices/list/ocr/letters/colleague-201304.pdf

Banyard, V. L. (2008). Measurement and correlates of prosocial bystander behavior: The case of interpersonal violence. *Violence and Victims, 23*(1), 83–97.

Banyard, V. L., Moynihan, M. M., & Crossman, M. T. (2009). Reducing sexual violence on campus: The role of student leaders as empowered bystanders. *Journal of College Student Development, 50*(4), 446–457.

Banyard, V. L., Moynihan, M. M., & Plante, E. G. (2007). Sexual violence prevention through bystander education: An experimental evaluation. *Journal of Community Psychology, 35*(4), 463–481.

Banyard, V. L., Moynihan, M., Walsh, W., Cohn, E., & Ward, S. (2010). Friends of survivors: The community impact of unwanted sexual experiences. *Journal of Interpersonal Violence, 25*(2), 242–256.

Banyard, V. L., Plante, E. G., & Moynihan, M. M. (2005). Rape prevention through bystander education: Bringing a broader community perspective to sexual violence prevention. Washington, DC: National Institute of Justice, Office of Justice Programs, U.S. Department of Justice.

Bennett, S., Banyard, V. L., & Garnhart, L. (2014). To act or not to act, that is the question? barriers and facilitators of bystander intervention. *Journal of Interpersonal Violence, 29*(3), 476.

Burn, S. M. (2009). A situational model of sexual assault prevention through bystander intervention. *Sex Roles, 60*(11–12), 779–792.

Campus Sexual Violence Elimination Act, H.R. 2016, 112th Cong. (2013).

Cantalupo, N. (2013). "Decriminalizing" campus institutional responses to peer sexual violence. In B. S. Fisher & J. J. Sloan III (Eds.), *Campus crime: Legal, social and policy perspectives* (pp. 90–118). Springfield, IL: Charles C. Thomas.

Clery Center for Security on Campus. (2012). The federal campus sexual assault victims' bill of rights. Retrieved from http://clerycenter.org/federal-campus-sexual-assault-victims'-bill-rights.

Coker, A. L., Cook-Craig, P. G., Williams, C. M., Fisher, B. S., Clear, E. R., Garcia, L. S., & Hegge, L. M. (2011). Evaluation of green dot: An active bystander intervention to reduce sexual violence on college campuses. *Violence Against Women, 17*(6), 777.

Coker, A. L., Fisher, B. S., Bush, H. M., Swan, S. C., Williams, C. M., Clear, E. R., & DeGue, S. (2014). Evaluation of the green dot bystander intervention to reduce interpersonal violence among college students across three campuses. *Violence Against Women, 17*(6), 1–21.

Farrell, G., & Bouloukos, A. C. (2001). International overview: A cross-national comparison of rates of repeat victimization. *Crime Prevention Studies, 12*, 5–25.

Fisher, B. S., Cullen, F. T., & Turner, M. G. (1999). *The extent and nature of sexual victimization among college women: A national-level analysis* (final report). Washington, DC: U.S. Department of Justice, National Institute of Justice.

Fisher, B. S., Daigle, L. E., & Cullen, F. T. (2010). What distinguishes single from recurrent sexual victims? The role of lifestyle-routine activities and first-incident characteristics. *Justice Quarterly, 27*(1), 102–129.

Fisher, B. S., Daigle, L. E., Cullen, F. T., & Turner, M. G. (2003). Reporting sexual victimization to the police and others: Results from a national-level study of college women. *Criminal Justice and Behavior: An International Journal, 30*(1), 6–38.

Fisher, B. S., Hartman, J. L., Cullen, F. T., & Turner, M. G. (2002). Making campuses safer for students: The Clery Act as a symbolic legal reform. *Stetson Law Review, 32*(1), 61–90.

Foubert, J. D. (2000). The longitudinal effects of a rape-prevention program on fraternity men's attitudes, behavioral intent, and behavior. *Journal of American College Health, 48*(4), 158–163.

Foubert, J. D., & Marriott, K. A. (1997). Effects of a sexual assault peer education program on men's belief in rape myths. *Sex Roles, 36*(3), 259–268.

Foubert, J., & Newberry, J. T. (2006). Effects of two versions of an empathy-based rape prevention program on fraternity men's survivor empathy, attitudes, and behavioral intent to commit rape or sexual assault. *Journal of College Student Development, 47*(2), 133–148.

Gidycz, C. A., Orchowski, L. M., & Berkowitz, A.D. (2011). Preventing sexual aggression among college men: An evaluation of a social norms and bystander intervention program. *Violence Against Women, 17*(6), 720.

Henriksen, C. B., Fisher, B. S., Williams, C. M. & Coker, A. L. (2014, November). *Bystander intervention: The mediating effect of gender.* Poster presented at the American Society of Criminology annual meeting, San Francisco, CA.

Hewitt, A., & Beauregard, E. (2014). Sexual crime and place: The impact of the environmental context on sexual assault outcomes. *Journal of Criminal Justice, 42*(5), 375.

Langhinrichsen-Rohling, J., Foubert, J. D., Brasfield, H. M., Hill, B., & Shelley-Tremblay, S. (2011). The men's program: Does it impact college men's self-reported bystander efficacy and willingness to intervene? *Violence Against Women, 17*(6), 743.

Latané, B., & Darley, J. M. (1970). *The unresponsive bystander: Why doesn't he help?* New York: Appleton-Century Crofts.

Lhamon, C. E. (2014, April 29). Questions and answers on Title IX and sexual violence. United States Department of Education Office for Civil Rights. Retrieved from http://www2.ed.gov/about/offices/list/ocr/docs/qa-201404-title-ix.pdf

Lindquist, C. H., Barrick, K., Krebs, C., Crosby, C. M., Lockard, A. J., & Sanders-Phillips, K. (2013). The context and consequences of sexual assault among undergraduate women at historically Black colleges and universities (HBCUs). *Journal of Interpersonal Violence, 28*(12), 2437–2461.

Katz, J., & Moore, J. (2013). Bystander education for campus sexual assault prevention: An initial meta-analysis. *Violence and Victims, 28*(6), 1054–1067.

Kilpatrick, D. G., Resnick, H. S., Ruggiero, K. J., Conoscenti, L. M., & McCauley, J. (2007). *Drug-facilitated, incapacitated, and forcible rape: A national study.* Charleston, NC: Medical University of South Carolina, National Crime Victims Research & Treatment Center.

Kirkpatrick, C., & Kanin, E. (1957). Male sex aggression on a university campus. *American Sociological Review, 22*(1), 52–58.

Koss, M. P., Gidycz, C. A., & Wisniewski, N. (1987). The scope of rape: Incidence and prevalence of sexual aggression and victimization in a national sample of higher education students. *Journal of Consulting and Clinical Psychology, 55*(2), 162–170.

Krebs, C. P., Lindquist, C. H., Warner, T. D., Fisher, B. S., & Martin, S. L. (2009). College women's experiences with physically forced, alcohol- or other drug-enabled, and drug-facilitated sexual assault before and since entering college. *Journal of American College Health, 57*(6), 639–647.

McMahon, S., & Banyard, V. L. (2012). When can I help? A conceptual framework for the prevention of sexual violence through bystander intervention. *Trauma, Violence & Abuse, 13*(1), 3–14.

McMahon, S., Postmus, J. L., Warrener, C., Martinez, J. A., & Spencer-Linzie, A. (2013). A statewide exploration of bystander and gender-role attitudes in New Jersey. *Affilia, 28*(3), 296–308.

Moynihan, M. M., Banyard, V. L., Arnold, J. S., Eckstein, R. P., & Stapleton, J. G. (2010). Engaging intercollegiate athletes in preventing and intervening in sexual and intimate partner violence. *Journal of American College Health, 59*(3), 197–204.

Moynihan, M. M., Banyard, V. L., Arnold, J. S., Eckstein, R. P., & Stapleton, J. G. (2011). Sisterhood may be powerful for reducing sexual and intimate partner violence: An evaluation of the bringing in the bystander in-person program with sorority members. *Violence Against Women, 17*(6), 703–719.

National Task Force to End Sexual Violence and Domestic Violence Against Women. (2013). The facts about VAWA. Retrieved from http://4vawa.org/the-facts-about-vawa/

Office for Civil Rights. (2001). Revised sexual harassment guidance: Harassment of students by school employees, other students, or third parties. Retrieved from http://www2. ed.gov/about/offices/list/ocr/docs/shguide.pdf

White House Council on Women and Girls. (2014). *Rape and sexual assault: A renewed call to action.* Washington, DC: Author.

White House Task Force to Protect Students From Sexual Assault. (2014). *Not alone: The first report of the White House task force to protect students from sexual assault.* Washington, DC: Author.

AFTERWORD

Questioning the Scripts of Sexual Misconduct

Tackling the issue of sexual violence in colleges and universities is a grueling task, and we commend the scholars, educators, and activists whose words are presented in this volume for their work and, no doubt, the emotional energy they poured into these chapters. We also commend them for their continued engagement with the very real struggles they face on their respective campuses and within their organizations. We also acknowledge and appreciate those whose voices are not heard in this volume, our readers and the many others who dedicate themselves to this movement. As Susan Marine states, "We're talking about rape here. It's distasteful. It's demeaning, and it's ugly." The willingness of those who confront rape and other forms of sexual violence and serve as much-needed support people for survivors on our campuses and beyond leaves us humbled and grateful. Thank you.

Within this volume, we appreciate the multiple ways that the authors look at a critically important topic for higher education today by intertwining theory and practice with critical analysis. While the book examines what exists, the authors of this book also look critically at what does not yet exist and who is not yet included in our understandings of and policies related to sexual assault prevention and response. We applaud the ways in which authors discuss not only the implementation of policy and construction of survivor-centered support structures but also the complexities encountered when implementing these policies and support structures. Finally, the authors pose questions about the ability of policy to fully address the issue of sexual violence and the ways in which support systems can better respond to the needs of survivors. In these ways, we find this book to be an important addition to the scholarship on combating sexual violence on our campuses. In this afterword, we comment briefly on a few particularly poignant aspects of the volume and pose the persistent questions that this volume has left in our minds.

Discursive Framings of "Sexual Misconduct"

We start with the very definition of "sexual misconduct." Colleges and universities are required to respond to sexual violence on campus—the responses must be compliant with federal and state laws and regulatory guidance. Yet, defining sexual violence on campus is not as easy as it may appear. Federal and state laws do not always agree and those disagreements leave colleges and universities to try to discern a mutually understandable space. Colleges are required to have policies against sexual assault, harassment, dating violence, domestic violence, and stalking; "sexual misconduct" is often used as an umbrella term. However, do the words we use to describe sexual violence allow for survivors to name their experience and find help? Does identifying rape as "sexual misconduct" help the community know that colleges take the issue seriously? Regardless of the names employed, most college or university policies hinge on the issue of consent, asking: Was there consent for the sexual activity in question? Popular culture definitions counter this framing, perpetuating a persistent myth that stranger rape is the real danger and that sexual assault by an acquaintance is a lesser crime. We are left to wonder: How do the myths and cultural beliefs students come in to college with influence their abilities to understand the realities of sexual violence? Furthermore, how does the language we use to describe sexual violence contribute to a particular framing of the issue?

Throughout the chapters in this volume, the concept of discourse played a prominent role. Sexual misconduct is a part of the discourse of higher education today. *The Chronicle of Higher Education* has regularly focused on sexual violence on campus throughout the last year as the terms of the discourse are contested by government actors, lawyers, college administrators, faculty members, activists, perpetrators, victim-survivors, and parents. While Susan Iverson carefully discusses the more specific and nuanced discourses that inform sexual misconduct policies, we think it is important to point out that many administrators, faculty members, and students are no longer surprised when we hear of or read about sexual misconduct in colleges and universities. It is part of our culture and, though many find it reprehensible, it is what we seem to have come to expect. At some level, it has become part of our normal.

Yet, there is not just one discourse that informs our thinking about sexual misconduct. Instead, many people and ideas are competing for meaning and dominance in this discourse. In this sense, it is useful to think about Susan Iverson's framing of "rape [and college's response to it] is conceived of as a script, rather than an event." We wonder: What are the scripts in the current sexual violence discourse and how do they operate to legitimate and reinforce certain potentials for institutional leadership and response as well as certain ways of being for educators and survivors?

Institutional Leadership and Response

The means by which colleges and universities respond to complaints of sexual misconduct reinforce a certain script. Cantalupo makes a strong argument for institutions to clearly separate their processes from criminal or civil ones, so as not to conflate the college process with a legal one. Colleges can only escape a criminal process script with deliberate attention and creative processes. While not elaborated on in this volume, research about college conduct processes is starting to challenge that criminal script. For example, there is a growing movement looking at how restorative justice processes might be an additional source of recourse for survivors (Brenner, 2013; Koss, Wilgus, & Williamsen, 2014). Traditional criminal justice systems leave many victims feeling unheard, unsupported, and re-victimized. In addition, the criminal justice system's racist, classist, and homophobic history make this path of recourse inaccessible to many victim-survivors. Some administrators are starting to ask: Can we move beyond a criminally based, punishment-focused system to one that is designed to facilitate healing, behavior change, and true accountability?

What are the scripts for current institutional leaders surrounding this issue? While colleges and universities are being called on, and legally mandated, to make changes on their campuses and to even name a "Title IX coordinator," what are the assumptions behind this leadership role and how does even the name "Title IX coordinator" frame the authority of those coordinators as campus leaders? This federally required role is supposed to oversee all of the issues outlined in this book, from policy and procedures, to prevention and staff training. To comply with the many (and ever changing) legal mandates, many colleges are hiring lawyers to lead them to compliance. However, leading to compliance narrows the agenda to one of following every changing rule rather than meeting the expressed needs of a community through compliant actions. While this may appear to be a small nuance, "compliance" is actually part of a powerful script.

I (Kaaren) am a Title IX coordinator with a background in prevention and campus administration. Some see this job as "neutral," assuming the script is one of merely assuring that the campus meets its compliance needs. However, when colleges choose to lead with compliance, they may be focusing only on the letter of the law, rather than the spirit of it. As Peter Lake (2014) explains, Title IX legislates the reduction and removal of barriers to education based in sex discrimination. This includes assuring fair processes for all parties involved and active prevention of sexual misconduct. However, does the prevailing leadership script about Title IX coordinators allow for the facilitation of real social change that actively seeks to prevent rape, not through individual acts of bystander intervention, but by wholesale culture change where sexual violence is neither encouraged nor tolerated? Or does the script actually reinforce the culture it is seeking to change?

These are questions that we are being called to ask. Compliance is not vision; compliance is the floor below which colleges are not to fall. We question the extent to which the scripts that emerge from campuses in this new era of attention to sexual violence allow for the enactment of transformational leadership and new visions that have the potential to lead to real changes in behavior, expectations, and campus response structures.

Educators

Scripts also exist for a variety of educators on our campuses. There exists one for facilitator or even savior who helps others who have been victimized. As Thomas-Card and Eichele point out, this script will be proliferated and diversified as colleges and universities are called to invest more in their responses to victim-survivors and as support systems hopefully become woven into the fabric of student services. Yet, how does the role of "savior" inadvertently construct images of survivors as merely victims without agency or power? Might our responses in higher education, however well meaning, reinforce society's understandings of survivors as powerless and without the ability to make decisions for themselves? Are there ways to interrupt the discourse of dependency, as Iverson discusses, in our sexual misconduct policies and responses? In addition, do these prevailing scripts assume that all victims of sexual violence are female identified? While we know that female students experience sexual violence at a higher rate than male students, they are not the only victims. Does our gendered script lock women in to always being victims and does it prevent male-identified, trans, and genderqueer students from seeing the support and response structures as means of assistance for themselves?

Educators who hold a variety of roles can be change agents in moving toward more effective systems as those who help others understand how negatively sexual violence affects individuals and communities (as Susan Marine describes). Alternatively, they can choose to read an old script that minimizes the seriousness of rape because "boys will be boys." This discourse calls on educators in all roles in colleges and universities to carefully assess their own positions on sexual violence *and* the educational, social, and emotional implications of those positions. While staff associated with student affairs, women's and/or gender centers, counseling centers, and victim advocacy centers have been involved with these issues for decades, others on campus are being called into service. Presidents are being called on to provide leadership and faculty are also implicated in helping to change the culture in relation to sexual misconduct on their campuses. Yet, these roles are not always clear. Persistent questions in higher education include: What is the role of faculty? Are they mandated reporters? Should they provide counsel to their students who may be victimized? A new organization, Faculty Against Rape, has recently formed to add to the conversation.

Survivors

There are also scripts for survivors. There are options to be strong agents, self-determined persons who make their own destiny in spite of the systematic barriers they might encounter. For women, though, this self-determination can be challenged when they are counseled to minimize or curtail their behavior or participation in public life because of the risk of violence. As was mentioned in the introduction, the Personal Empowerment Through Self Awareness (PETSA) program at the University of Montana appears to imply that if women merely work hard as individuals to be aware of themselves and choose "safe" behaviors, they can prevent sexual violence. Yet, is there any sexual violence that occurs outside of a culture in which such violence is comprehensible? What is a strong, self-determined woman to do with this script?

There may be an obligation for survivors to fulfill the script of the "responsible victim" where they dutifully report their assault through the proper channels, comply with their institution's investigation procedures, and seek out institutional support resources. The script for a responsible victim is closely connected to the script for a "good victim." I (Kaaren) have heard from many victims that they don't feel entitled to campus adjudication because they feel at fault, whether it was because they were drinking, didn't scream, froze in the moment, or had any number of responses that counters the "good victim" script, which is powerful and can impede perceived and actual access to resources. In addition, if institutions fail to provide federally mandated support and response structures, it is now a victim's responsibility to be the whistle-blower and to report their institution to the Office for Civil Rights. Where alternate scripts for survivors exist, how do they support and sustain current victim hierarchies alluded to by many of this book's authors? For example, how do the stories getting press now uphold the common narrative of White women getting raped at fraternities or by athletes and serve to delegitimize survivor experiences that fall outside of this experience? In addition, how do these scripts continue to uphold certain paths for redress as legitimate, while positioning others as incomprehensible, ineffective, or inappropriate?

Where are the scripts that acknowledge the intersectional identities that likely shape how and why people experience the various aspects of this sexual assault discourse? How do these scripts silence those working to decolonize the sexual assault movement and challenge our White supremacist society? In my (Garrett's) work as a crisis counselor for a small rape crisis center, I work to support indigenous advocates and advocates of color as they deconstruct dominant colonizer narratives that frame brown and black bodies as inherently rape-able. (How) do any of our scripts include and legitimate the voices and experiences of people of color who often face particular racialized upbringings around issues of sexuality and sexual violence?

Where are the parts in this current script for LGBTQ people to play? We notice that most essays in this volume reify the heterosexist discourse of sexual violence that Sara Wooten points out and, as noted previously, assume a female-identified victim. Does this focus, which leaves LGBTQ victim-survivors out of these scripts, lead some to doubt the legitimacy of their experiences? While this form of violence is disproportionately perpetrated against women by men, it is not exclusively so. Educators and policymakers need to ensure that the scripts we create allow for LGBTQ people to acknowledge, name, and address their experiences of sexual violence, which are affected by and intertwined with their gender identities and sexual orientations. The needs of a male-identified survivor may also conflict with the needs of a female-identified survivor. In a survivor support circle for example, the presence of a male-identified survivor can trigger other survivors. Educators and policymakers must wrestle with these and other issues involving multiple and intersecting identities to ensure that people can get their needs met.

Conclusion

Sexual violence on campus does not exist in a vacuum. The tragedy of persistent and pervasive sexual violence exists just as much outside of the academy as within it. Given this reality, if we are to reduce sexual violence in our campus communities, we must also pay attention to the issue outside of our walls and to the education and indoctrination our students, faculty, and staff receive before arriving at our doors. In addition, we need to continue to work with community and governmental organizations addressing rape and other forms of sexual violence in different communities. While this volume thoroughly addresses many issues integral to consider while working on combating sexual violence in higher education, our hope is that, as a movement, we continue to look within as well as outside of our field to inform our practice. For example, there is a wealth of information about sexual offenders that rarely gets seen in higher education policy and prevention work (Karp & Wilson, 2015). We also need to honor and educate ourselves on support and systems of accountability for those living and working outside of academe.

Power, knowledge, language, and difference shape discourses and, within discourses, possibilities for change. Using these lenses, what can we learn about the discourses in which sexual violence is possible? In a world in which gendered power structures still exist, heteronormativity is prevalent, and Whiteness is the standard to which all others are compared, how do victim-survivors with multiple complex identities have power as individuals and as a group? While it seems that best practices and governmental expectations about heterosexual misconduct are increasingly articulated, we know and share much less about prevention or about how LGBTQ people experience sexual misconduct. As Susan Iverson pointed out in her chapter, we use language associated with managing risks, dependency, and rationality, while avoiding naming the subject—in policies we use words like "perpetrator" and "assault" and "rapist" less regularly. As Alison Kiss and Kiersten Feeney White pointed out, we also have cultures in which silence around sexual misconduct is chosen or encouraged. Finally, in a world in which gender as a socially constructed category is dichotomized as women and men, rather than as one facet of a multi-faceted and fluid identity, we are likely to oversimplify our responses to sexual assault because we will have limited understandings in the ways in which it can be perpetuated and experienced.

Recently, I (Rebecca) researched gender equity policies in Austria. At the end of long conversations focusing on gender, I asked what leaders, scholars, and educators would change if they had the power to change one thing to promote equity. Many answered in a way that surprised me. They noted that they wished they could deconstruct the hierarchies that normalize dehumanizing relations between people in ways that go well beyond the needs and functions of the organization. Sexual violence is happening and being addressed within a larger context of hierarchies in our society and on our campuses. We hope that as we continue to address this issue, we examine that larger culture and the ways in which our power structures make certain discourses around our relations with others possible and impossible.

Rebecca Ropers-Huilman, Kaaren M. Williamsen,
and Garrett Drew Hoffman

References

Brenner, A. (2013). Transforming campus culture to prevent rape: The possibility and promise of restorative justice as a response to campus sexual violence. *Harvard Journal of Law and Gender.* Retrieved from http://harvardjlg.com/2013/10/transforming-campus-culture-to-prevent-rape-the-possibility-and-promise-of-restorative-justice-as-a-response-to-campus-sexual-violence/

Karp, D., & Wilson, R. J. (2015, February). *Circles of support and accountability.* Workshop conducted from the Association of Student Conduct Administration Annual Conference, St. Petersburg Beach, FL.

Koss, M. P., Wilgus, J., & Williamsen, K. (2014). Campus sexual misconduct: Restorative justice approaches to enhance compliance with Title IX guidance. *Trauma, Violence, & Abuse, 15*(3), 242–257.

Lake, P. (2014, November). *Title IX compliance institute.* Workshop conducted in Orlando, FL.

CONTRIBUTOR BIOGRAPHIES

Nancy Chi Cantalupo, Esq., is currently associate vice president of equity, inclusion, and violence prevention at NASPA–Student Affairs Administrators in Higher Education. She received her J.D. from Georgetown Law, and she has worked to combat sexual harassment and violence in education for 20 years through use of Title IX and the Clery Act. Her research focuses upon the use of U.S. civil rights, common law, international, and comparative legal regimes to combat discriminatory, particularly gender-based, violence and has appeared in the *Maryland Law Review, Journal of College and University Law*, and *Campus Crime: Legal, Social, and Policy Perspectives.*

Todd W. Crosset is an associate professor in the Mark H. McCormack Department of Sport Management in the Isenberg School of Management at the University of Massachusetts, Amherst. He has been writing, teaching, and reaching the topic of collegiate athlete sexual assault for 25 years. Prior to arriving at the University of Massachusetts, he held positions as a collegiate head coach of swimming (Northeastern University) and assistant athletic director (Dartmouth College), and was an All-American swimmer (University of Texas).

Katie Eichele is the director of the Aurora Center for Advocacy & Education at the University of Minnesota–Twin Cities. She has served the UMN since 2004 in roles such as the coordinator of judicial affairs for housing and residential life before providing leadership at the Aurora Center around issues of sexual assault, relationship violence, and stalking. She received her B.S. in mass communications and her M.S. in marketing, public relations, and advertising from North Dakota State University and her professional experience stems from university student conduct, student development, social justice, and crisis management.

Bonnie S. Fisher is professor in the School of Criminal Justice at the University of Cincinnati. She served on the National Academy of Sciences Panel on Measuring Rape and Sexual Assault in Bureau of Justice Statistics Household Surveys during 2011–2013. In 2015, she was the Co-PI (with David Cantor at Westat) working with the American Association of Universities Campus Climate Survey on Sexual Assault and Sexual Misconduct Design Team. Her published articles and chapters span the field of victimology, and her primary research area has been on violence against women, from domestic violence to stalking to sexual assault, with an emphasis on college women.

Caitlin B. Henriksen is a Ph.D. candidate at the University of Cincinnati in Criminal Justice. Her research interests include victimology, specifically recurring victimization, cyber-victimization, and bystander intervention.

Susan V. Iverson is associate professor of higher education administration and student personnel at Kent State University, where she is also an affiliated faculty member with the KSU women's studies program. Prior to becoming faculty, Iverson worked in student affairs administration for more than 10 years, most recently at University of Maine, as associate director of Safe Campus Project, a federally grant-funded initiative to address interpersonal violence on campus. Iverson's research interests focus on: equity and diversity, the status of women in higher education, critical pedagogy, and feminist and poststructural approaches to inquiry.

Alison Kiss is the executive director of the Clery Center for Security on Campus, a national nonprofit focusing on issues of campus safety. Alison is currently working on a dissertation focused on college and university leadership and institutionalization of sexual assault prevention programs. She most recently served as a member of the Department of Education negotiated rule-making committee for the Violence Against Women Act amendments to the Clery Act and has been influential in policy around campus sexual assault.

W. Scott Lewis, J.D., is a partner with the NCHERM Group. He is a cofounder and past president of NaBITA.org, a cofounder of ATIXA.org and weareSCOPE.org, as well as past president of ASCA. He currently serves as the president of SACCA.org. Over his 20 years in education, he has been on faculty, served as dean and associate vice provost, and as special counsel. He has also served as a consultant with the White House, the OCR, the USOC, and the Departments of Justice and Education; he is also author and editor of numerous publications. He lives in Denver, Colorado, with his family.

Susan Marine, Ph.D., is assistant professor and director of the higher education graduate program at Merrimack College. Over the last two decades, Susan has led numerous initiatives related to the advancement of women and LGBTQ students in higher education, while being active in the movement to end sexual and domestic violence. Susan has written extensively on LGB and trans* student agency and belonging, and the evolution of feminist change in the academy.

Kelsey L. Mattick is a Ph.D. candidate in criminal justice at the University of Cincinnati. She is currently in her second year of the doctoral program with a concentration in corrections. Her research interests include correctional rehabilitation, community corrections, and victimology.

Roland W. Mitchell is interim associate dean of research engagement and graduate studies and associate professor of higher education in the School of Education at Louisiana State University. He has a B.A. in history from Fisk University, a M.Ed. in higher education from Vanderbilt University, and a Ph.D. in educational research from the University of Alabama. He teaches courses that focus on the history of higher education and college teaching, and his articles have appeared in leading education journals such as *Urban Education, International Journal of Qualitative Studies in Education*, and the *Review of Education Pedagogy and Cultural Studies*. Roland is the editor of the *College Student Affairs Journal*, higher education section editor of the *Journal of Curriculum Theorizing*, a member of the leadership team of the Bergamo Conference on Curriculum Theory and Classroom Practice and director of the Louisiana State University Writing Project's Teaching African American Boys Summer Institute. His current research interests include theorizing the impact of historical and communal knowledge on pedagogy.

Saundra K. Schuster is a Partner with the NCHERM Group, LLC (National Center for Higher Education Risk Management), a national risk management legal consulting firm, and executive director of Student Affairs Community College Administrators (SACCA). Ms. Schuster is a recognized expert in preventive and civil rights law for education. She previously served as the general counsel for Sinclair Community College; senior assistant attorney general for the State of Ohio; and as the associate general counsel for the University of Toledo. In addition to her legal work in higher education, Ms. Schuster has over 25 years of experience in college administration and teaching, including serving as a Student Affairs Dean at the Ohio State University. Ms. Schuster is coauthor of "The First Amendment: A Guide for College Administrators," and contributing author to "Campus Conduct Practice" and "The Book on BIT: Forming and Operating Effective Behavioral Intervention Teams of College Campuses."

Brett A. Sokolow is the president and CEO of the NCHERM Group, LLC, a Philadelphia-area law firm serving more than 70 colleges and universities as legal counsel. The firm has consulted with more than 3,000 colleges and universities across the country and operates four associations (SCOPE, ATIXA, NaBITA, and SACCA) with more than 4,000 members.

Daniel C. Swinton, J.D., Ed.D., is managing partner of the NCHERM Group, LLC, a Philadelphia-area law firm serving more than 70 colleges and universities as legal counsel. He is also associate executive director of the Association of Title IX Administrators (ATIXA), a membership association dedicated to providing training, resources and professional development to college and university and K–12 Title IX administrators. Daniel is a past president of the Association of Student Conduct Administrators (ASCA) and a member of the Tennessee State Bar.

Traci Thomas-Card is the Prevention Program Coordinator for the Aurora Center for Advocacy & Education and Boynton Health Service at the University of Minnesota–Twin Cities. She began her work in sexual violence prevention in 2004 and is responsible for education and outreach to the campus community on bystander intervention, consent, and general issues surrounding sexual assault, relationship violence, and stalking prevention. Traci earned her B.A. in comprehensive English literature and her M.A. in English from the University of Wisconsin–Eau Claire and is currently pursuing her Ed.D. in higher education through the department of Organizational Leadership, Policy, and Development at the University of Minnesota. Her current research interests include the LGBTQ college student population, intersectionality, student development, and violence prevention.

Kiersten N. Feeney White, Ed.D., is assistant vice president for student life at Saint Joseph's University in Philadelphia, Pennsylvania, and has worked as a consultant and trainer for the Clery Center for Security on Campus, Inc. Prior to her current administrative role, Kiersten worked in community standards, student activities and also served as the *NASPA Journal* editorial assistant. She holds a B.S. in sociology, a M.S. in training and organizational development, and an Ed.D. in educational leadership from Saint Joseph's University; her dissertation focus was ethical commitment to campus safety and the Clery Act.

Sara Carrigan Wooten is a doctoral candidate in educational leadership and research at Louisiana State University. She completed her B.A. in women's studies at Purdue University and received a M.A. in sociology and women's and gender studies from Brandeis University and an additional master's degree in educational studies from Tufts University. Wooten's dissertation is centered on lesbian, gay, bisexual, transgender, and queer students' experiences of sexual violence in higher education. Her research interests include heterosexism and heteronormativity in sexual violence prevention and response resources, critical discourse analysis, and higher education policy development.

INDEX